INSCRIBED IN REMEMBRANCE
Gravemarker lettering: form, function and recording

George Thomson

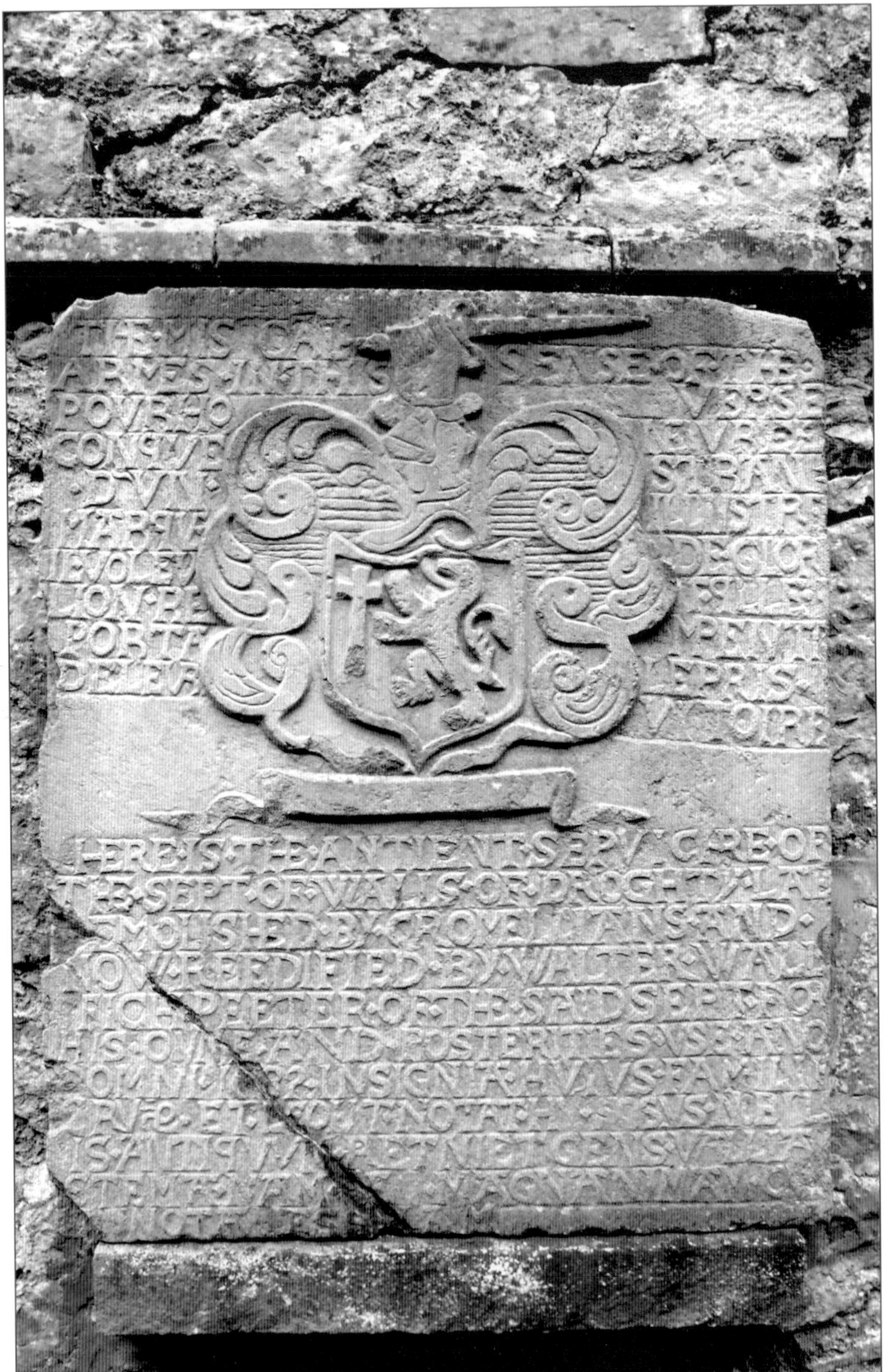

Mural memorial, Athenry Priory, Co. Galway, Ireland (1682)

INSCRIBED IN REMEMBRANCE

Gravemarker lettering: form, function and recording

George Thomson

Wordwell

WORDWELL LTD

Published by
Wordwell Ltd
Media House, South County Business Park, Leopardstown, Dublin 18,
Ireland
www.wordwellbooks.com

First published 2009

ISBN 978 1 905569 35 9

British Library Cataloguing-in-Publication Data.
A catalogue record for this book is available from the British Library.

Printed in Spain by Graficas Castuera, Pamplona

Cover design: George Thomson
Copy-editing: Emer Condit

CONTENTS

PREFACE

In what now seems like prehistory, a group of young school friends would tease each other about ghosts and ghouls in the local burial grounds and nervously glare at the skull and crossbones on a headstone in the local churchyard, taunting each other about its meaning, stories of pirates, what might lie beneath and what might rise from the soil. That image travelled with me over the Scottish borderlands to Cumbria, the English Cotswolds and thence to Ireland. It accompanied me to Europe, where it rested on some gravestones in north Germany, the Netherlands, Brittany and the Basque Regions of France and Spain, before flying to North America, returning more than 50 years later to its original home, where it was photographed and placed in an archive for posterity.

I must have explored several thousand graveyards, churchyards, cemeteries and other burial grounds since then, in more than twenty countries. Much of the time, the majority of other visitors to these places are friends and relatives of the deceased, paying their respects. Some, like me, are there for other reasons: studying gravemarkers, recording genealogical information, reading the intriguing, humorous and sometimes even cruel epitaphs, puzzling over the enigmatic iconography, or simply enjoying the unique, usually peaceful atmosphere of the place. On occasion, my antics—taking up strange prostrate positions, measuring minute details of obscure parts of headstones or hurriedly rushing from one gravemarker to another, camera in hand—have attracted some curiosity. The question inevitably arises, 'Are you looking for someone in particular?' When I say that I am undertaking research on gravemarker lettering, I get a not-unexpected look that combines bewilderment with mild cynicism.

The best way to respond is not easy. Referring to my work as a study of gravemarker lettering suggests something rather shallow to the non-specialist, but I avoid the temptation to call it research in inscriptional palaeography, as that would sound pedantic. To rescue the situation, I point out some features of interest, such as ligatures, layout misjudgements and just a little bit about letterform. The bemused onlooker takes his leave, hopefully seeing the inscriptions in quite a different light.

I am passionate about calligraphy, lettering and typography. Those of us who are fascinated by the alphabet and its forms are sometimes criticised and occasionally even derided for our over-enthusiasm for the subject. But, in spite of the increased use of iconography in ever more pervasive electronic gadgets and such things as buddicons, smilicons and emoticons, the written and printed word is still paramount as our principal means of visual communication. Even in the days of widespread illiteracy, the use of symbolism on gravemarkers was almost invariably accompanied by an inscription, no matter how well or how badly it may have been cut. The development of our alphabet, how it has been used and how it has been interpreted by different societies in the west informs and enhances our knowledge of what has come to be known as material culture. Lettering is a vitally important part of our everyday experience. Without it we would be much the poorer.

Lettering studies have tended to be the Cinderella in the field of design research. For example, in spite of the dramatic changes resulting from developments in digital typography and font design, very little research into the legibility of print has been published since the 1950s. Perhaps it is not surprising that lettering on gravemarkers is an even more poorly researched field. When the majority of books and other published material on sepulchral memorials, gravemarkers and other funerary artefacts tend to focus on a single theme, geographical region or country, often with little contextualisation, and these, in turn, give little space to palaeography, the consequence is a serious hiatus in the literature. Possibly another contributing factor is that a study of gravemarker lettering spans several disciplines, including history, archaeology, palaeography, art and design, and specialists in these fields may feel uncomfortable about moving beyond their own area of expertise. One of the very few books that takes a comprehensive and contextual view of the subject of funerary art in some depth is Hueppi's *Kunst und Kult der Grabstätten* (1968).

I have unashamedly drawn on several of my papers published in academic journals and used some illustrations and diagrams from them. This should make that material more widely available to the non-specialist.

To paraphrase several writers of such prefaces as this, the definitive book of gravemarker lettering has yet to be written. This is not it. Hopefully, what I have offered and introduced here will encourage others to engage in gravemarker lettering research, to develop some of the concepts that are presented and to further research in this fascinating subject. At the very least, I hope it will encourage historians, genealogists and others who already enjoy a range of pursuits in burial grounds to see lettering on gravemarkers from an entirely different perspective.

Acknowledgements

I have been greatly assisted by numerous individuals who have willingly contributed their time, help, expertise and knowledge or engaged in constructive discussion on material included in this book. They include Chris Fanos (England), Herbert van Hasselt (Netherlands), the late John Higgitt (Scotland), Bill Kreuger (USA), Ruth Lawler (Ireland), Julian Litten (England), Mike McNerney (USA), Martin Mitov (Bulgaria), Louise McKeever (Ireland), Jaak Nijssen (Belgium), Isabel von Papen (Germany), Andrew Thomson (Canada) and Harry Tummers (Netherlands). I thank them for their help and cooperation. Dr Roger Dennis (England) read sections of the book and provided helpful suggestions, especially for the section on recording and analysis. The University of Cumbria, Faculty of the Arts, provided financial support towards publication from the Research Capability Fund. I thank my wife Elizabeth for her ongoing support, both moral and physical, throughout the years, trekking from one burial ground to the next, usually without complaint, frequently pointing me in the direction of interesting gravemarkers that otherwise I would have missed. Finally, I thank the many anonymous individuals in various countries who were approached and asked for the locations of burial sites that, without local knowledge, I would never have found.

GRAVEMARKER LETTERING: A NATION'S HERITAGE

Gravemarkers are an important and often overlooked part of a nation's heritage. They record the lives of the country's past inhabitants and tell us much about those who erected the monuments in their memory. Perhaps it is because they remind us of our mortality that the attitude towards burial grounds is either total avoidance or fascination. Those who appreciate the unique atmosphere of a churchyard often become absorbed in an interest in the epitaphs, sculpturing, symbolism or genealogical associations of the memorials, a fascination that frequently develops into a lifetime pursuit.

On older gravestones, through epitaphs and symbolic carvings, we see evidence of the level of respect in which the individuals were held and an appreciation of the contribution they made to the community. We find both morbidity and humour. As the purpose of a tombstone is to remember the deceased, the inscription is, in some respects, the most important part. Arguably, without inscription memorials are meaningless to all but those by whom they were erected. In parts of Germany, gravemarkers are called *sprechende Steine*, 'speaking stones'. They speak to us not only by the form in which the memorial is crafted but also through the words of the inscription. But how much attention was paid to the lettering itself? What consideration was given to the choice of style, size, layout and final execution of the inscription? Who made the decisions? And, most importantly, what significance has the lettering as an element and indicator of a regional or national culture? These are questions we seek to answer in this book.

Very little study has been made of gravemarker lettering on inscribed memorials of the post-medieval period. Current and past palaeographic and epigraphic studies tend to focus on the Middle Ages and earlier, although a few art historians have given some attention to the lettering on 'significant' medieval memorials.[1] *Tombstone lettering in the British Isles* by Alan Bartram is the only work dedicated to the subject of lettering on post-medieval gravestones. This is almost entirely focused on England, with a few examples from Wales, Ireland and Scotland. His approach is more typographical than palaeographical, dealing almost exclusively with inscriptions on materials such as slate or 'hard northern stone.'[2] Short sections on gravemarker lettering appear in Mary Timoney's *Had me made* and Lionel Gilbert's *A grave look at history*. A few paragraphs on lettering are included in Frederick Burgess' *English churchyard memorials*, Hilary Lees' *Hallowed ground—churchyards of Gloucestershire and the Cotswolds*, Diedrich Steilen's *Norddeutsche Grabmalkunst*, Wolfgang Runge's *Sprechende Steine*, Louis Colas' *La tombe Basque*, Betty Willsher's *Understanding Scottish graveyards* (new edition), and in the classic work by Betty Willsher and Doreen Hunter, *Stones—a guide to some remarkable eighteenth century gravestones*, now sadly out of print.[3] Even the extensive papers on graveyard memorials in serial publications make only casual reference to lettering style.[4]

It is surprising that this subject has been overlooked. Research on gravemarker lettering can make a considerable contribution to studies of material culture, archaeology and history. It is a unique and relatively untouched research resource that ranges from folk art to a highly skilled craft. The material included in publications on post-medieval gravemarkers, both book and serial, is usually limited to a very specific region or country, without consideration of a more extensive geographical or cultural context, and with little or no mention of memorials in materials other than stone.[5] The large number of post-medieval exterior brass plates, found mostly in England, is virtually ignored by all but the publications of the Monumental Brass Society.[6] Some of the most interesting and important collections of gravemarkers are found in Scotland, England, Ireland, western Germany, France (Brittany and the Basque Region), the USA and Canada. This book focuses on examples from these areas, as they are where we find the most varied and culturally significant examples of inscriptional lettering. It is hoped that such an approach demonstrates the importance of studying gravemarker lettering beyond narrow parochial and material boundaries. Also, the clear relationship between gravemarkers and other inscribed memorial lettering, including that cut in stone and engraved on metal, is not ignored here.

But why study lettering on gravemarkers? One of our primary means of communication is through words. The way we write, print or cut inscriptions tells us something about ourselves. Through lettering we can determine aspects of cultural identity. We can identify tastes and fashions of the time. We can learn about the changing techniques and methodologies of a craft that spans many centuries. We can learn a lot about contemporary standards of education and the abilities of the individuals who cut the lettering. We can identify creativity and ingenuity. We can find evidence of human fallibility in the many mistakes in the inscriptions that have been cut in such a permanent medium that future generations can see and enjoy.

It is important here to recognise the differences between commercial memorials made and incised by professional masons and rustic vernacular memorials cut by untrained individuals. In practice, this is sometimes not easy and, to a certain extent, rather artificial. There is a continuum from the large formal memorials made by the most skilful craftsmen to the rough stones erected, made and inscribed by untrained amateurs. Culture embedded in tombstone inscriptions is often most strongly expressed in the less formal gravemarkers.[7] It is the sheer variety and number of these artefacts that make the cultural record so unique.

From the end of the eighteenth century, copybooks and type catalogues were widely used as source material for lettering by masons. By the middle of the nineteenth century, in much of western Europe and North America, mechanical methods of gravestone manufacture had made their appearance. These factors resulted in a degree of standardisation of the inscriptions, even although lettering was still mostly hand-cut until relatively recently.[8] The individuality that reflected local culture and that had been a feature for many centuries before in Britain, Ireland, the USA and Canada was almost entirely obliterated. In Germany, however, the tradition of good hand-cut lettering was maintained to some extent and the craft is still thriving there today. The focus in this book is more on memorial lettering from before the middle of the nineteenth century, without neglecting the notable examples of more recent times.

Aesthetic or quality judgements of gravemarker lettering have been avoided as far as possible. Introducing biases and prejudices based on such assessment would impair the objectivity of a study of cultural differences and their historical significance. In a palaeographic study of this sort, the work of the untrained craftsman is as important as that of the master mason. Adjectives such as ‘beautiful’ and ‘crude’ are sometimes difficult to avoid when discussing the skill of the mason who inscribed the stone. When these epithets are used they are not employed as a reasoned aesthetic assessment of the artistic quality of the lettering but as a comment qualifying an analytical conclusion. Similarly, it is not easy to ignore the idiosyncratic treatment of lettering, spelling or layout, much of which contributes to our understanding of those who cut the inscriptions, and that represents the complete antithesis of our regulated lives today.

This book is the outcome of extensive palaeographic studies of gravemarker lettering in the Latin alphabet, mainly of the post-medieval period. In practice, this encompasses central and western Europe, including Britain and Ireland, and North America. Some contextual material is discussed where relevant. For example, the extremely interesting gravemarkers from Bulgaria, inscribed in Cyrillic, are compared with memorial forms in Ireland.[9] These in turn may have derived from some Ottoman forms similar to those of the fourteenth century and before in Turkey.[10]

I have deliberately used the term 'gravemarker' for any memorial that marks the site of a burial. This includes an extensive range of artefacts to which many authors apply more specific, but frequently misleading, epithets. Although the choice of nomenclature is, to some extent, a semantic argument, there are some problems with several terms currently used. The most common of these are 'gravestone' and 'tombstone', both often applied to any funerary memorial, irrespective of the material from which it is fashioned. It is inappropriate to call something a 'stone' that is made from cast iron, brass or some other non-lithic material. The term 'marker' has come to be applied to small, often uninscribed memorials. Why this should be is unclear and it is not easy to justify restricting the term to memorials of that sort. 'Gravemarker', therefore, includes gravestones, memorial mural monuments, brass memorial plates and any other funerary or sepulchral artefact that marks the site of a grave, irrespective of its form, size or the material from which it is made. It can even be applied to living organisms such as trees, for example the dendroglyphs carved in *Eucalyptus* by the Aboriginal people of Australia. Increasingly, trees are being used as memorials in Europe and North America. The only complication that arises with the term gravemarker is when the body of the deceased is interred in a different place from where the memorial is sited, as was sometimes the case in the nineteenth century in New England during the 'urn-and-willow' period. In this situation, the artefact is a memorial. Similar ambiguous terminology is regularly used to describe burial sites, with significant differences in use between Britain, Ireland and elsewhere. A burial site is anywhere that a burial has or burials have taken place. A burial ground is a specific area set aside for interments. A graveyard is a yard or area of land in which graves have been or will be established and is, in effect, synonymous with a burial ground. A churchyard (kirkyard in Scotland) is an area adjacent to or surrounding a church, abbey or cathedral. Although often used for burials, it may never have been intended for that purpose. In Britain and Ireland the term 'cemetery', that translates literally as 'sleeping place', tends to be applied to sites specifically established for the purposes of burials, usually by a local council or civic authority. In the USA the term is often also used for older burial grounds, even if they are associated with an ecclesiastical structure, such as a church, chapel or meeting-house. In France and Germany the terms *cimetière* and *Kirchhof* are used for any interment site. In the Netherlands, *begraafplaats* means cemetery or burial ground. The generic term 'burial ground' or 'burial site' is much preferred, and more specific descriptions, such as 'churchyard', can be applied as appropriate. This avoids ambiguity and complications introduced as a consequence of linguistic interpretation, and the terms can be applied irrespective of national or cultural context.

Throughout the text, I have used the term 'Roman' with a capital R when applied to the people, places or artefacts of that classical period. The term 'roman' with a small or lower-case 'r' is used to denote the lettering style.

Some of the outcomes of my studies have been published in specialist journals.[11] It is timely, however, to bring together the outcomes of research to date so that it is accessible to a wider readership. It is my aim to raise the profile of the subject in the hope that it will stimulate interest, promote and suggest methods of recording and analysis, encourage research and conservation, and open eyes on an aspect of gravemarkers that has not been considered in detail before.

Fig. 1—The floor of L'Église Saint Exupere, Brittany, France, covered with early post-medieval graveslabs.

Fig. 2—The cemetery (now churchyard) of Greyfriers Kirk, Edinburgh, Scotland.

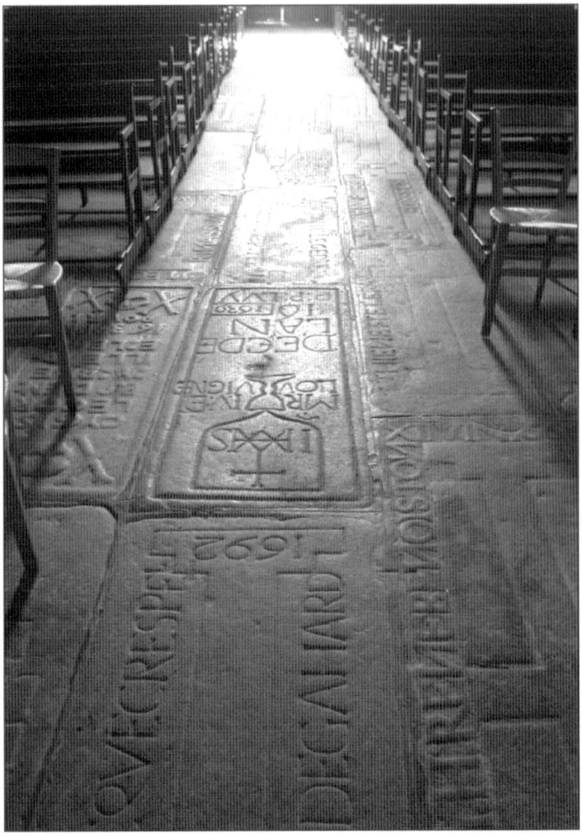

Figure 1

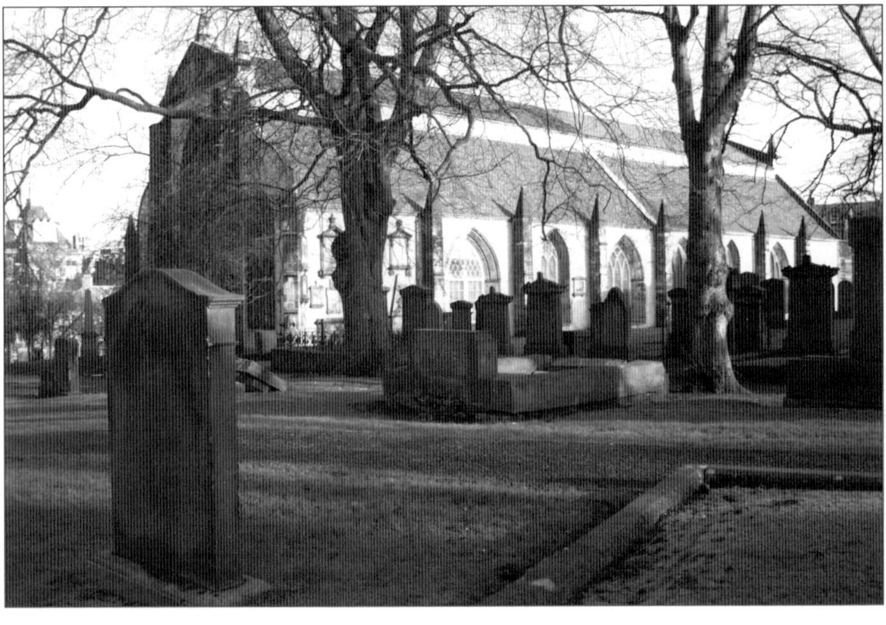

Figure 2

BURIALS AND BURIAL SITES

In much of western Europe and Canada, before the widespread establishment of civic cemeteries from early in the nineteenth century, most burials were on religious sites, initially within churches, cathedrals, abbeys and friaries, and later in the surrounding churchyards.[12] The turbulent history of religion in Europe has left us with the legacy of a wealth of ecclesiastical buildings, some still functioning as places of worship, others picturesque ruins. Denominational disruption and disputes between religious groups fostered diversity in the approach to both ecclesiastical architecture and the design of artefacts, including gravemarkers. This was especially so in Ireland and Germany and, to a lesser extent, in the USA. The drop in church attendance in mainland Britain in the last few decades, and consequent financial considerations, has resulted in many of these buildings being converted for other uses and they no longer function as religious establishments. Few new churches have been built in Scotland, England or Wales in recent years. Most of those that have been erected are Roman Catholic, many of which are innovative in their design but have no burial sites connected with them.

Even before the so-called 'modern cemetery movement', not all churches, cathedrals, abbeys or friaries had associated churchyards and not all burial grounds were associated with church buildings. There are several instances where the reasons for this are obvious. For example, in Scotland, England and Wales early churchyards with tombstones beside Roman Catholic chapels are extremely rare. After the Reformation, Roman Catholicism was suppressed and graveyards were not permitted. Anyone who retained their allegiance kept it as an utmost secret and buried their kin in such a way that they would not be identified as Roman Catholic. By the time the Roman Catholic hierarchy was restored in 1870, public non-denominational cemeteries had been widely established.[13] Braemar

Fig. 3—A small section of the massive, beautifully landscaped Varel Cemetery, Oldenburgerland, Germany.

Fig. 4—The crowded burial ground of the church at Lissewege, Belgium.

Fig. 5—Display of modern gravemarkers, Museum für Sepulkralkultur, Kassel, Hessen, Germany.

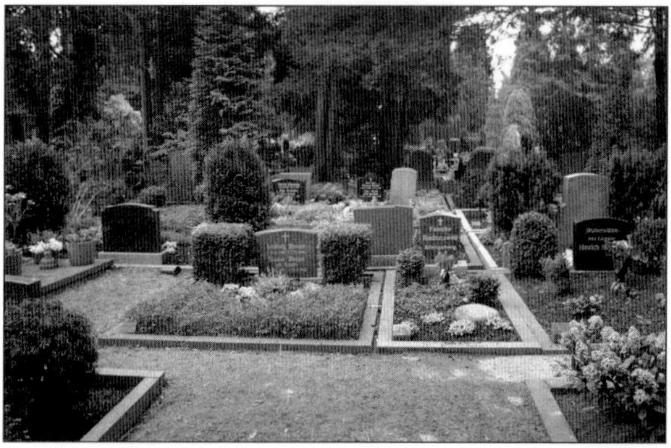

Figure 3

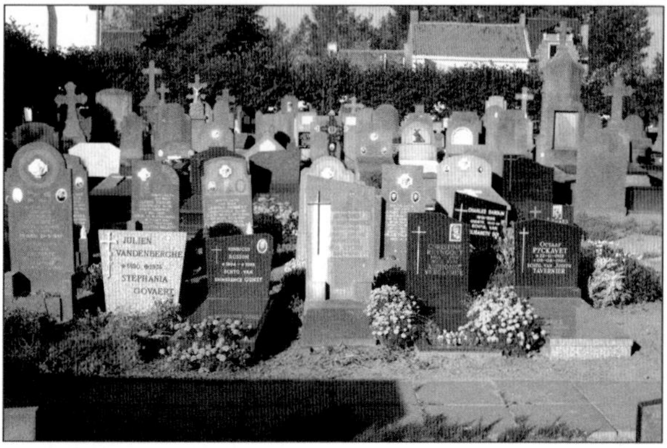

Figure 4

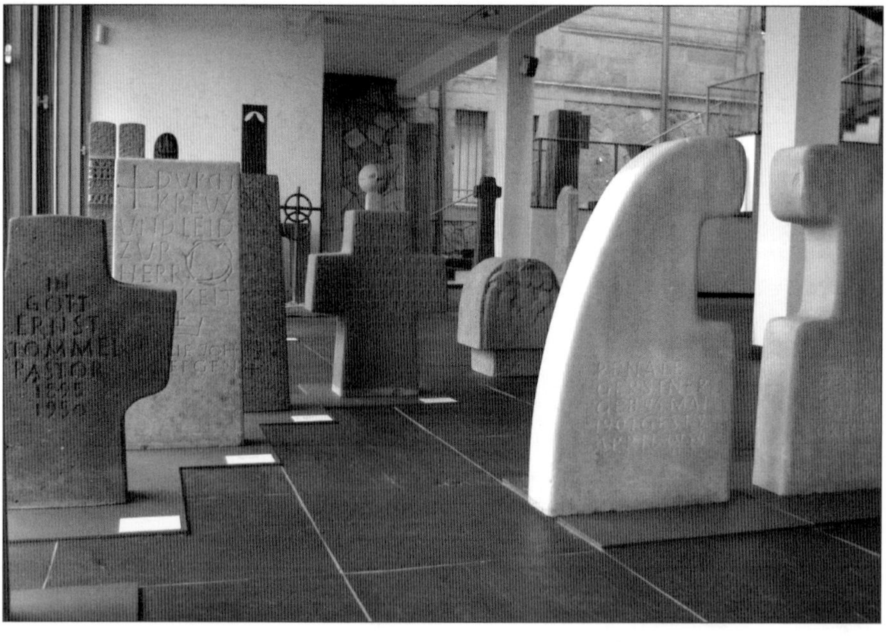

Figure 5

Kirkyard, Aberdeenshire, Scotland, is one exception with eighteenth-century burials of Roman Catholic priests, although the church building has long since disappeared.

Until the end of the eighteenth century, in much of western Europe interment within the church building was commonplace, although restricted to the clergy or the wealthy. In Ireland this was largely a Roman Catholic and Church of Ireland practice.[14] In some instances, the entire floor area of cathedrals and churches, such as the Oude Kerk, Amsterdam, with 2,500 slabs, L'Église Saint-Sauveur, Dinan, Brittany, and L'Église Saint Exupere, also in Brittany, France, are covered by memorials, frequently inscribed (Fig. 1). Even some smaller churches have numerous inscribed graveslabs serving as the floor surface. In Scotland burial within churches was outlawed by decree in 1588, mainly through lack of space, although many interior funerary monuments dated long after that can be found, as the gentry found means by which the law could be evaded. In London, burial within new churches was declared illegal from 1711. Before the unification of Germany in 1871, bans on burials in church buildings and within towns and cities were introduced by the *Josephinische Begraebnisreformen* in Austria in 1788 and the *Preussische Begraebnisreformen* in 1794 in Prussia for hygienic reasons.[15] This concern for the insanitary aspects of burials near human habitation was to change the face of burial practice throughout western Europe from the end of the eighteenth century. The Burial Act of 1855 tightened up the regulations for interment in what was then the 'United Kingdom of Great Britain and Ireland', which included the present Republic.

In Scotland, the church building was usually located at the northern end of the site. Few burials were made in the shadow of the church to the north, as this was considered to be a sign of shame and interments found there are usually of the illegitimate or those who were in debt. When space permitted and soil depths were appropriate, burials were made on the other three sides of the church. Sometimes, special areas or sites were set aside for particular categories of deceased, especially in the case of epidemics, including 'cholera grounds'. These can be found in many churchyards. More often than not, the graves were not commemorated with a marker. In Britain, and even more so in Ireland, there are known burial sites with no trace of gravemarkers. The Famine burial grounds in Ireland are examples of this.

Although interment in churches and churchyards was the norm from at least the medieval period until the end of the eighteenth century, a separate burial ground was established at Pisa, Italy, in the thirteenth century.[16] In many parts of seventeenth-century Europe, the risk to health from burials in close proximity to human habitation was becoming evident, although divorcing burial grounds from churches was strongly resisted by the clergy. The advent of the modern civic cemetery really began with the founding of Greyfriers Cemetery (Scotland) by Edinburgh Town Council in 1562, although it was adjacent to the Old Greyfriers Kirk (Fig. 2). By the end of the eighteenth century, churchyards were rapidly running out of burial space and the need for alternative sites was pressing. This resulted in the establishment of numerous cemeteries from the early nineteenth century onwards, many of which were considered as recreational areas or parks. For example, Greenock Cemetery, near Glasgow, Scotland, was completed in 1846 at a cost of £2,967.15.0. This sum included 'the expense of forming two ornamental Ponds, of considerable extent, which have been stocked with choice aquatic plants'. In Ireland, civic burials began under the Public Health Act (Ireland) in 1878 and bye-laws controlled those that continued in churches. Where land was available, the new cemeteries were built alongside existing churchyards. The larger ones, especially those serving an urban community, were created on sites some distance from any church or population centre, hence the term 'rural cemetery movement' in the USA and Canada.[17] In the USA burial sites were sometimes located near to religious meeting-houses, less commonly churches.

The smallest burial grounds have a single or only a few gravemarkers. The tiny burial ground at Gorestown, Co. Tyrone, Ireland, is a good example. In Britain these are often private vaults, such as that at Albie in Dumfriesshire, Scotland. Many large city cemeteries have thousands of lairs or plots, as in the Ohlsdorf Cemetery in Hamburg, Germany, the largest in the world, Brookwood Cemetery, near Woking in Surrey, the largest in England, the Glasnevin Cemetery in Dublin, Crown Hill Cemetery in Indianapolis, the largest in the USA, and the Père-Lachaise Cemetery in Paris (Fig. 3). Scottish and Irish churchyards usually have many more gravestones per unit area than their counterparts in England. There are exceptions. Some churchyards in Sussex and Surrey approach similar gravemarker densities to Scotland. Also, some English churchyards in the more northern counties and also in parts of Wales are closer to the Scottish pattern than elsewhere. In those heavily used churchyards, it is not unusual to have row after row of closely adjacent headstones, each row barely far enough apart for two people to pass. In England, Canada and the USA, memorials are usually more widely scattered. In European countries that are predominantly Roman Catholic, more modern churchyards are frequently almost entirely covered by gravemarkers, with only narrow paths between the rows of graves (Fig. 4). In parts of Europe, there is a widespread practice of reusing lairs. Consequently, in these areas and in all but the older churchyards and other burial grounds, memorials are mostly of a relatively recent date. In Germany, burial plots can be reused and the gravemarkers removed, sometimes to museums, after only fifteen to 25 years. In the Museum für Sepulkralkultur at Kassel, several modern sculptural gravestones are on display, one with a date as recent as 1991 (Fig. 5).

The number of older gravemarkers that have survived from before 1800 in churchyards and burial grounds varies a great deal across western Europe. Britain, Ireland, south-west France, north Brittany, north Holland and north Germany are particularly rich in this respect. Conversely, in

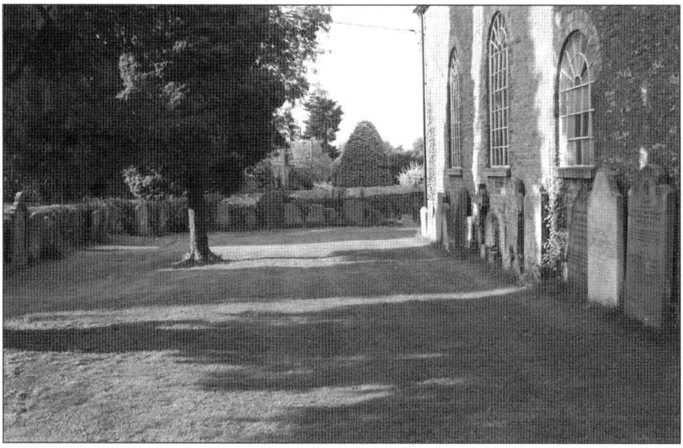

Fig. 6—Headstones relocated against the church and perimeter wall, Carey Baptist Church, Moulton, Northamptonshire, England.

parts of south-east Germany, much of Scandinavia, and the Flemish regions of Belgium and the Netherlands, older post-medieval gravemarkers are extremely rare or totally absent. To some extent this is due to differential survival, often influenced by burial site management policy. Differences in burial practices have also contributed to this disparity.

Sometimes a chronology of burials can be identified, more so in more recent times, where lairs were allocated in a logical row-on-row manner. More often memorials of vastly different dates can be found side by side. Very old tombstones located between or behind more recent ones can easily be overlooked in a churchyard dominated by large Victorian headstones. For some time in much of western Europe, however, it has been the practice to remove older headstones from their original locations and to reuse the material for building or other purposes. Sometimes a few stones are retained and fixed against church walls or displayed in the interior of the building. The paucity of remaining early gravemarkers in most of Belgium, southern Holland and parts of southern Germany is regrettable. In many cases an entire corpus of cultural information has been lost. Unfortunately, the total removal of headstones or, at best, their relocation on graveyard perimeters is becoming more common in England and Ireland (Fig. 6). This is not a new phenomenon. In Britain and Ireland, seventeenth- and eighteenth-century gravemarkers were built into walls in the nineteenth and early twentieth centuries.

It has been Christian practice for centuries to bury the dead with the head to the west and feet to the east, although this custom was not adhered to in every case, especially when space was at a premium. This orientation means that the lettered face of the gravemarker faces east. In Ireland it is believed that the inscriptional face of the headstones of ministers or priests faces west towards the congregation. In Scotland and Germany, however, both faces of the marker often bear inscriptions. The practice is much less common in England, Ireland and North America. The characteristic discoid gravemarkers of west Ulster in Ireland never have inscriptions on the reverse side, which is usually devoted to mortality symbols. Many memorials have more than one inscription, cut at various times and on any face of the stone, including the edge. Consequently, even a modestly sized churchyard can have several hundred inscriptions varying in date and style, providing an invaluable resource for research.

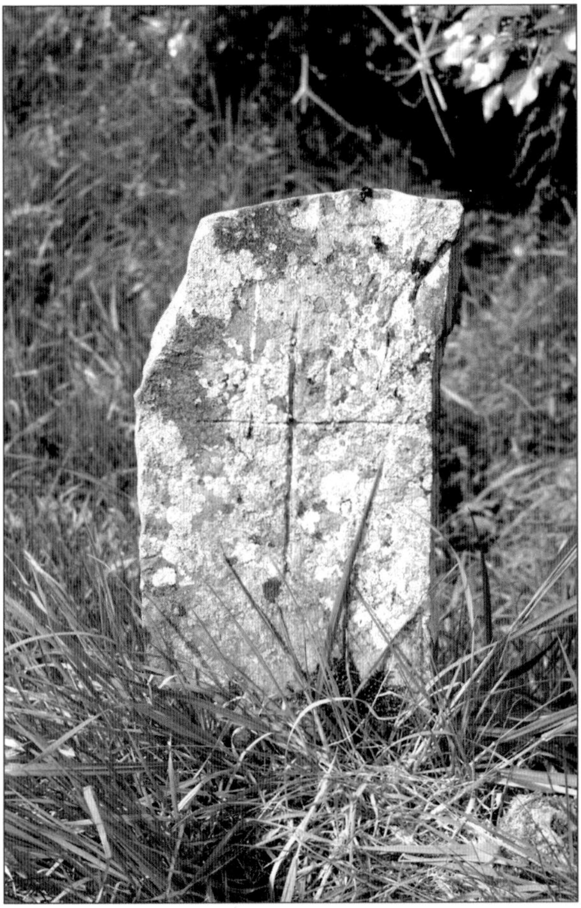

Figure 7

Fig. 7—Field stone with incised cross, Kilmore Old Burial Ground, Co. Down, Ireland.

MEMORIAL FORMS

The great variety of gravemarker designs is reflected in the fact that Burgess lists no less than 32 variants of post-medieval types, excluding non-lithic gravemarkers, such as those in metal, that are not gravestones as such.[18] The classifications of other authors are generally more modest and their taxonomy is rather more generic.[19] From a lettering perspective, we need not be too concerned about the more subtle differences between the various structures, except where these clearly impact on the choice, use or layout of lettering. The most obvious effect that the memorial design can have on lettering is the size and shape of the area available on the monument for the inscription (Fig. 8). This is determined by the relative importance that the sculptor, mason or client places on the shape and size of the monument itself, the sculptural details and the text. We see many instances where massive, highly ornate tombstones or other memorials, such as the large, exuberant and expensive monuments erected for and by those who could afford them, have inscriptions restricted to small inconspicuous panels. Conversely, many of the more modest headstones of the seventeenth and early eighteenth centuries are dominated by lettering, at least on one side, sometimes with mortality symbols and other sculpturing confined to the reverse of the stone or, at most, restricted to a smaller area at the top of the main face.

There was usually a contemporary tradition or fashion for a particular form of memorial, although this was not always followed for cost or other reasons. From the Neolithic period field stones, boulders, stone mounds over wedge tombs and chambered cairns marked burial sites. Field stones have been used when a formal memorial could not be afforded, a practice that has persisted even to the present day.[20] Throughout the Christian era some of these often roughly shaped stones were identified as burial markers by an incised cross or, at most, a very simple, often unsophisticated,

Fig. 8—
Memorial forms indicating the areas usually occupied by the inscription.

A: graveslab
B: monumental brass
C: body stone
D: table stone
E: chest tomb
F: bale tomb
G: headstone
H: head and shaft headstone
I: pedestal memorial
J: cross
K: graveboard
L: wall tomb
M: canopy tomb
N: brass plate

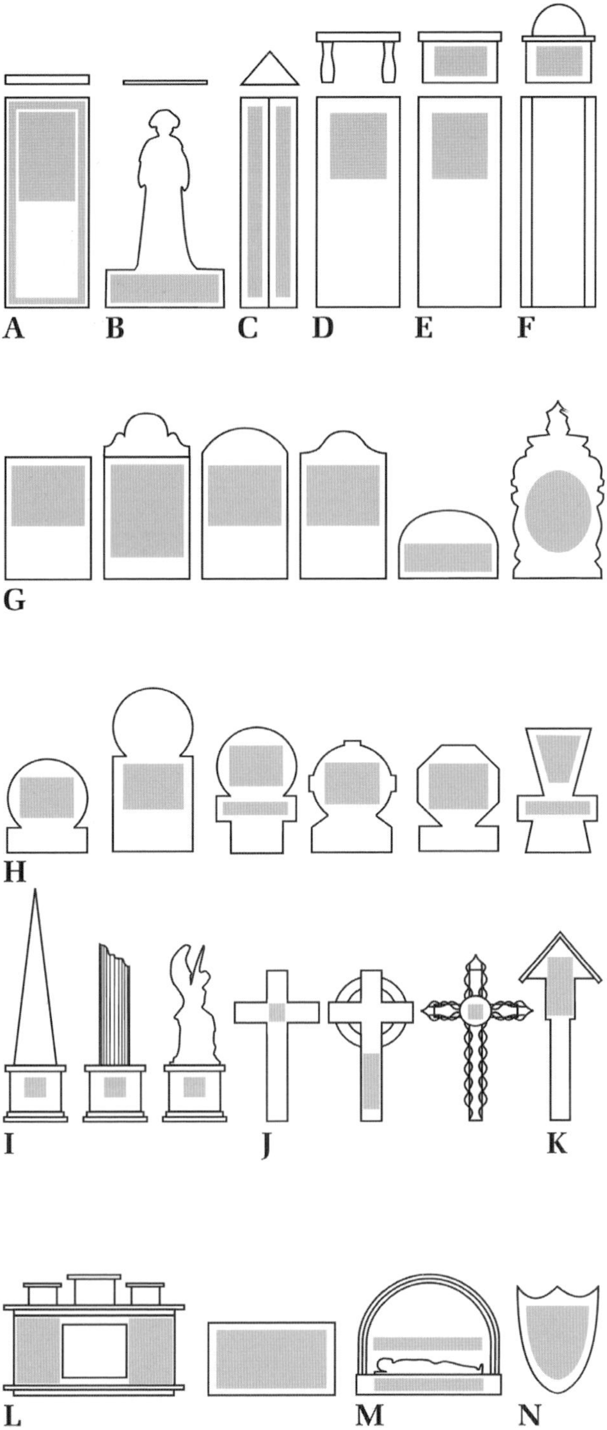

Figure 8

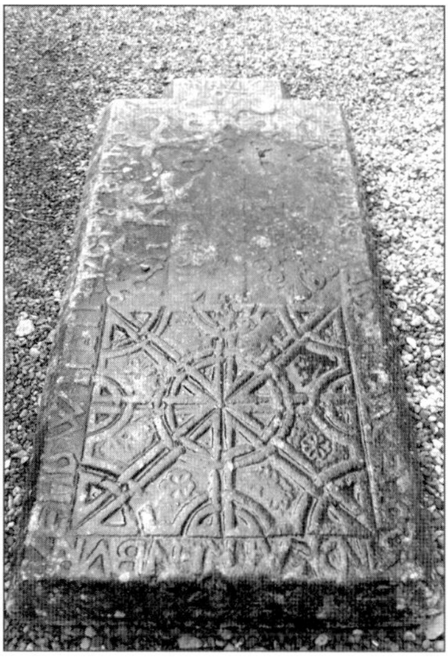

Figure 9

Fig. 9—Graveslab, Athenry Priory, Co. Galway, Ireland (1627).

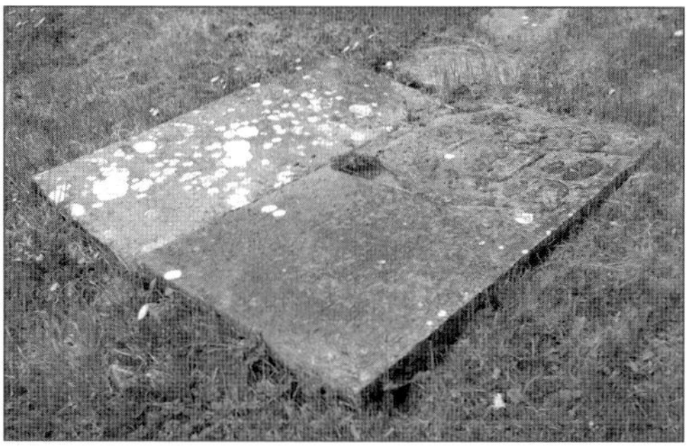

Figure 10

Fig. 10—Ledgers, Ardagh, Co. Longford, Ireland (eighteenth century).

inscription (Fig. 7).

In medieval and early post-medieval western Europe it was the practice to place recumbent memorials over the grave in the form of stone graveslabs or monumental brasses within the church buildings (Fig. 9). The exterior post-medieval forms of stone graveslabs are usually referred to as ledgers (Fig. 10). Graveslabs and some monumental brasses were made large enough to cover the entire grave. Some smaller monumental brasses or plaques were mounted on full-sized stone slabs (Fig. 13). The scale of these memorials provided the masons with an extensive area for both inscription and iconography, and some of the most creative and elaborate designs in the field of funerary art can be found on this type of artefact. The term 'body stone' has been used by different authors for a variety of recumbent gravemarkers, including early simple, narrow stones running the full length of the grave or coped stones between headstones and footstones (Fig. 12). In a more recent form, up to at least the end of the nineteenth century, it is a long, narrow, plain or coped slab, often with lettering running along its full length.

Raised slab memorials include table stones and box or chest tombs. Table stones, flat stones set on four or six pillars, appeared about the middle of the seventeenth century and were used until the nineteenth (Fig. 11). An eighteenth-century variant of the table stone is the chest or box tomb, a large stone casket in which the body of the deceased was deposited, covered by a flat stone slab (Fig. 14). In the Cotswolds region of England a bale tomb is a chest tomb with a richly sculpted, inverted, semi-cylindrical cover, reminiscent of Lycian tombs of the classical era in southern Turkey (Fig. 15).[21]

The predominance of particular memorial forms at different times and in different regions or countries changed markedly from the middle of the

Fig. 11—Table stone, Sweetheart Abbey, Dumfriesshire, Scotland.

Fig. 12—Monumental brass on graveslab, St Andrew's Church, Greystoke, Cumbria, England (1526).

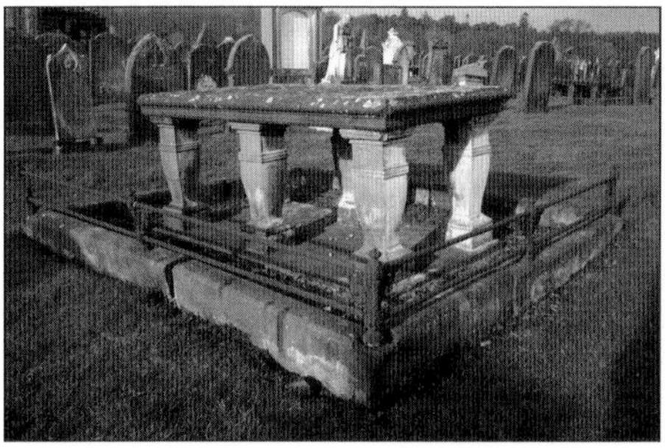

Figure 11

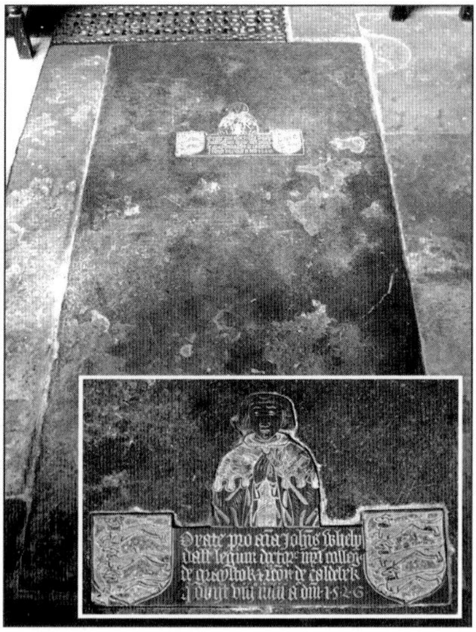

Figure 12

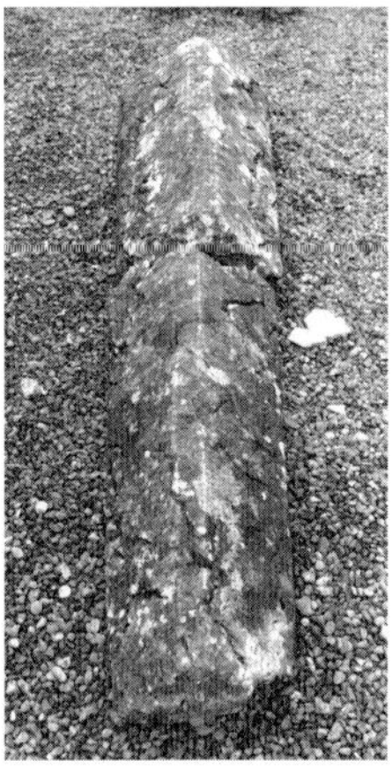

Figure 13

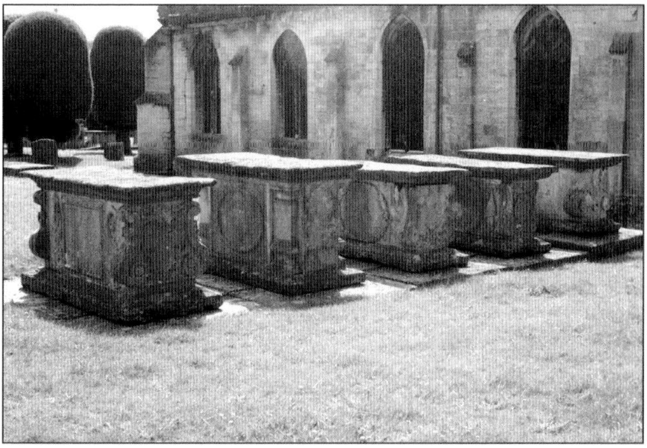

Figure 14

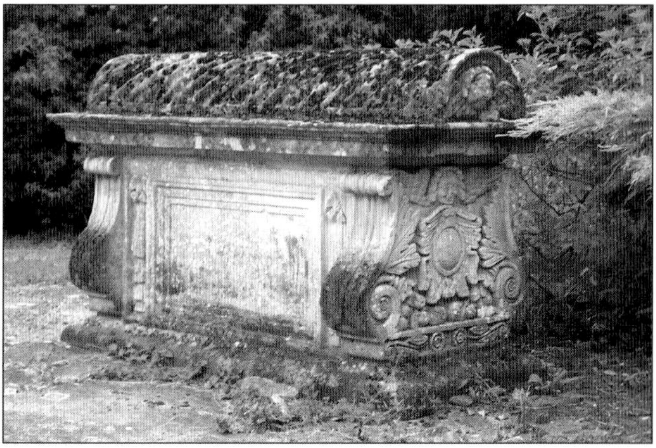

Figure 15

Fig. 13—Body stone, Athenry Priory, Co, Galway, Ireland (date unknown).

Fig. 14—Box tombs, Painswick, Gloucestershire, England.

Fig. 15—Bale tomb, Quennington, Gloucestershire, England.

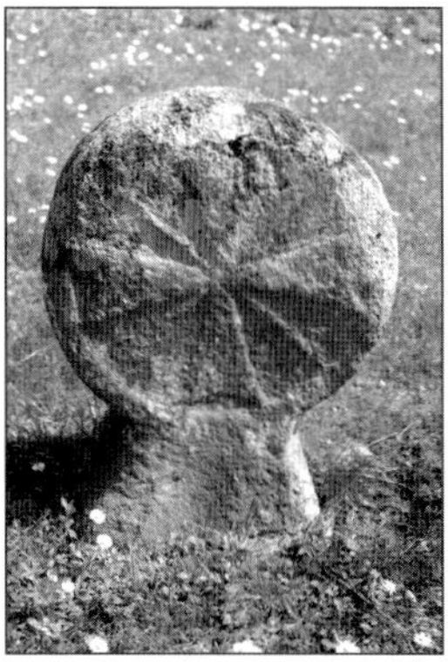

Figure 16

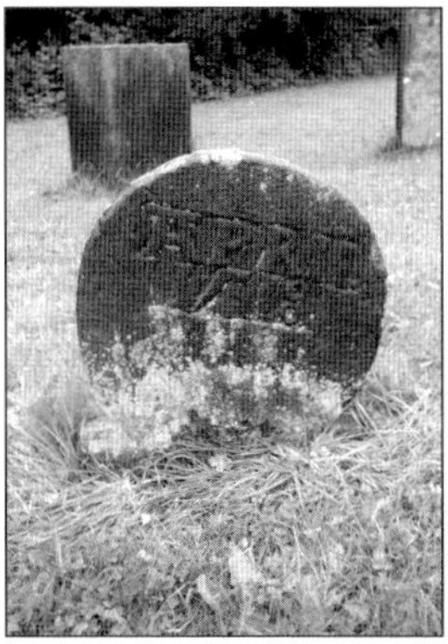

Figure 17

Fig. 16—Discoid gravemarker, Espelette, Pyrénées Atlantique, France (possibly thirteenth century).

Fig. 17—The earliest post-medieval headstone in England, Alstonefield, Staffordshire (1518).

sixteenth century, when the headstone became the dominant funerary memorial. Gravestones, in the form of discoid markers, had been erected from the twelfth century in the Basque Regions of southern France and Spain, and, less commonly, in Portugal, the Luxembourg area of Belgium and England (Fig. 16).[22] A few discoid medieval gravemarkers of a similar form can be found elsewhere.[23] The earliest dated headstone in England is a discoid marker inscribed 'April 1518' at Alstonefield, Staffordshire (Fig. 17). Scottish headstones are said to have made their appearance in the second decade of the seventeenth century, although there is a memorial that was once a headstone set in the wall of Canonbie Churchyard, Dumfriesshire, dated 1593.[24] They became very popular by 1700 in Britain, although, unusually, the slab or table stone remained predominant in the north of Scotland until the end of the eighteenth century. As far as we can tell from the few surviving examples, a similar chronology was followed in the rest of Europe. There is a headstone dated 1576 at Marburg, apparently the earliest in Germany. The earliest date on a New England headstone is 1633 on a rather insignificant and easily overlooked gravemarker at Cambridge, Massachusetts. Annapolis Royal, Nova Scotia, has the oldest Canadian headstone, dated 1720, although this memorial was almost certainly imported from Boston, Massachusetts.[25] Although not yet fully researched, the headstone in Ireland probably dates from the middle of the seventeenth century. The earliest may be a discoid gravemarker at Magheraculmoney, Co. Tyrone, dated 1679. The date on Australia's earliest headstone is 1788. With the notable exception of the impressive headstones in the far north of Germany, the earliest were small and the size increased until we find the largest early in the twentieth century. The headstone is the standard offering from monumental masons today in most of Europe and North America. Rarely is much creative thought now given to the

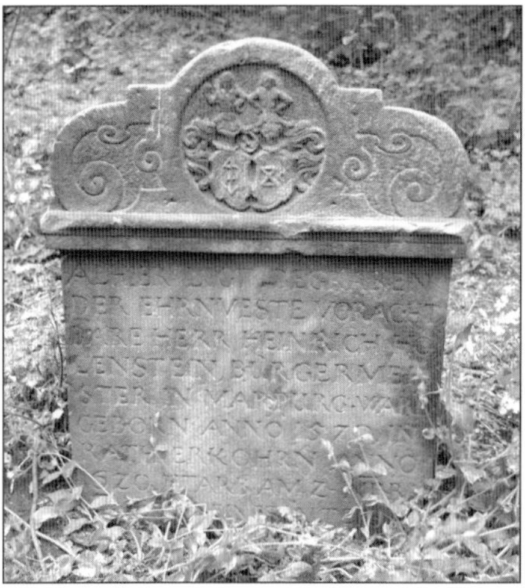

Figure 18

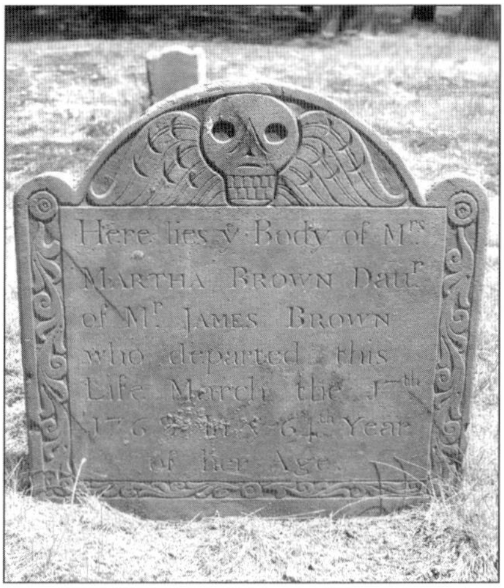

Figure 19

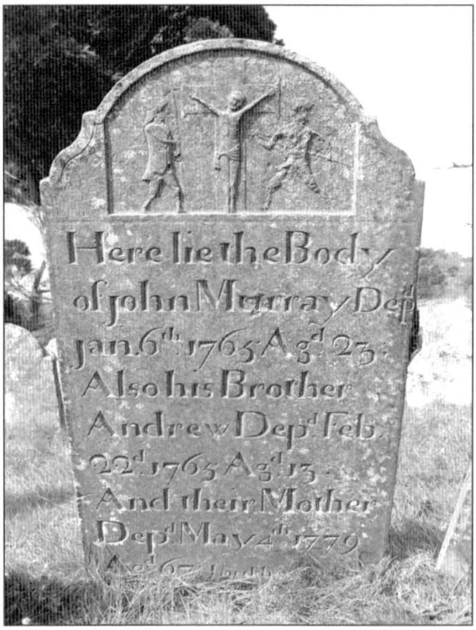

Figure 20

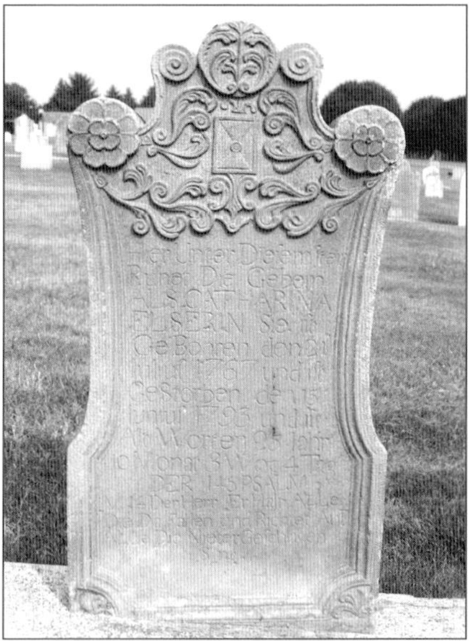

Figure 21

Fig. 18—Headstone, St Michael's Church, Marburg, Hessen, Germany (1620 or later).

Fig. 19—A typical New England headstone, Wellfleet, Massachusetts, USA (1762).

Fig. 20—Pedimented headstone, Glendalough, Co. Wicklow, Ireland (1779).

Fig. 21—German Pennsylvanian headstone, Brickersville, Pennsylvania, USA (1793).

Fig. 22—Painted headstone with background removed, Noordbroek, Groningen Province, Netherlands (1898).

Fig. 23—Anthropomorphic headstone, Huisduinen, North Holland Province, Netherlands (mid-nineteenth century).

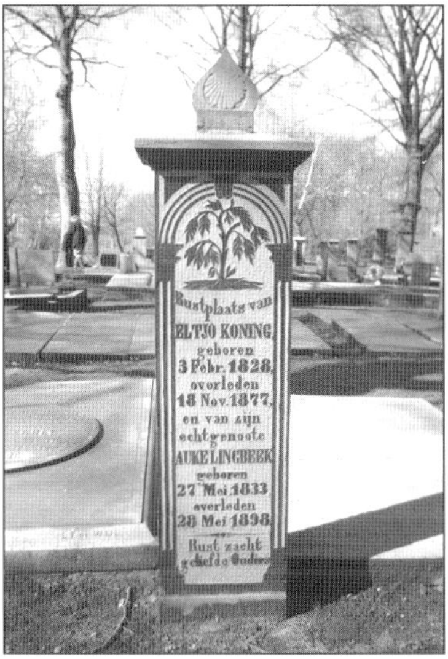

Figure 22

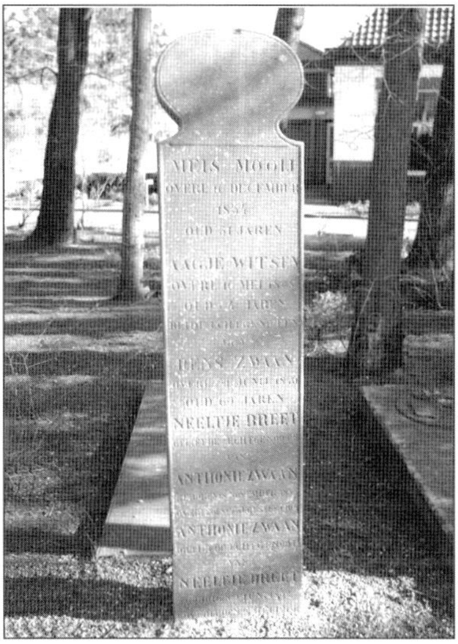

Figure 23

layout or letterform.

Because of their abundance, it is not surprising that headstones have been sculpted in a great diversity of forms, probably more so than any other funerary memorial, from the smallest marker to the large Baroque and Neoclassical vertical monuments. They also afford the most valuable assemblage of inscriptional lettering. The relatively simple rectangular vertical headstone, with or without a shaped pediment, is by far the most common form in much of western Europe, the USA and Canada (Fig. 18). In some Irish counties (Wicklow, Wexford, South Tipperary, Cork and, to a lesser extent, Roscommon) and in north-west Germany (Oldenburgerland and the Friesian Islands) the tympanum is elaborately carved with crucifixion and/or other religious scenes and iconography (Fig. 20).[26] Some other styles are characteristic of geographical regions. The small headstones of New England, especially Massachusetts, are distinctive (Fig. 19).[27] The richly ornamented Baroque-style headstones of the German regions of Hessen and the north Rhineland-Palatinate are also found in Pennsylvania, the memorial design and decoration imported by the immigrants from their homeland (Fig. 21).[28] A local style of tall, narrow, black-painted headstones with the background cut away to leave the dark lettering in relief against the pale grey stone has been used frequently from the end of the nineteenth century in the Groningen Province of the Netherlands (Fig. 22). Interestingly, this technique was also occasionally used in the Basque Region of France. Even slimmer anthropomorphic gravemarkers with a discoid or semi-discoid head are characteristic of headstones in the Province of North Holland (Fig. 23).

Head and shaft gravemarkers comprise a very distinctive group. They include discoid headstones and other markers in which the main part of the memorial surmounts a simple, often rectangular base (Fig. 24). Discoid

Fig. 24—Discoid headstone, Killeevan, Co. Monaghan, Ireland (1747).

Fig. 25—Key memorial, St George Churchyard, Trebuch, Bulgaria (date unknown, before the fourteenth century) (photograph Martin Mitov).

Fig. 26—Key headstone, Desertmartin, Co. Derry, Ireland (1720s).

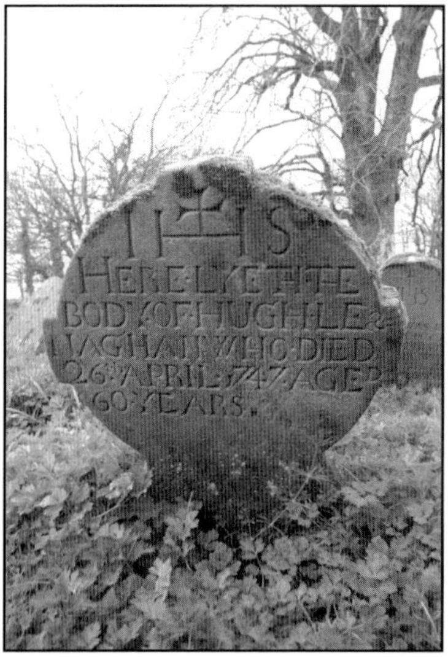

Figure 24

gravemarkers, and the morphologically related discoid wayside markers of Cornwall and Brittany, are culturally important artefacts. The influence on and meaning of memorials of this form have been disputed for some time.[29] One view is that they are anthropomorphic, representing the human figure, and there should be little doubt that this is so in the case of many seventeenth- and eighteenth-century North Holland headstones. Some late eighteenth- and nineteenth-century gravemarkers from Bulgaria are known to represent husband and wife, or male and female, the discoid form being female and a form in which the head is an inverted triangle, referred to as a 'key' memorial, representing the male (Fig. 25).[30] Curiously, this trapezoidal type is found nowhere else in Europe, other than in a few burial grounds in the south of County Derry in Ireland and a medieval fragment in Lowther Church, Cumbria (Fig. 26). Some discoid gravemarkers in North Carolina are also considered to be anthropomorphic.[31] Some authors suggest that they are based on a cross, mainly because of the 'arms' or other cruciform structures that are present on some, but not all, discoid memorials. These appendages can be found on the discoid gravemarkers of West Ulster in Ireland and the discoid markers of Kentucky and North Carolina (Fig. 27).[32] Another view is that the discoid element is a legacy of ancient sun-worshipping cults or simply a fixation with the circle.[33] Discoid markers, even when they have cruciform elements, should not be confused with Celtic crosses, with which they have no evolutionary relationship. It has been demonstrated that the Irish discoid markers have evolved from a distinctive form in County Tyrone.[34] Neither is it easy or justified to consider the discoid markers in isolation from other head and shaft types, including ovoid, hexagonal and other forms to which they are morphologically related.

It could be argued that crosses used as gravemarkers are variants of

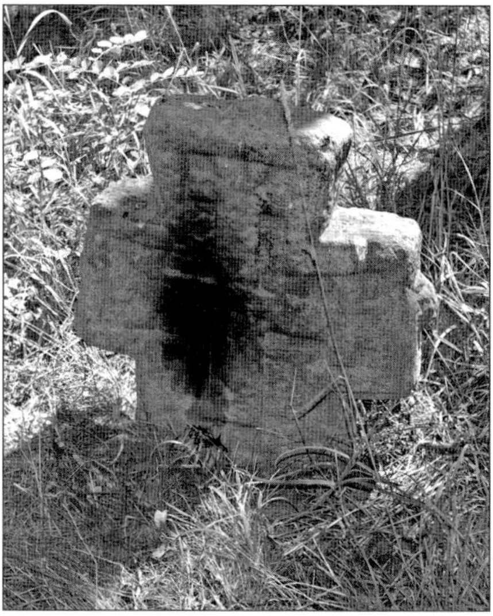

Figure 25

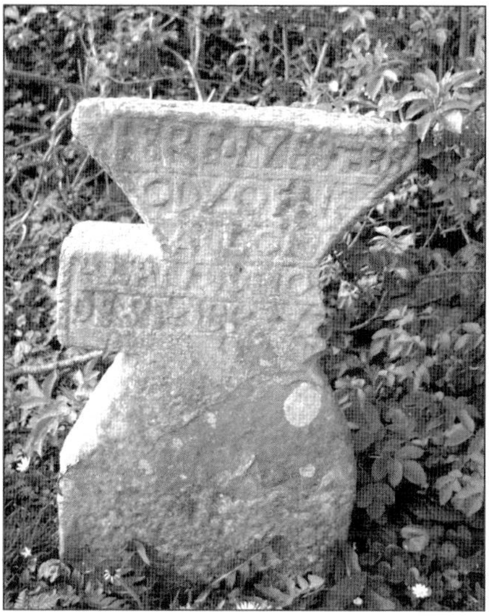

Figure 26

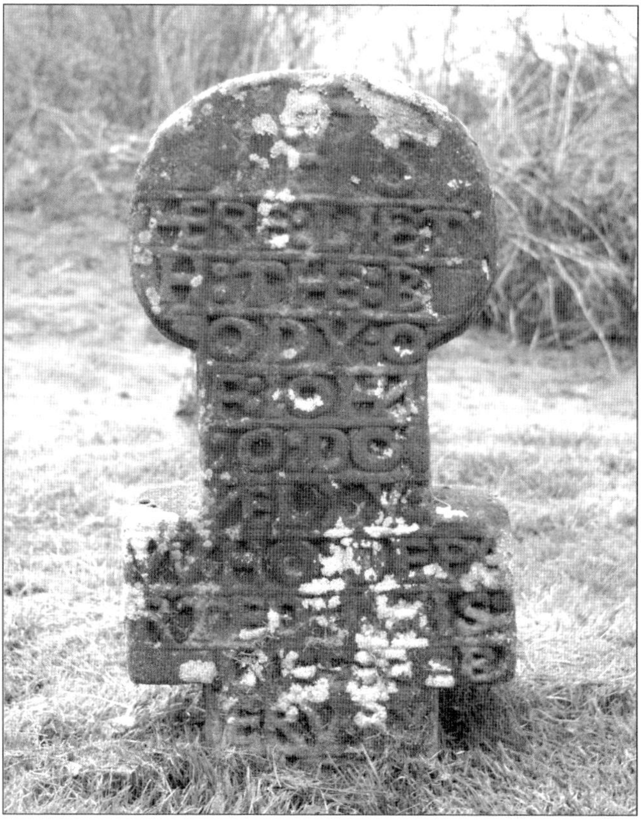

Figure 27

Fig. 27—Discoid gravemarker with 'arms', Ballynascreen, Co. Derry, Ireland (seventeenth–eighteenth century).

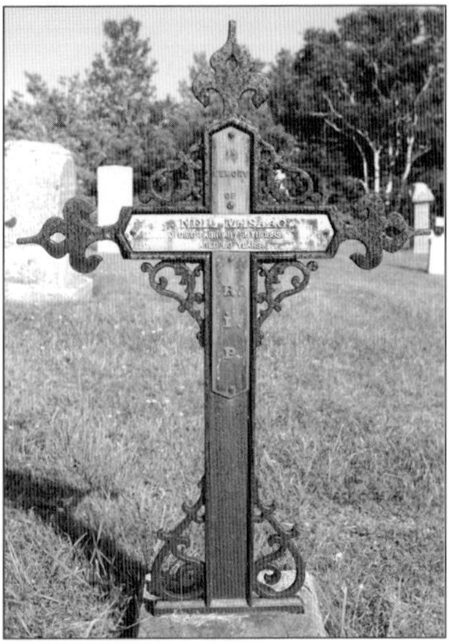

Figure 28

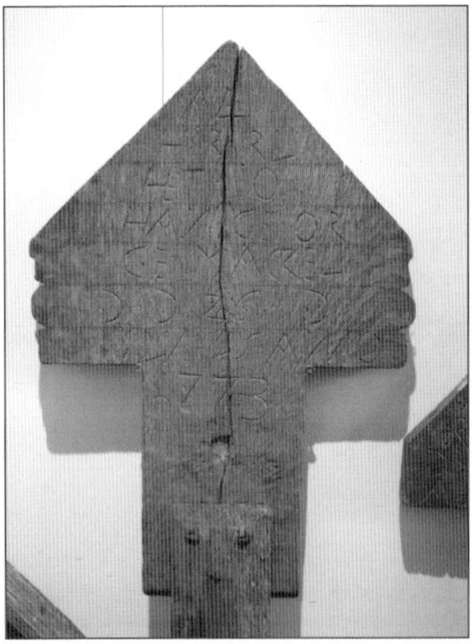

Figure 29

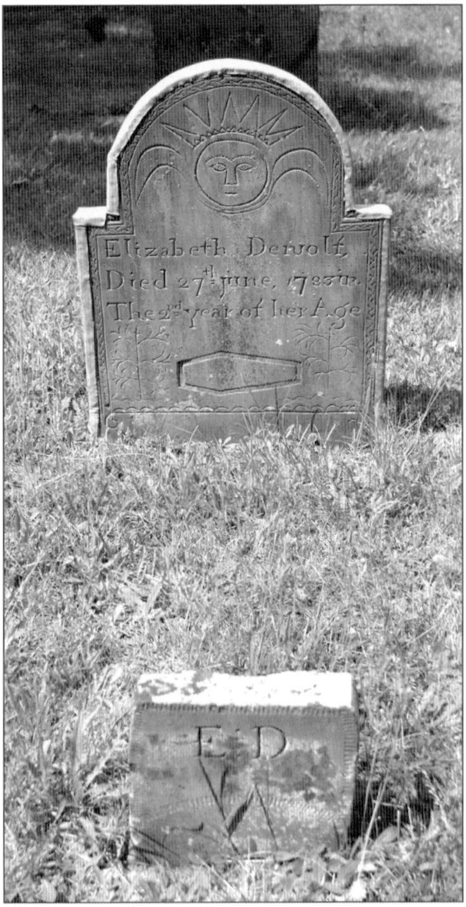

Figure 30

Fig. 28—Cast-iron cross gravemarker, Mabou, Nova Scotia, Canada (1883).

Fig. 29—Wooden gravemarker in the Museum für Sepulkralkultur, Kassel, Hessen, Germany (1773).

Fig. 30—Headstone and footstone, Wolfville, Nova Scotia, Canada (1783).

Fig. 31—Marble memorial in female form, Chebogue, Nova Scotia, Canada (1864).

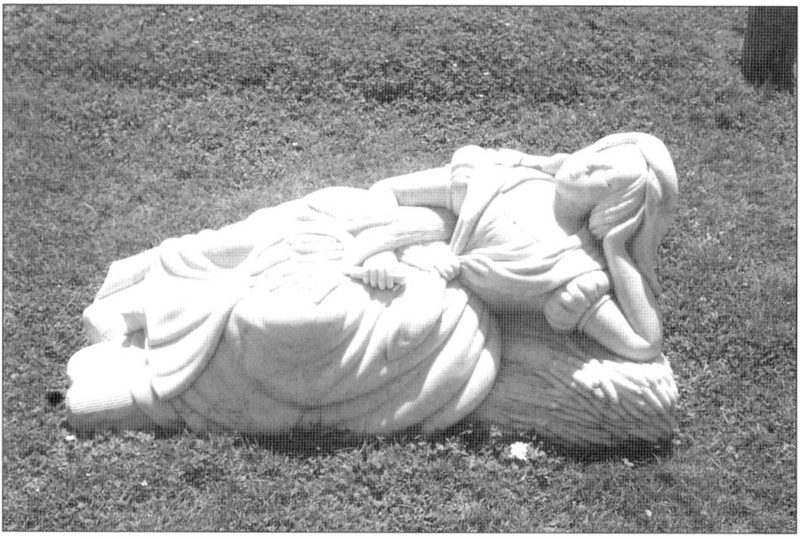

Figure 31

head and shaft memorials, especially when they are in the form of 'ringed' or 'wheel' crosses. The principal concept of crosses is the dominance of the vertical and horizontal arms and not the ring or circle formed in the counters of the cruciform shape. Discoid and cruciform gravemarkers are not functionally synonymous with wayside crosses or churchyard crosses that do not mark the site of a burial. In practice, this distinction is not always easy to make, especially when the artefact has been moved from its original site, its provenance is uncertain and it may have been reused as a gravemarker.[35] Metal crosses are common in Roman Catholic burial grounds, especially in Italy, France, south Belgium, Ireland and Nova Scotia (Fig. 28). Although they are mostly nineteenth- and twentieth-century in date, some German examples date from the sixteenth century. They are frequently elaborate and a small plate with the memorial inscription is usually affixed. There is a distinctive group of 61 Protestant iron crosses at Pojo in Finland dating from the very end of the eighteenth century.[36]

Gravemarkers analogous to headstones but made from other materials, especially wood and cast iron, are less common than those made from stone. Neither of these materials withstands the elements for any length of time and relatively few have survived intact. Nevertheless, enough of them have lasted to show that many wooden gravemarkers had very distinctive forms. The inscriptions on some that are protected in German museums have also been preserved (Fig. 29) and a few more recent ones can still be seen in Australia.[37] The very few surviving headboards in Britain and Ireland are of similar form to the headstones in the same regions, as are headboards in North Carolina and Tennessee, other than those accredited to the Native American culture.[38]

The practice of placing a headstone at the top of the grave and a footstone at the bottom was widespread in Europe and America (Fig. 30).

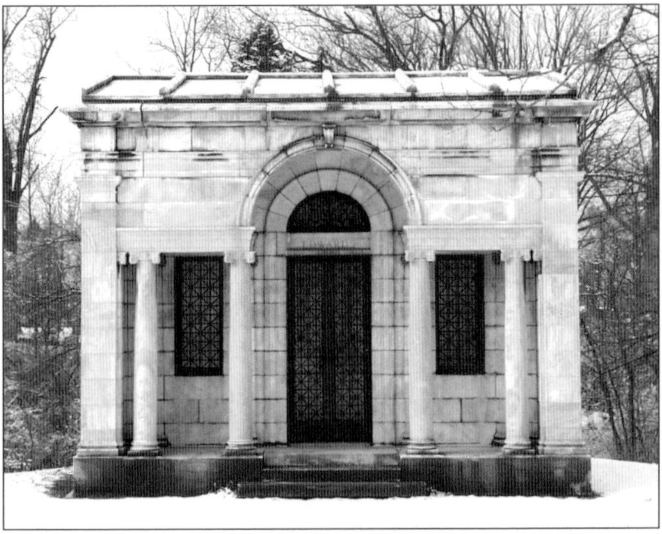

Figure 32

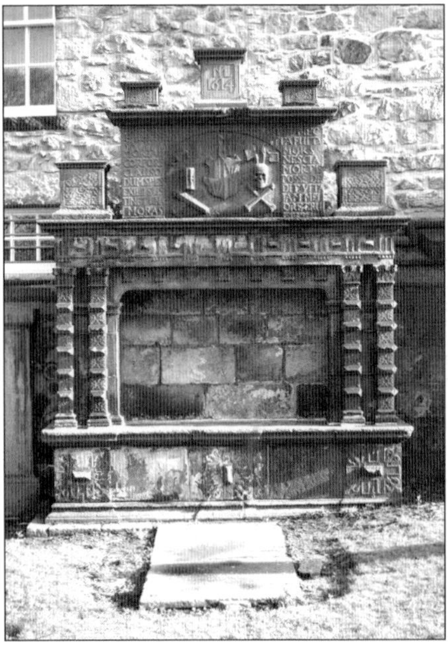

Figure 33

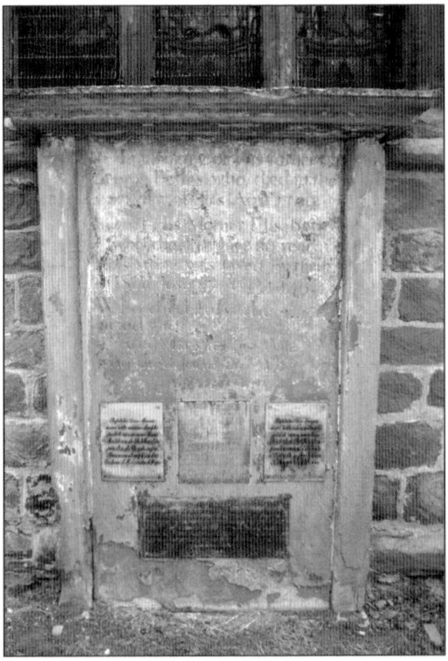

Figure 34

Fig. 32—Architectural mausoleum, Oakwood Cemetery, Syracuse, New York, USA (nineteenth–twentieth century).

Fig. 33—Mural monument in Greyfriers Churchyard, Edinburgh, Scotland.

Fig. 34—Exterior brass plates, Long Marton, Cumbria, England (seventeenth–eighteenth century).

Wooden headboards with footboards are also known to have been erected.[39] A body stone was sometimes placed between the headstone and footstone. Often both the headstone and the footstone are inscribed, the latter usually with initials only and, perhaps, a date.

Post-medieval pedestal gravemarkers are principally a nineteenth- and early twentieth-century phenomenon, most abundant in the Victorian period in England. In France, Spain and Italy they follow a Renaissance or Baroque tradition. Many are nostalgic and include such fantasies as broken columns, obelisks and other sculptural forms inspired by classical models. The most spectacular of these are figurative monuments carved with considerable realism. They are more often female than male (Fig. 31).[40] From a palaeographic perspective, however, these memorials are relatively unimportant as the inscription is usually very much secondary to the sculpture.

Architectural memorials include mausoleums, vaults and American gravehouses.[41] These are burial chambers for one or more individuals. Inscriptions are cut either on memorial plaques or incised directly on the structure. There are massive mausoleums in many large city cemeteries, such as the Oakwood Cemetery, Syracuse, New York State, or the Père-Lachaise Cemetery in Paris (Fig. 32). Although these memorials are often historically important, the cultural significance of the inscriptions is doubtful.

Wall memorials include a diverse range of artefacts. Because of their location, wall memorials do not necessarily mark the exact site of the burial. Strictly speaking, not all of them are gravemarkers. Those that are funerary monuments are functionally related to them and are considered as an integrated element of the same culture. Wall tombs and canopy tombs, often with an effigy, can be found in many medieval cathedrals, abbeys and churches. Mural tablets were also frequently carved at this time. Mural monuments, often sited on the walls of churchyards, were usually erected for and by the aristocracy (Fig. 33). All the wall memorial types provide a rich source of palaeographic material. A quite different form of wall gravemarker is the memorial brass plate, mounted on the interior of the church building or mounted on a headstone, table stone or chest tomb in the churchyard (Fig. 34). Exterior brass plates from before the middle of the nineteenth century are found almost exclusively in England, with a few in Scotland, continental Europe and elsewhere. The lettering on these brass plates has been shown to be an important cultural marker.[42]

There is a spectrum of memorial forms that may or may not fit into one of the above categories. In addition to older forms, some are now produced by monumental masons. These include 'die', an upright headstone on a base; 'slant', a gravemarker of triangular section with the lettered face at about 60 degrees; 'bevel', similar to a slant but with the angle of the lettered face much reduced; and 'kerb set', a stone kerb or surround around the burial plot with a vertical headstone at one end.

Other non-funerary memorials include menhirs or standing stones,

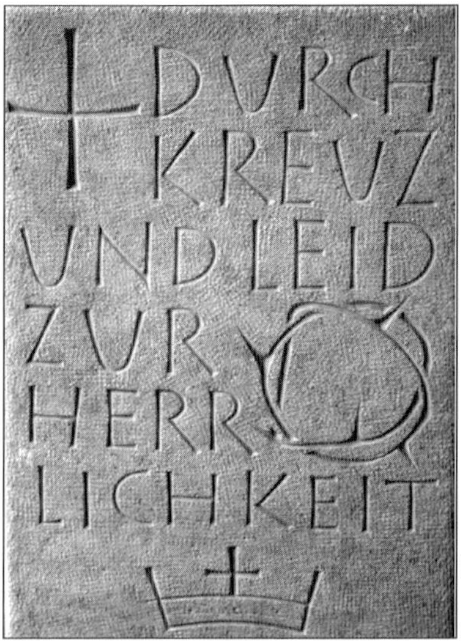

Fig. 35—An example of good modern letter-cutting in stone by Karl Josef Schneider, Museum für Sepulkralkultur, Kassel, Hessen, Germany (1959).

Figure 35

Celtic and churchyard crosses, wayside crosses and lintels. Some of these occasionally have lettering of a style contemporary with that on gravemarkers and each can contribute to an understanding of the other.[43]

Flowers have long been placed on graves or the site of a death, sometimes in the form of an immortelle, a glass dome containing the plants. Gardens of Remembrance at crematoria and the recent trend towards memorial trees, flowerbeds and benches, with little more than simple, industrially produced plaques, do not contribute to or develop lettering craft tradition. They tell us little or nothing about culture at local, regional, national or international level. Occasionally, however, a truly creative sculptural memorial is enhanced with lettering of real quality, and good examples of this can be seen in Germany and elsewhere (Fig. 35).[44]

In 1999 Scott Mindrum established a website called 'Making everlasting memories', to which memorial messages and images could be submitted. The year before, he had patented a video device to be used as a memorial on headstones but had never produced it, in the belief that it would not be viable. This innovative concept in funerary commemoration has been resurrected by Sergio Aguirre in 2004 in the form of 'serenity panels', solar-powered video memorials fixed to headstones or other gravemarkers, that allow the graveside visitor to observe and celebrate the life of the deceased. They are marketed by Vidstone of Miami, Florida. If and when lettering is used on these, its cultural context is more appropriately located in the field of digital typographic history than palaeography *per se*.

A SHORT HISTORY OF LETTERING

Written communication can be traced back to the picture writing of early peoples in the Middle East about 20,000 years ago. Its origins are thought to be pictographs, sometimes referred to as pictograms. This 'picture writing', painted or scratched on cave walls or pebbles, appeared contemporaneously in other parts of the world. It was used by some cultures in North America and Australia until recent times. Through a gradual process of simplification and abstraction, sometime about the fifth millennium BC, pictographs evolved into non-alphabetic scripts. Cuneiform, the earliest surviving form of 'true' writing, dates from about 4,000 BC. It was written by making impressions on clay tablets with the end of a square-sectioned strip of wood or embryonic stylus. Mesopotamia, the land between the Tigris and Euphrates rivers, was the centre of this innovation. There are examples carved in stone and impressed in precious metals, but no pen-written examples are known, although they may have been scribed on perishable material, such as papyrus, and could have been lost through time (Fig. 37).[45]

Egyptian hieroglyphics of the Nile Valley post-date cuneiform by a little less than a thousand years. The ancient Egyptians used two other forms of writing, hieratic for more formal papyri and demotic for other documents, both written with a reed pen or brush. These scripts were particularly important, as they were the first that show the influence of the pen on the letterform.[46] Writing on papyrus with a reed pen cut to a straight chisel-shaped writing tip (the square or broad-edged pen) produced thick and thin lines (Fig. 38). The interplay between inscriptional and written forms was a dynamic relationship that influenced the development of our alphabet through history.

The Semitic cultures of the eastern Mediterranean developed the first truly alphabotic writing. Surviving examples are mostly on papyrus.

ROMAN INSCRIPTIONALS

uncials

VERSAL CAPITALS

Humanist minuscules

Gothic rotunda

Gothic textura

Italic

Copperplate script

SANS-SERIF

Figure 36

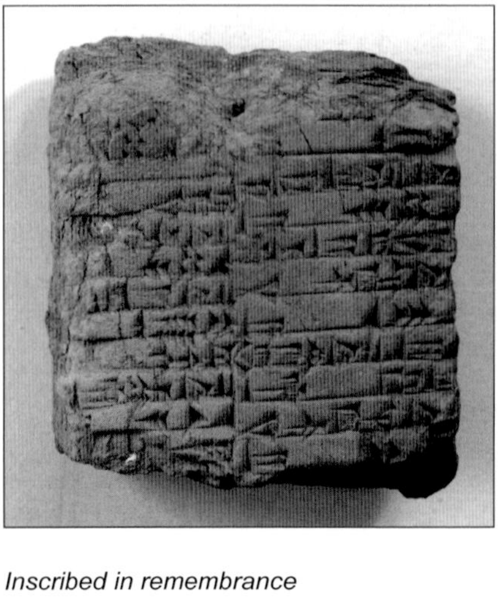

Figure 37

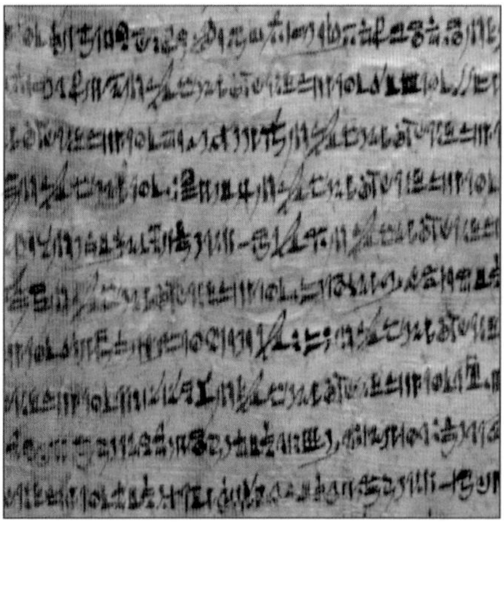

Figure 38

Inscribed in remembrance

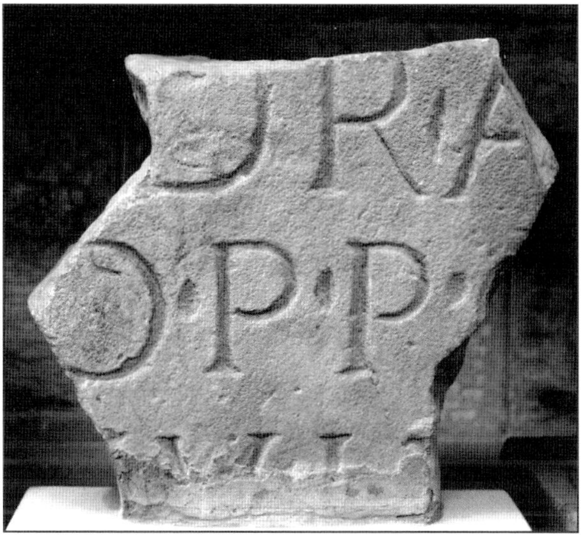

Figure 39

Fig. 36—Some principal historical lettering styles from Roman inscriptional capitals to sans-serif.

Fig. 37—Cuneiform tablet (*c.* 3500 BC) (author's collection).

Fig. 38—Egyptian hieratic writing (*c.* 1000 BC) (author's collection).

Fig. 39—Fragment of dedication slab, Chesters, Northumberland, England (AD 136–161).

There are very few examples of inscriptional forms. It is thought that the Phoenicians brought the north Semitic scripts westwards, to be developed into the alphabetic characters we use today, firstly by the Greeks about the eighth or seventh century BC, and eventually, through Etruscan and Hellenistic forms, by the Romans, about the third century BC.

The Romans introduced vowels that were missing from earlier scripts. They also developed the form of the serif, which had appeared in rudimentary incised archaic Greek lettering, as an important element of inscriptional capitals (Fig. 39).[47] According to Edward Catich, roman inscriptional letters, and in particular serifs, owe much to the use of a brush. He recognised that the roman capitals were first painted before being cut with the chisel.[48] The basic designs of the roman capitals that we use today have changed little from the inscriptional forms that first appeared about the fourth century BC in Italy, although they did not reach maturity until two or three hundred years later. While the majority of Roman inscriptions were incised on stone, letters cut from sheet bronze, probably gilded, were also used. Sockets, into which the letters were fixed, can be seen on the Arch of Titus in Rome. Like the Egyptians, the Romans used several scripts. In addition to inscriptional capitals, which can be seen in museums and archaeological sites throughout Europe and the Middle East, they used square and rustic forms. The square capital was a more regularly proportioned version of the inscriptional capitals, and pen-written versions on papyrus have survived. The truly calligraphic rustic capitals, written with a broad-edged pen or brush, were also occasionally cut in stone. The Romans used cursive writing in almost unrecognisable variants of the inscriptional capitals for informal documents and letters. This was written with a metal stylus on wax or a rather crude metal point or nib with ink on papyrus.

Inscriptions on buildings were important as elements of Mesopotamian, Egyptian and classical Roman cultures. They were usually integral to the structures. The Romans erected stelae or mural monuments with formal memorial inscriptions to commemorate the achievements of Caesars and generals. They inscribed epitaphs to the dead on the walls of catacombs and on stone gravemarkers. The use of stone-cut lettering was widespread throughout the Middle and Near East up to the end of the fifth century AD. The Early Christian era heralded a decline in the use of mural inscriptions. Incised lettering did not entirely disappear and it continued to be used, more so in Italy than elsewhere, as well as being applied to a range of artefacts, including memorials and Christian crosses.

Sometime before the end of the Roman Empire with the fall of Constantinople in AD 751, and probably as early as the fifth century, uncials emerged as a new style of writing. This is a manuscript form that was the beginning of a development that led to our lower-case or small letters, with embryonic ascenders and descenders on letters such as d and p. It origins are uncertain. In the fifth century the uncial letterform was brought to the far west of Europe and the Celtic regions, where it reached its peak with the great illuminated manuscript books, including the Book of Kells and the Lindisfarne Gospels, written with a goose-quill pen on a type of parchment called vellum, made from calfskin. Variants of uncial lettering, often of hybrid character, were used on graveslabs and crosses. These are often closer to another contemporary style called versal, a beautiful form that has an entices or tapering of the vertical lines, bulging curves and long, thin serifs. The lettering on these artefacts is often referred to by the inappropriate term 'Lombardic'. There was a short period of experimentation from the tenth to the twelfth century, especially in Romanesque Spain and France, when new forms appeared that were quite different from other contemporary scripts.[49]

Carolingian minuscules (named after the Emperor Charlemagne) of the eighth and ninth centuries represent the first script in which the forms, both capital and minuscule or lower-case, are similar to those we use today. It was common practice to use Carolingian capitals, variants of roman capitals, as initial letters. A later expression of this minuscule form in the fifteenth century is referred to as 'humanist'. A number of convergent factors in the thirteenth and fourteenth centuries, including economic conditions (the shortage of parchment) and other medieval influences, such as architectural style, led to the development of rotunda, textura (gothic 'black letter') and other gothic forms that were adopted and used for three centuries in all but the far south of Europe. The width of letters was gradually reduced, as more words could be compressed into each line. The characters also acquired a more angular form, echoing the pointed arches of medieval churches. Cursive scripts, based on gothic forms, were written up to the early nineteenth century, either as 'court' or 'secretary' hands, used mainly on legal and business documents. When Johannes Gutenberg developed printing using movable type about 1450, his first

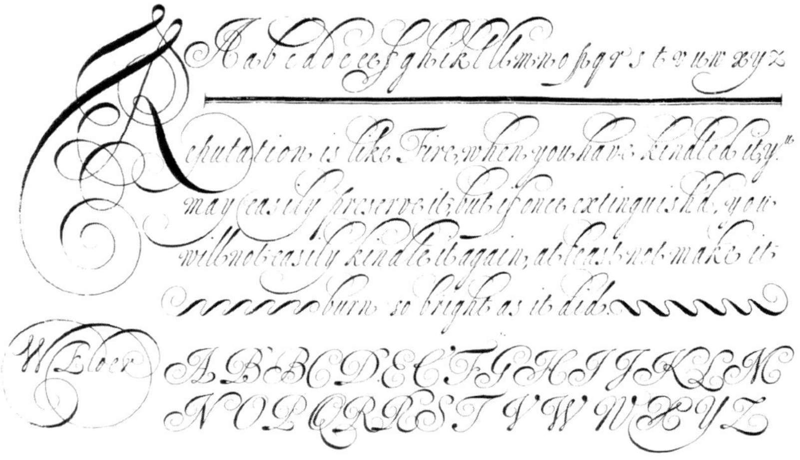

figure 40

Fig. 40—Copperplate writing from *The modish penman* by William Elder (*c.* 1691) (author's collection).

book, the 42-line Bible, used a type form based on the gothic textura.

Although lettering was frequently inscribed on gothic buildings, especially cathedrals and abbeys, the Renaissance saw an increase in the use of architectural lettering, mostly on civic structures but also on domestic buildings in the south of France and northern Spain, and carved or painted on wood-built houses in Germany, Switzerland, Austria and Flanders. By the middle of the seventeenth century the most widespread use of inscriptional lettering was on gravemarkers.

In Italy, the Carolingian minuscule was not abandoned. By the later fifteenth century this humanist script had become more cursive, written freely rather than constructed with a series of separate pen strokes. This new 'italic' writing style was used in the Renaissance writing books of the three Italian writing masters Ludovico Arrighi, Giovanantonio Tagliente and Giovanbattista Palatino. For those who could afford them, these manuals or copybooks encouraged and supported the spread of handwriting, which had largely been the preserve of scribes and monks. From the seventeenth to the nineteenth century, many copybooks were produced. The manuals in German proposed the use of gothic forms. Those in France, Britain and the USA suggested a variety of running script hands. The early copybooks were printed from wood engravings, copied from handwritten originals, and the later ones from engravings on copper, giving the term 'copperplate' to some of the florid styles of writing that evolved. Gradually, the engraver through his skill strongly influenced the letterforms. The engraving tool works very differently from the quill pen. The writer had to cut the quill to a sharp, flexible point so that the samples in the writing manuals, with their flourishes and idiosyncratic thicks, thins and blobs, could be copied accurately. Penmanship had a high profile in society and the copybook cursives were used on silver and gold artefacts,

Fig. 41—Title-page of Fry's type specimen-book (1828) (author's collection).

Fig. 42—Display typefaces similar to lettering on nineteenth-century gravemarkers.

Fig. 43—An illustration from Butterfield's *Instrumenta ecclesiastica* (1847).

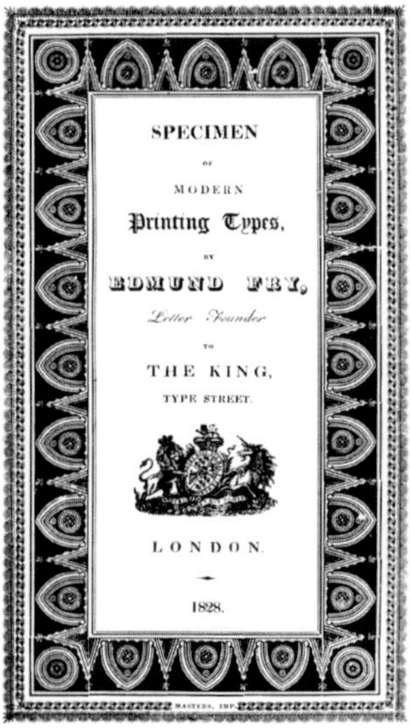

SPECIMEN

OF

MODERN

Printing Types,

BY

EDMUND FRY,

Letter Founder

TO

THE KING,

TYPE STREET.

LONDON.

1828.

Figure 41

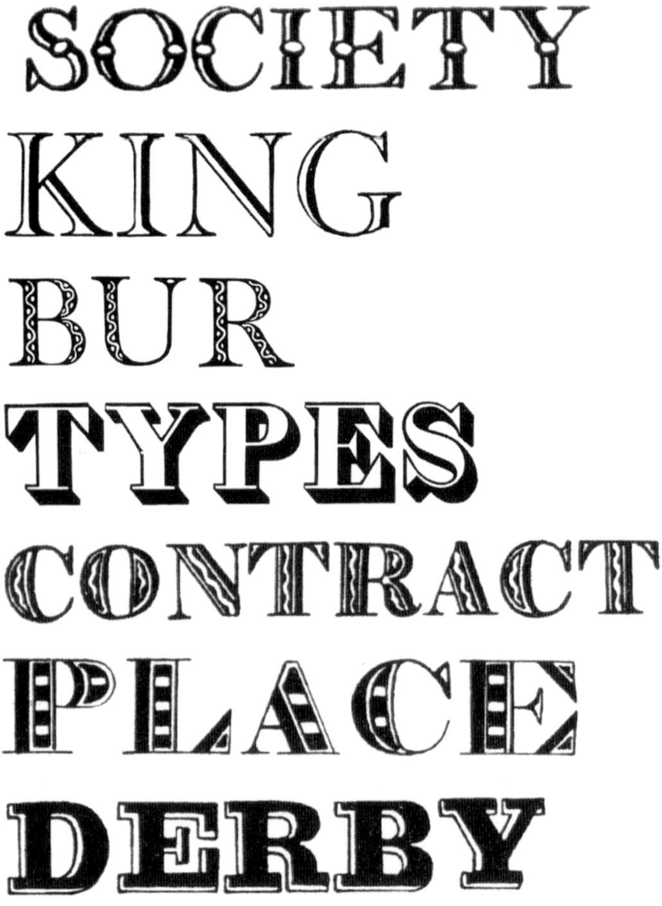

Figure 42

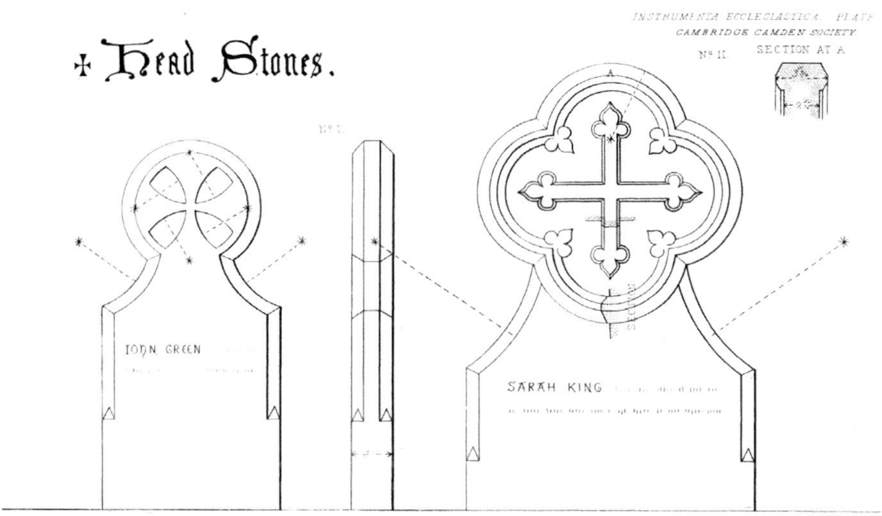

Figure 43

as well as in embroidery and on stone.[50] No longer did the letterforms emanate from the technical qualities of the pen or the kinaesthetics of its use. While there is no doubting the skill of many of the writing masters such as George Bickham, William Elder and Edward Cocker, arguably, by the middle of the nineteenth century, writing had lost character, form and legibility (Fig. 40).

The Renaissance that followed the Middle Ages and inspired new learning throughout Europe was consolidated. By the end of the eighteenth century, the printing legacy of Gutenberg had flourished. The rate at which books were being published rose dramatically and they were becoming more affordable. An increasing number of typefaces were being cut and used, especially so-called decorative 'display faces' (Fig. 42). In Britain, Ireland, the USA and Canada by the middle of the nineteenth century masons were taking advantage of the variety of designs available to printers. From at least as early as the beginning of the nineteenth century these often-florid typefaces were advertised through type manuals, specimen-books and sample sheets (Fig. 43). The letter-cutters utilised the typefaces in these books, modifying them with great skill and dexterity for their purposes on gravemarkers. They also used memorial design manuals and books, very few of which have survived. A work that is known to have been used extensively is that by Butterfield, published in 1847, usually referred to as *Instrumenta ecclesiastica*, which also included designs for other religious artefacts (Fig. 43).[51] Mixing letter styles, often inappropriately, was characteristic of that period. To some extent, the spirit and individuality that was so characteristic of the previous two decades was diluted by this over-reliance on type forms. The masons' exuberance was not embraced to the same extent in continental Europe, where the approach to gravemarker lettering at that time was more restrained and based on tradition. Art

Fig. 44—Art Nouveau lettering on a headstone, Varel cemetery, Oldenburgerland, Germany (1912).

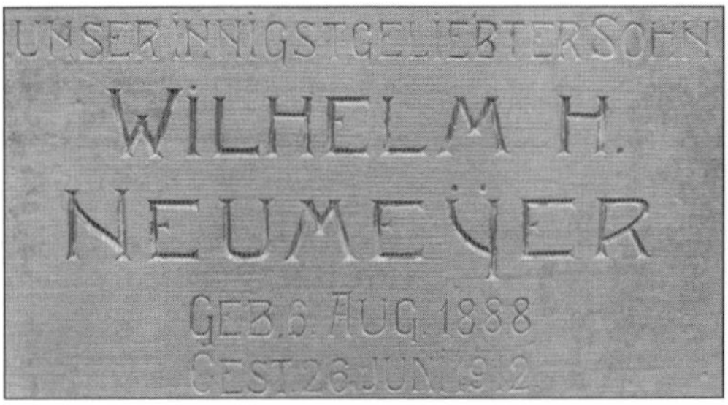

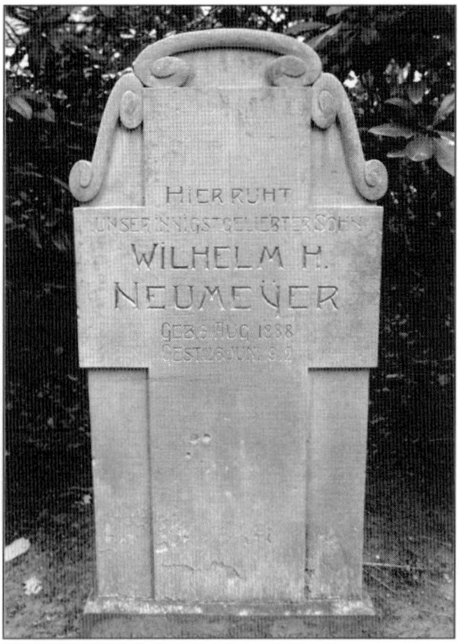

Figure 44

Nouveau lettering, frequently used in printed matter, was occasionally modified for use on early twentieth-century German gravemarkers, but rarely elsewhere (Fig. 44).

The influence of the German Bauhaus, established in Weimar in 1919, encouraged designers in all fields to reconsider the principles on which they based their ideas, suggesting that form should be determined by the function of the product.[52] While the edicts and influences of the Bauhaus changed the future path of type design and other visual arts, the extent to which they influenced gravemarker lettering, even in Germany, is unclear. Nevertheless, from the beginning of the 1930s in Britain, Ireland, the USA and Canada, the extensive use of mixed styles based on Victorian typefaces virtually ended and lettering used on most headstones was a simple, incised sans-serif or roman form, often infilled with lead. The post-war period in Britain and Ireland, and to a lesser extent in the USA and Canada, heralded an even more sober approach to gravemarker design. Most memorials became very modest artefacts. Many British, American and Canadian civic authorities imposed regulations on the size, design and material of memorials in cemeteries, based on practicality rather than aesthetics. Even on more elaborate gravemarkers, lettering was relegated to typeface designs or characterless inscriptional forms, some of which had become almost a masons' cliché.

THE INSCRIPTIONAL PERSPECTIVE

The influence that inscriptional lettering has had on the development of our alphabet and on the design of the lettering styles that we use today in print, electronic media and elsewhere cannot be overestimated. Although we are concerned here with memorials in the Latin alphabet, some aspects of archaic Greek letter-cutting deserve attention. Early Greek inscriptions are monolinear. Any variation in line width is due more to chance than intention. It is possible that the embryonic serifs, already cited, represent the beginnings of their development that reaches its height with the roman capitals. It is unlikely, however, that the Romans were aware of the Greek models. There is no material evidence of serifs on Greek letters in the intervening period until much more recent times.[53] The strict geometry of archaic Greek inscriptions is further expressed in some that are arranged in a layout called *stocheidon*, in which the letters are aligned both vertically and horizontally. Dots or lines as word separators appear in early Greek memorials and other inscriptions, a practice that was adopted by the Romans and later seen on medieval and post-medieval gravemarkers.

The development of the roman inscriptional capitals had the most profound and long-lasting effect on our alphabet's historical development. It was the foundation of all subsequent lettering and writing styles that use the Latin alphabet and a form that was utilised in print, inscribed in stone and carved in wood for over 2,000 years. Classical Roman inscriptions were incised and never cut as relief letters (Fig. 45). In the most refined form, the C, O, D, M, N and G are round and wide. Other letters, including B, E, P, R and S, are narrow. The A occasionally has a horizontal line on top and the crossbar is sometimes in the form of an inverted V. The central V of the M reaches the baseline. The letter proportions are determined by aesthetic judgement and not by geometric construct. The Romans erected inscribed stone memorials, both funerary and dedicatory. Epitaphs usually began

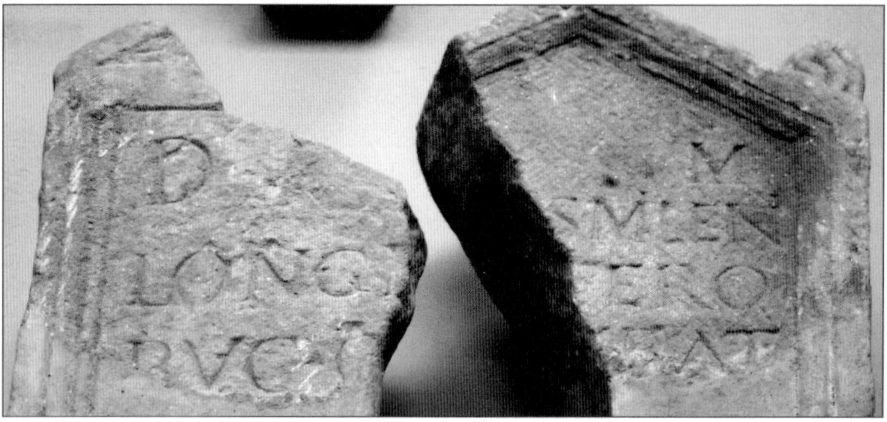

Figure 45

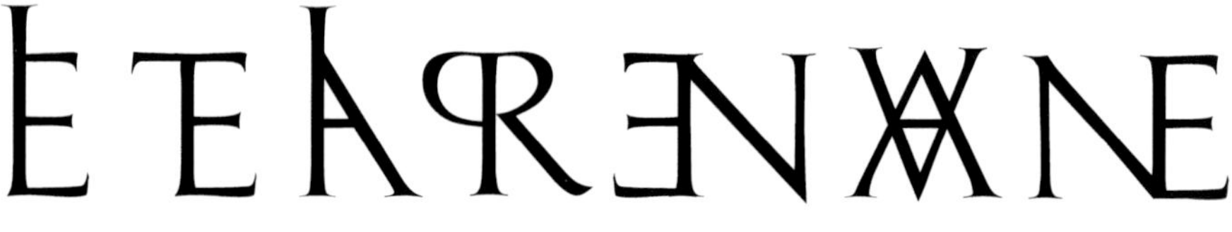

Figure 46

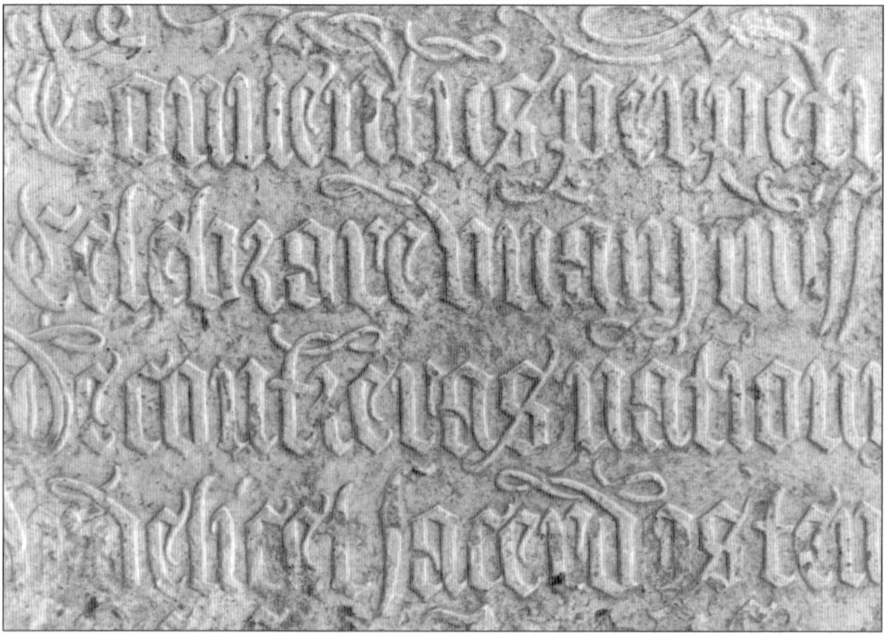

Figure 47

Fig. 45—Roman inscriptions on two tombstone fragments, Chesters, Northumberland, England (first–fourth century AD).

Fig. 46—Some ligatures used in Roman inscriptions.

Fig. 47—Medieval gothic inscription, Brugge, Belgium (probably fourteenth century).

with DM, an abbreviation of DIS MANIBUS ('to the spirit of the dead'). They used local stone and, as the empire spread from the Middle East and North Africa to the western fringes of mainland Britain, the available material included marbles, slates, limestones and sandstones. Although marbles and harder limestones were conducive to fine letter-cutting, the grainier sandstones were not. In consequence, the quality of surviving inscriptions varies widely, determined by the suitability of the stone, the skill of the mason and the extent to which they have been eroded by wind, rain and pollution.

The significance of the Trajan inscription in Rome, cut in AD 114, as the archetypal example of roman capitals tends to distract our attention from the many memorial inscriptions, cut in the first five centuries of the Christian era, that exhibit an extensive range of interpretations of the basic style. The inventiveness of some masons who cut them is apparent in the lettering on many gravemarkers of the fifth to ninth centuries. We see variation in letter proportion and letters that are at considerable variance from the classic model. In both formal and more vernacular provincial memorial inscriptions, the use of ligatures was fairly common and frequently novel (Fig. 46). Sometimes letters were mirrored, apparently to make a more interesting combined character. There are inscriptions where letter height was increased or letter size reduced, occasionally by half, to make the letters fit more effectively. Letters were sometimes placed within other letters. We find these practices reappearing in post-medieval gravemarker inscriptions.

Variants of the roman capitals were incised for many centuries after the Roman Empire was extinguished. There were several evolutionary developments, some subtle, some more substantial. Most of the inscriptions that survive from the five centuries following the Roman period are in southern Europe, however, especially Italy, Spain and the south of France, although some examples can be seen at least as far north as Germany. A few inscriptions in variants of roman capitals were cut in England. Although inscriptional lettering in the fourth to sixth centuries was in decline, there are many early Christian epitaphs, including those in the Catacombs, Rome. These detail the name of the deceased, the month and day but, curiously, not the year. They often include the words *in pace*, *bene meriti* or *hic requiescit*. The varied inscriptions in roman lettering and its derivatives from the end of the fourth century until the so-called Carolingian Renaissance in the ninth are often crudely cut, usually with far less skill than many of their classical predecessors. Many are epitaphs and are always in capitals. Most palaeographers and art historians dismiss the aesthetic value of this lettering as naïve or rustic.[54] Nevertheless, although they are often unquestionably poorly crafted, they exhibit a great creativity and innovation that are often missing in more formal inscriptions.

The Romans never conquered Ireland, so their influence on lettering was negligible there. Much surviving stone-cut lettering from the fifth to the eleventh centuries in Ireland, Scotland, Wales and some of the

Fig. 48—The round 'Gothic' capital, often called 'Lombardic'.

Fig. 49—Uncio-versal, Clonmacnoise, Co. Offaly, Ireland (eighth–twelfth century).

Fig. 50—Raised archaic roman, Annan Old Burial Ground, Dumfriesshire, Scotland (1720).

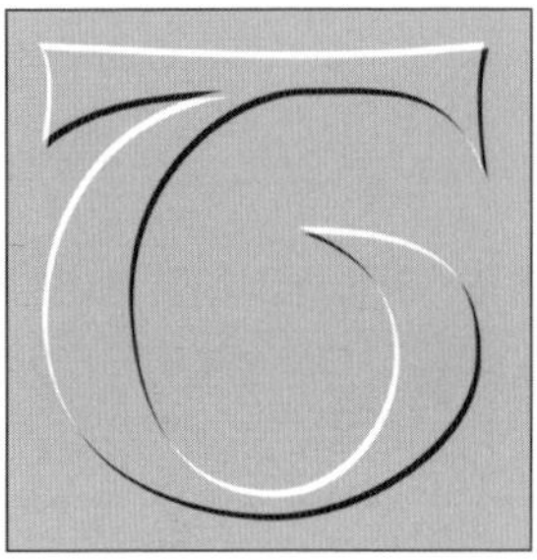

Figure 48

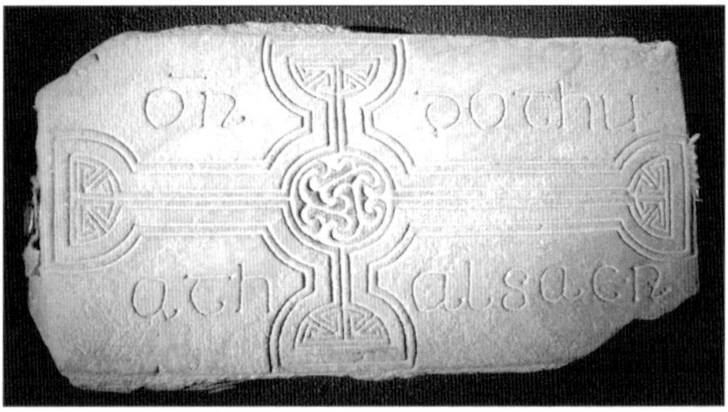

Figure 49

western counties of England is on crosses and in a form adopted by the Celts intermediate between uncial and versal. The letters were almost invariably in relief. There are two inscriptions, one relief, the other incised, in the collection of the National Museum of Scotland, Edinburgh, in a letterform similar to that in the incipit pages of the Book of Kells and the Lindisfarne Gospels. This distinctive and very geometric form, comprised entirely of straight lines, was also used in some French manuscripts. Stone inscriptions of this period, other than in roman or uncio-versal, are extremely rare.

From the twelfth to the early sixteenth century, the predominant inscriptional style in central and western Europe was gothic, appearing in both relief and incised forms. The principal use of gothic lettering was on manuscripts but it was also chosen for memorial plaques on church walls, sepulchral slabs and on other funerary monuments (Fig. 47). In southern Europe roman inscriptions still predominated. Elsewhere, lettering in a form of modified uncials or versals was also used on graveslabs and crosses (Fig. 49). This was the letterform called 'Lombardic' by archaeologists and some palaeographers and the 'Gothic capital' by Nicolette Gray.[55] It was designed to accompany textura and, with its large counters and elegant curves, was most appropriate as the canvas for the illuminator and miniature illustrator of medieval manuscripts (Fig. 48). A similar style became popular with the Victorians in Britain and for a short time afterwards, often infilled or applied as relief lead letters.

In the context of gravemarkers, the sixteenth century is a significant time in the history of inscriptional lettering. The adoption of the post-medieval-style graveslabs and headstones towards the end of the century advanced the use of memorial texts. Europe was split by the Reformation. In some provinces this inhibited the development of funerary memorial design and

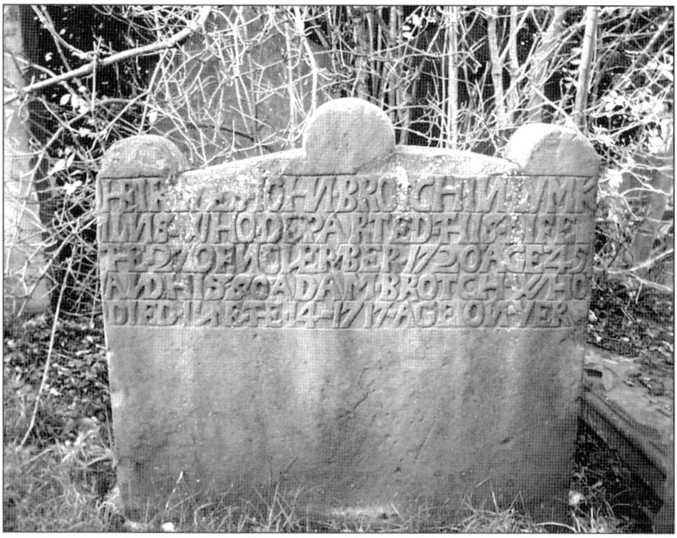

Figure 50

inscription. In others it promoted it. The exponential increase in burials marked by inscribed gravemarkers in the seventeenth century provided masons with the opportunity to utilise their letter-cutting skills and others to satisfy their need to mark the memory of their dead with a cut, painted or even crudely scratched inscription on a stone or wooden gravemarker. It is throughout the sixteenth, seventeenth and eighteenth centuries that we see the flourishing of the letter-cutter's craft, a powerful eruption of creativity in gravemarker inscriptions and the use of letter styles other than roman, including cursives and gothics. This was the heyday of memorial sculpturing and gravemarker lettering in the central and northern parts of western Europe and North America, including Britain, Ireland, France, the USA and Canada. In the post-medieval period, for religious and cultural reasons, the use of lettering on memorials as a vehicle for the letter-cutter's art did not extend to parts of southern and eastern Europe to the same extent. The renaissance in the use of lettering on funerary memorials was not restricted to gravemarkers. Lettering was cut on external and interior structural timbers and on lintels in much of Europe, including Britain and Ireland. Lettering became an important architectural feature.

Inscriptional roman letterforms of the sixteenth and early seventeenth centuries did not blindly follow the classic roman canon. In Spain, Germany, England, Scotland and Ireland we find heavy, relief lettering with rudimentary serifs and changes to some letters and numerals (Fig. 50). In the Basque Region of southern France and north-eastern Spain, some very distinctive roman-based forms were cut on gravemarkers, lintels above doorways and in wood on fireplaces. Whether these were sufficiently distinct to justify the name 'Basque Style', a somewhat exaggerated form designed by typographers in the twentieth century, is debatable. All the forms can be seen either in roman inscriptions or in relief archaic roman

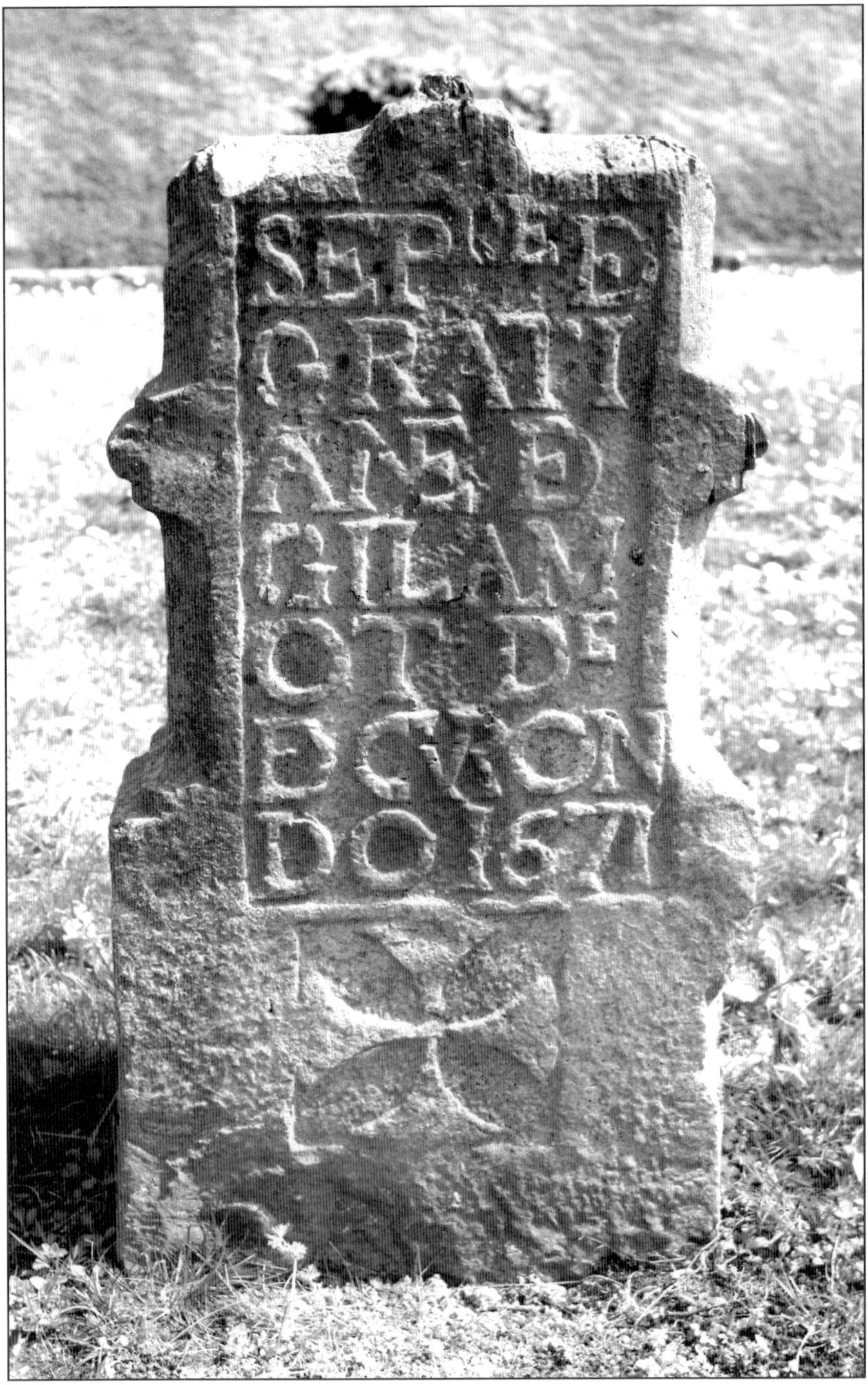

Figure 51

Fig. 51—Basque lettering on *stèle tabulaire*, Espelette, Pyrénées Atlantique, France (1671).

Inscribed in remembrance

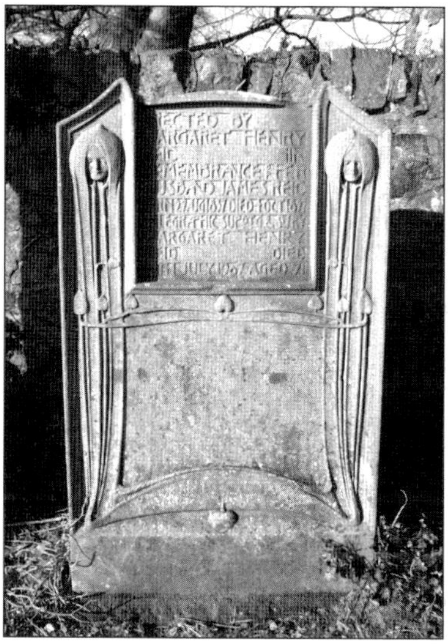

Fig. 52—Headstone designed by Charles Rennie Mackintosh, Kilmacolm, Renfrewshire, Scotland (1905–6).

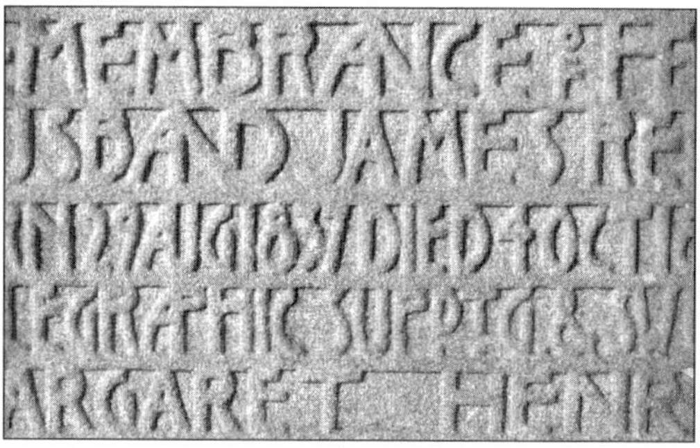

Figure 52

texts elsewhere in Europe.[56] This even includes the capital D with the interjected E that is a very common Basque ligature (Fig. 51).

Later, variations of the roman letterform on gravemarkers were limitless. Masons delighted in modifying the form and imposing their own ideas on the classical model, as well as introducing ligatures, flourishes and other enhancements. But roman was not the only form to be given a creative treatment. Cursive, script and, towards the end of the period, italic lettering contributed to the variety of inscriptions that we see at this time.

All this creativity was to be eclipsed, in part, by the political upheavals of the twentieth century. The use of power tools in the manufacture of gravemarkers and other memorials was established, although lettering was still hand-cut well into the twentieth century. In other design and craft fields, the Arts and Crafts Movement, the Aesthetic Movement and Art Nouveau were intrinsically rich and varied in their approach. Other than in Germany, little influence of these movements can be identified in gravemarker lettering, although a very few memorials in relief lettering in copper and bronze have some elements in common. The Scottish architect/designer Charles Rennie Mackintosh designed several memorials, including two gravestones, one at Kilmacolm, Renfrewshire (1898), and the other at East Wemyss, Fife (1905–6), on which a restrained version of his distinctive lettering was used. It is neither Arts and Crafts nor Art Nouveau, but to some extent borrows from both, especially the use of high and low horizontals on A, F and H. It also incorporates some elements from the past, especially in the use of ligatures, variable letter height and relatively simple basic forms (Fig. 52).[57] Slightly later, art deco was rather more severe, and in Germany Dada and constructivism totally rejected the past. There is little evidence that any of these trends were reflected to any extent in gravemarker inscriptions. In England, Eric Gill suggested a rethink of the craft of letter-cutting and promoted the use of a roman style based on the Trajan inscription. It was taught in almost every art college in Britain, and this roman inscriptional style inevitably found its way onto gravemarkers for some decades in the twentieth century. A similar influence in the USA was that of John Howard Benson from Newport, Rhode Island, who demonstrated great skill in cutting roman gravemarker lettering.

In the second half of the twentieth century, few clients were prepared to pay the cost of a skilled letter-cutter to incise their memorials, resulting in the dominance of the banal sans-serif that was first used with other styles early in the nineteenth century and that, together with a simple roman, became the most commonly used letterform by the 1930s (Fig. 53). The invention of machines that can incise lettering, the adoption of inexpensive shot-blasting using computer-cut stencils and the use of advanced laser engravers have changed the face of the mason's trade. No longer do we find the creative genius of the vernacular carver, the skilfully sculpted memorial inscriptions of the craft mason, or the exuberant lettering of the Victorian headstones. Typefaces, many of which are unsuited to gravemarker inscription, have become the standard lettering palette of the mason. The use of these new technologies should not be an impediment to creativity. It is a great pity that masons have not embraced the challenge and used these advanced techniques as an aid to innovative inscriptional design. The demise of creative gravemarker lettering in both the USA and Canada, where the political and religious environment was different from and the economic situation more favourable than that in Europe, may suggest that there was a change in attitude towards the importance of the inscription and its place in commemoration. Some gravemarker inscriptions are still cut by hand, but the dichotomy between most commercially produced headstones and the work of many highly skilled letter-cutters has never been greater than it is today.[58]

Fig. 53—Typical nineteenth–twentieth-century sans-serif on headstone, St Mary's Church, Dumfries, Dumfriesshire, Scotland (1905–27).

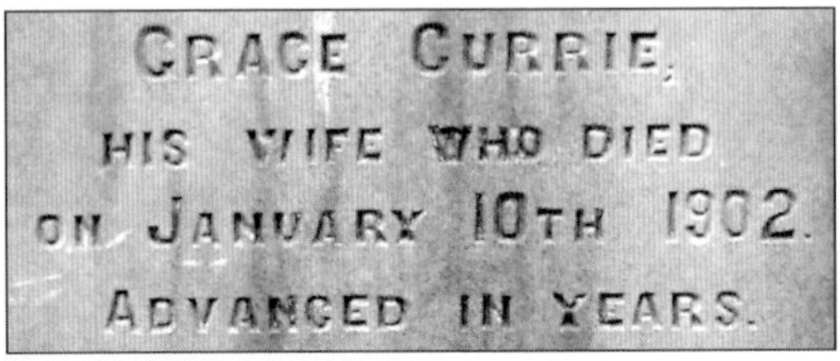

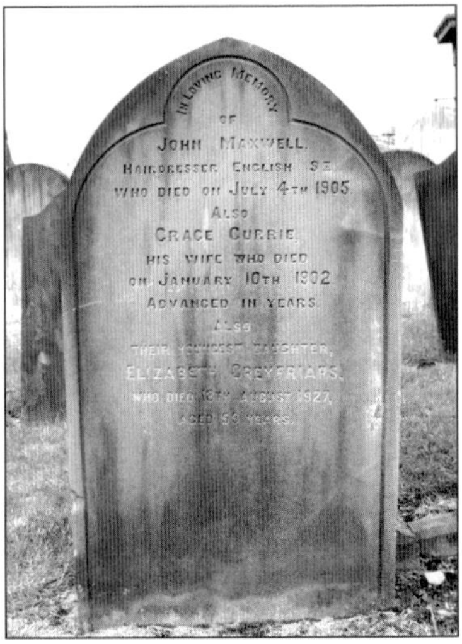

Figure 53

THE MASONS

Tombstones speak volumes about the individuals who fashioned them and cut the inscriptions thereon. The ability of the mason who can shape and inscribe a stone with great skill and dexterity is clear for all to see in his work. The poor work of an untalented, though perhaps well-meaning, handyman is equally apparent. This wide range of masonry skill can be observed in contemporaneous memorials. Little makes an interesting and useful distinction between what she calls 'traditional' and 'commercial' gravemarkers, the former being vernacular and the latter those made by trained, professional masons.[59] Skill differentials can also be seen in gravemarkers from different regions and historical periods. Changes in the organisation of the trade, especially in relation to training and apprenticeships, traditions and technology all played their part in determining standards. In assessing the skill with which a memorial or its inscription has been made we must make some allowances for the extent to which the artefact has deteriorated through exposure to the atmosphere and other hazards to which tombstones are subject. Inscriptions are particularly vulnerable and it is easy to attribute the blame to poor letter-cutting when, in reality, erosion has been responsible for loss of form. It is significant that stones that had obviously been cut by unskilled individuals generally exhibit the same attributes as those in contemporary formal skilled mason's monuments in the same district.[60] This is clear evidence of an awareness of stylistic traditions. Local traditions were probably very important.

Master masons have always been held in high regard. They constituted an important part of the Roman legionary force. They built the monasteries, cathedrals and abbeys. They carved memorials, including gravemarkers and inscriptions. In seventeenth- and eighteenth-century Britain, the master masons continued the medieval practice of combining building work with carving.[61] We often find that the mason was also a farmer or

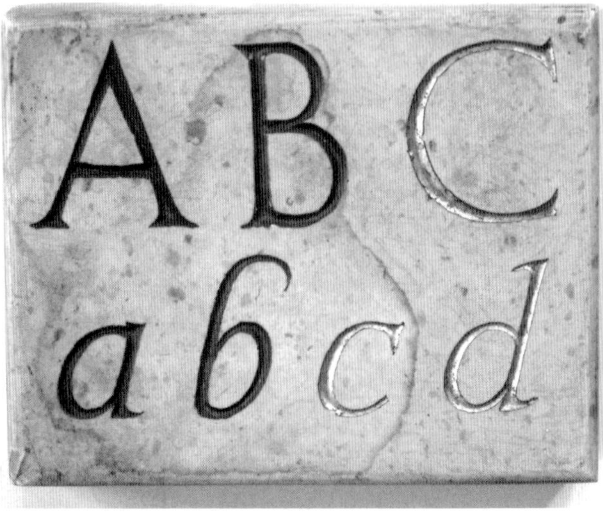

Fig. 54—A trial or sample piece with incised and gilded lettering on marble, probably made by John Coles of Thrapston, Northamptonshire, England (eighteenth century) (author's collection).

Figure 54

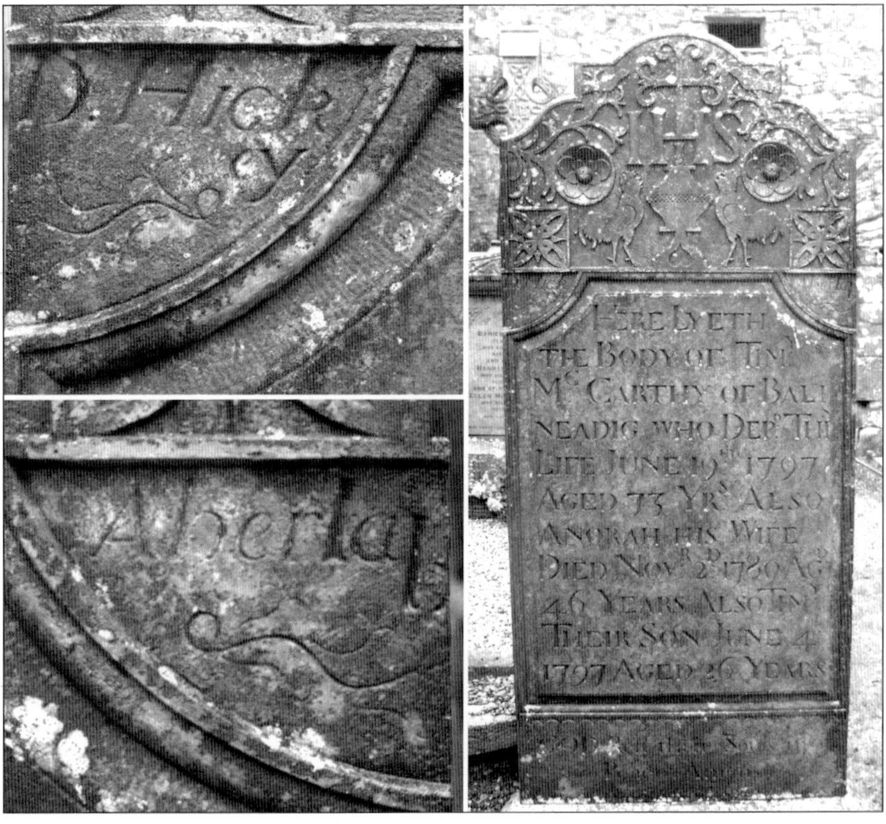

Figure 55

Fig. 55—Headstone signed 'D. Hickey / Aherla', Kilcrea Friary, Co. Cork, Ireland (1789 with addition 1797).

Inscribed in remembrance

participated in some other trade. In New England, probably all early gravestone-carvers were originally engaged in other stonework.[62] The craft ran in families and was passed down from generation to generation. Burgess lists seven classes of monumental craftsmen working in the middle of the eighteenth century in England, ranging from the master mason and town statuary to the casual worker who turned his hand to making headstones 'for pocket money or recreation.'[63] In England, the training of a professional mason involved an apprenticeship of seven years. As part of their education the masons would produce small trial items with incised and gilded lettering. Masons also produced samples in marble to show clients. An example is the small piece probably carved by John Coles of Thrapston, Northamptonshire (1736–1816) (Fig. 54).

In the medieval period, masons sometimes travelled around the country or emigrated to find work. From the late sixteenth century onwards the extent to which masons travelled to undertake their craft is not known. Relocation potentially could have diluted local traditions in letter-cutting. This was probably limited and certainly more likely in the case of highly skilled craftsmen whose reputations would put them in great demand. Duval and Rigby, referring to New England, suggest that most masons practised near their birthplace.[64] In the USA, however, there appears to have been a significant trade in ready-made headstones, many being sold to clients several hundred miles away. Also, it is known that masons emigrated to North America and exercised their trade where they settled. For example, it is believed that some Scottish masons practised their craft in New England.[65] James Hay of Halifax, Nova Scotia, was described as a 'stonecarver lately from Scotland'.

Burgess lists 577 memorial masons working in England before 1900, who were known either from signed gravemarkers or from archives. Of this number, 112 were certainly operating before 1800 and no less than thirteen were working before 1700. The earliest recorded post-medieval carver in England appears to be John Hemings of Stratford-on-Avon (1632–83).[66] In Ireland, several early masons are known from their signatures on headstones. Examples include the eighteenth-century stone-carvers Denis Cullen of Monaseed, Miles Brien, James Byrne, J. Butler, Hugh Rogan, David Doyle, Martin O'Connor and D. Hickey (Fig. 55).[67] William Kidwell is known to have come from London to work in Waterford. In the USA, a surprising number of early makers of gravemarkers have been recorded, principally from the north-eastern states. Several seventeenth-century carvers are known from Boston, including William Mumford, J. N., the Lamsons of Charlestown and the Fosters of Dorchester, as well as others from the New England states.[68] A headstone of 1744 at Chebogue, Nova Scotia, is signed 'Abraham Codner Next to the Drawbridge Boston', although the first known Canadian gravestone-maker was James Hay, who was working in 1775. He was the first of the family to continue a masonry tradition.[69] In Germany few stones were signed before 1800. There are two memorials by Johann Ordemann in Ganderkesse, Oldenburgerland, signed 'Fecit Johann Ordemann' (1771) and 'Fecit Ordemann' (1782).[70] Some headstones in Australia signed 'Shea' are dated between 1855 and 1858.

Considering the heritage of gravemarkers with which Scotland is blessed, it is remarkable that we do not know the names of any post-medieval Scottish headstone masons until the end of the eighteenth century at the earliest, with the exception of Duncan Haggart of Perthshire and possibly James Faichney, who cut the family memorial of 1707 at Innerpeffray in the same county.[71] Some masons began to sign their headstones from the late 1860s onwards. Research to identify early Scottish gravestone-cutters is much needed and would undoubtedly reveal many more. As we have seen, this gap in our knowledge is in stark contrast with parts of England, for example the Vales of Belvoir and Evesham, west Devon and north Cornwall, as well as New England, where eighteenth-century signed headstones are not uncommon.[72]

In Massachusetts, Connecticut and New Hampshire, where many headstones exhibit a naïvety in the use of lettering, there is often a close correspondence between the skills of the mason who fashioned the stones, created the symbolic carvings and applied the decoration, and the letter-carver who cut the inscription. To some extent this is rather surprising when it is known that the trade practice of memorial masonry there was based on selling pre-sculpted headstones to which the inscription was added at a later date.[73] Obviously, this may have been cut by the same mason or workshop on occasion. Similarly, in England, Wales, Ireland and Canada, the skill seen in the sculpturing of the headstone is usually echoed in the cutting of the inscription. In Scotland the tradition of gravestone production was somewhat different from elsewhere. It was common practice to split the task of making the gravestone between the skilled or master mason who shaped the stone and carved the motifs and the more humble assistant who cut the inscription.[74] Evidence from many tombstones dated before 1800 indicates that their shaping and sculpturing were considered to be of much more importance than the lettering.[75] Although there are numerous simple gravestones with lettering only, the relatively crude cutting and proportionally small area of the stone used for the inscription on many memorials suggest that lettering was not seen as a priority, often cut by a less skilled partner. It is certainly sometimes not given as much attention as other elements on the stone. The consequence of this in Scotland is the mass of skilfully carved elaborate headstones with extremely naïve inscriptional lettering. This approach to the production of gravemarkers has left Scotland with a legacy of lively vernacular lettering, rivalled only in Ireland, that is a consequence of rural craftsmanship, raw creativity and, sometimes, even a disregard for all lettering conventions of time and place.

It is known from British local history and from signed brasses that many, if not most, were not made locally and were imported from major centres such as London and Birmingham.[76] There were exceptions. Lack *et al.* report that many external brasses in the Cotswolds were made in Cirencester, King's Stanley, Minchinhampton, Stroud and, according to local tradition, in Bristol.[77] The high proportion of imports means that any geographical trends detected in lettering design are due more to client preference and instruction rather than local craft traditions. Bertram recognised that geographic trends in the design of monumental brasses were blurred for the same reason. This is in stark contrast with the very subtle local differences that can be detected in lettering on gravestones and that reflect cultural diversity.[78]

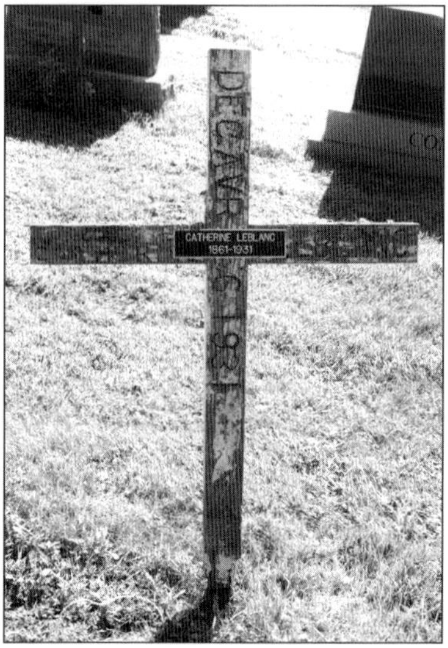

Figure 56

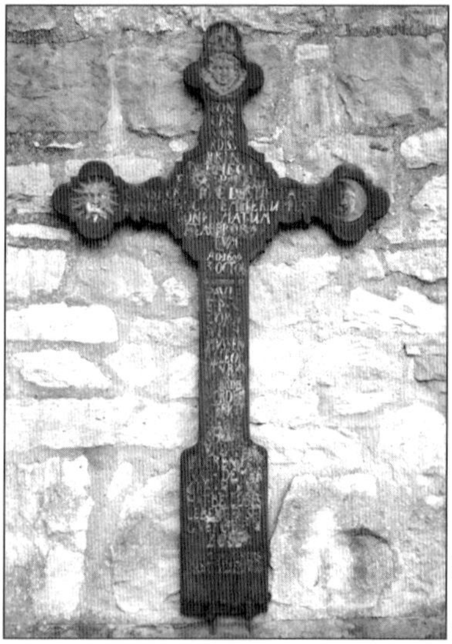

Figure 57

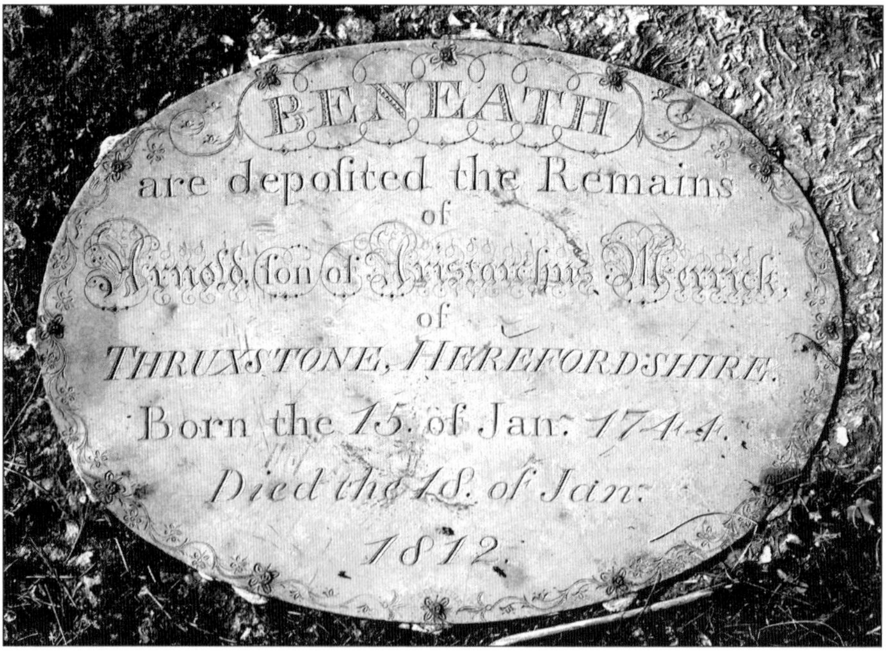

Figure 58

Fig. 56—Wooden cross with metal plaque, Church Point, Clare County, Nova Scotia, Canada (1931).

Fig. 57—Early iron cross with gilt lettering, Peckelsheim, Hessen, Germany (1609).

Fig. 58—Exterior memorial brass plate, Sapperton, Gloucestershire, England (1812).

Inscribed in remembrance

MATERIALS AND TECHNIQUES

The cultural dimension of commemorative practice no doubt was, and to some extent still is, the major determining factor that influenced the choice of materials from which gravemarkers were made. In some traditions permanence was clearly not an important consideration and the use of transient wooden markers was considered appropriate.[79] Most western societies, however, see the gravemarker as something permanent, something timeless, that reflects their beliefs in an eternal afterlife and that will sustain the memory of the deceased. Of course, availability of raw materials played its part. In communities where it was not economical or practical to import stone from a distance, memorials would be made from whatever was to hand. Yet there is an anomaly in some countries. In Germany the practice of removing gravemarkers after only a few years appears to be at odds with the effort made and expense incurred by those who erected them.

In Europe and North America stone has been the principal material of choice for as long as gravemarkers and other memorials have been erected. It has been perceived as a permanent substance by the ancient Greeks and the Romans, during the Early Christian period, throughout the Dark Ages and Middle Ages, and the entire post-medieval period up to the present day. There are few populated places on earth where stone is not readily available. Four stone types have been used more than others: sandstone, limestone, slate and marble. None of these have a standard consistency, varying in textural qualities and suitability for letter-cutting. Nor are they uniform in their ability to withstand weathering or environmental pollution.

Sandstone is a sedimentary rock, comprised mainly of quartz and/or feldspar. It varies greatly in durability. Some sandstones are very resistant to erosion but others, usually the coarser-grained varieties, weather and erode in just a few years. Sandstone varies in colour, from dark terracotta to pale grey. For many centuries, sandstone gravemarkers were probably the most common and widespread, being used for medieval graveslabs and the majority of headstones until the mid-nineteenth century.

Many limestones are relatively hard, especially those from the dark-coloured Carboniferous stratas. The geologically more recent ones do not stand up well to the elements. The harder limestones carve well and are compatible with detailed letter-cutting. Limestone is mineral calcite (a crystalline form of calcium carbonate), usually formed from the deposit of marine organisms.

Some of the most delicate lettering and detailed flourished decoration was cut in slate in the first half of the nineteenth century. Slate is a homogeneous metamorphic rock derived from shale-type sediments of clay or volcanic ash. Because of its sedimentary origin, some types are prone to flaking. Eighteenth- and nineteenth-century slate headstones are common in parts of Ireland, the English Midlands, Yorkshire, Devon, Cornwall and Wales. Many early New England gravemarkers, and a proportion of those in New York State and Pennsylvania, were cut from slate.

Although there are nineteenth-century granite gravemarkers in Europe, it is in the last 50 years that this material has become the most commonly used stone for memorials. In the last few decades its increased use has been accelerated by the availability of relatively inexpensive stone from sources in the Far East, especially China and India, where quarries not only supply raw materials but also produce ready-made headstones and other gravemarkers for the European and American markets. Granite is an igneous rock comprising quartz and feldspar grains of various sizes and in varying proportions, together with some mica and other intrusions. In some granites the individual grains are prominent. In others the grains are so fine that the stone is almost indistinguishable in appearance from slate. The lettered surface is usually ground to a high polish. Its colour varies from pink or pale grey through various greens to jet black.

Marble was used by the ancient Greeks and Romans for their sculptures and many of their sepulchral artefacts. It was widely used for formal, interior funerary memorials from medieval times until the Renaissance, and for exterior pedestal gravemarkers by the Victorians, who saw it as an appropriate material to represent affluence and status. In the nineteenth century, 'white stone' (marble) headstones became widespread in the eastern USA and Canada. Some of the marble was imported from Europe. Although variable in quality, some marble, especially the dolomitic variety, is not a durable material in an external environment, evidenced by the erosion on many nineteenth-century headstones made from it in North America.[80] It is a metamorphosed rock comprising mostly calcite or dolomite that also contains magnesium. A similar material, alabaster, a product of gypsum (anhydrous sulphate of calcium) or calcite, was very occasionally used.

In parts of central Scotland and the north of England there are many seventeenth- and eighteenth-century headstones and other gravemarkers cut from a very hard, dark grey basalt, locally referred to as 'whinstone'. The memorials made from basalt are extremely well preserved. Some Afro-Americans utilised quartzite for their gravemarkers, although many are simple unmarked field stones. Some gravemarkers were made from other local stones.

Wooden gravemarkers of the nineteenth century or earlier are rare. This is not surprising, as wood decays much more rapidly than most other materials used for memorials. They may have been much more common and widespread than now, and may even have been used as temporary markers before more permanent ones were erected. Some wooden examples are on display in European museums. A few groups of wooden gravemarkers survive in North Carolina burial grounds, and others survive as individuals in churchyards in Britain and Ireland. More recently, wooden crosses with small metal plaques have been used, especially in Ireland and Canada (Fig. 56).

Gravemarkers in various metals represent a minority of European and North American memorials. The most notable of these are the medieval brasses that can be seen in churches, cathedrals and abbeys throughout Europe.[81] Small brass plates were commonly used as memorials in some English and Welsh churches, and less frequently elsewhere in Europe. There are 57 in the Oude Kerk, Amsterdam, with dates ranging from 1772 to 1863. Between the late sixteenth and the early twentieth centuries in the English counties of Gloucestershire, Oxfordshire, Cumbria and Yorkshire there was a practice of fixing a small, engraved memorial plate to a headstone, ledger, table stone, chest tomb or the church wall.[82] A few external brass plates are found elsewhere in England, with some in other countries, including Scotland and Canada but apparently not in Ireland. It is thought that these were used in areas where the stone was unsuitable for the inscription. They are found alongside inscriptions on the stones and are absent from many other areas where the stone has suffered considerable erosion. Although these plates are called 'brass', they are actually made from a material closer to bronze (Fig. 58).[83]

Cast-iron gravemarkers are not common. Many of those that can still be found date from the late eighteenth to the early twentieth century, although there is a very early iron cross with gilt lettering at Peckelsheim, Germany, dated 1609 (Fig. 57). In countries with a damp climate, the gravemarkers are considerably corroded and the inscriptions have rarely survived. They have fared better in Canada than elsewhere.[84] Wrought-iron markers, usually in the form of crosses, are a more recent phenomenon. A small, simply inscribed brass plate is usually fixed to the memorial. They are very common in Roman Catholic burial grounds in continental Europe and are frequent in Ireland and Canada. The 'white bronze' gravemarker, usually in the form of an obelisk or short, vertical slab headstone, appears to be an almost entirely Canadian artefact (Fig. 59). They were produced by hollow casting in the late 1880s and early 1890s and can be seen throughout

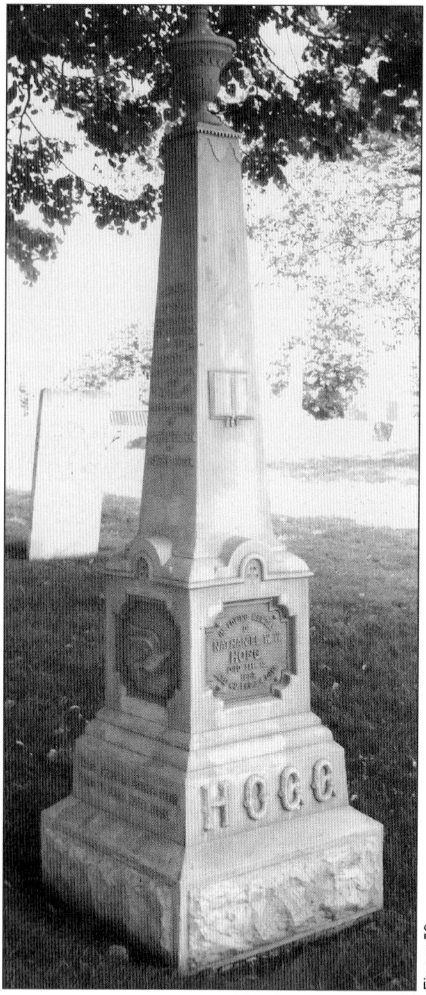

Figure 59

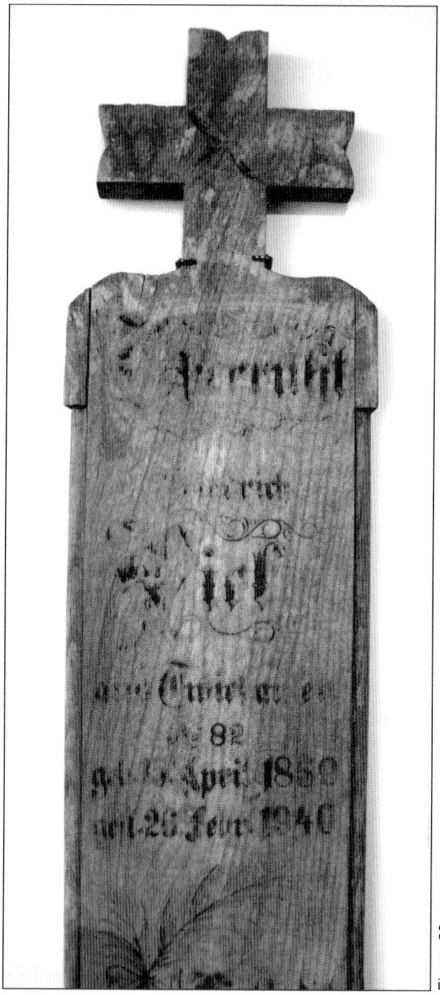

Figure 60

Fig. 59—'White bronze' memorial, Chebogue, Nova Scotia, Canada (1887).

Fig. 60—Painted wooden graveboard, Museum für Sepulkralkultur, Kassel, Hessen, Germany (1859).

Fig. 61—Headstone with lettering painted on a white-painted background, Meeden, Groningen Province, Netherlands (1916).

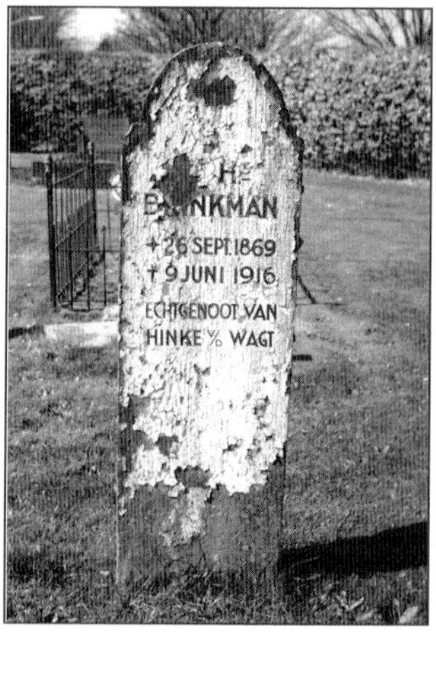

Figure 61

Nova Scotia. In spite of their name, these simulated stone memorials are not bronze but are made from a material whose main constituent is zinc. The alloy is virtually indestructible and, according to a contemporary advertisement, will not corrode, change colour or absorb moisture; it is not affected by frost and moss will not grow on it.[85] A separate small panel was often attached for the inscription.

Other materials have been, and are being, used for gravemarkers, but much less commonly than the traditional stone. The introduction of concrete memorials about the beginning of the twentieth century arguably was due more to economics than aesthetics. Crosses in the Celtic style and small cruciform gravemarkers were amongst the designs produced in this material. The soft mix could be cast in the same way as iron, with the inscription included in the mould or cut afterwards. Stained glass or mosaic was sometimes incorporated into the design. Ceramic gravemarkers and those made from tiles are rare.[86] Brick memorials are probably more common in Australia than elsewhere. Fibreglass (fibre-reinforced polymer or FRP) has not been widely accepted as a material for the manufacture of gravemarkers, in spite of its durability. Electroplated metalised plastic plaques are used in some modern cemeteries. The use of such innovative materials and processes could become more common in future.

Painting lettering is by far the simplest and most economical way to apply an inscription. Most memorials on which the lettering has been painted are vernacular wooden gravemarkers and in most instances the inscriptions have all but disappeared. Some graveboards with very well-drawn gothic lettering are preserved in the Museum für Sepulkralkultur in Kassel. Even although these date from the 1930s and 1940s, the deterioration in the lettering is evident (Fig. 60). In Australia there are wooden gravemarkers of the second half of the nineteenth and very early twentieth centuries with engraved lettering that has been painted. Some stone gravemarkers in the northern part of the Netherlands have the inscription painted black on a white-painted background. These date from the mid-nineteenth to the early twentieth century and are extremely rare (Fig. 61).

The technique of cutting lettering in stone by hand and the tools employed have changed little since Roman times. Even before that, the ancient Greeks incised letters in stone in a similar way. The basic equipment used by the lettering sculptor includes chisels of various sizes, with the cutting edge ranging from about 5mm (¼in.) to 25mm (1in.), a 'dummy' or mallet weighing a little over 500g (1¼lbs), a heavy hammer and sharpening stones. Chisels were originally made from tempered steel, but the modern tungsten-tipped version stays sharp longer and is sometimes preferred. The technique of letter-cutting in wood is similar to that in stone except that the craftsman has to take account of the grain of the material and curved gouges are used in addition to chisels. The sequence of letter-carving in stone or engraving in wood is relatively straightforward but requires skill, patience and a degree of physical effort.

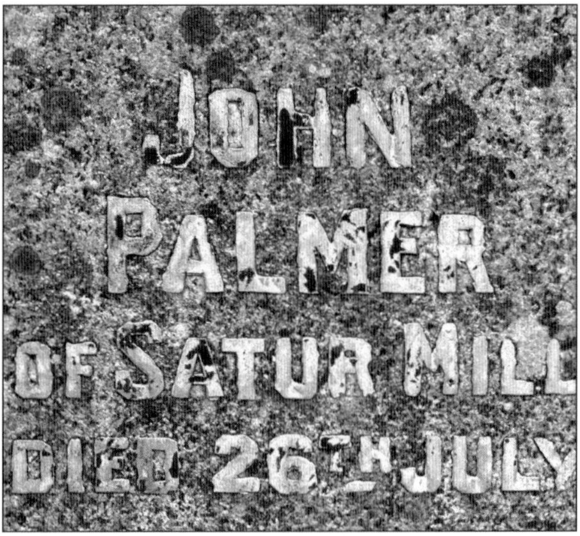

Fig. 62—Lead lettering set in granite, Middlebie Cemetery, Dumfriesshire, Scotland (1932).

Figure 62

Before the advent of power cutters and pneumatic chisels, stones had to be shaped by hand. Once the surface on which the inscription is to be incised has been prepared, guidelines and outlines of the letters are drawn or lightly incised. Guidelines can still be seen on some eighteenth-century headstones. An alternative technique, similar to that which it is thought the Romans employed, is to paint the letters with a brush. Chiselling each side alternately to an angle of 45 degrees makes a V-shaped cut. Raised or relief lettering, where the background is removed to leave the letters standing proud, requires much more work. This is probably why it became less popular from the seventeenth century onwards, even though it is easier to cut a good letter in relief.

The Romans probably painted most of their inscribed lettering on sandstone with a red pigment. Incised letters on marble and, more rarely, slate tombstone memorials were often painted or gilded, but this practice is virtually unknown on medieval and post-medieval tombstones made from softer, grainier materials. Colouring, occasionally found in post-medieval headstone inscriptions, may not be contemporary with the cutting of the lettering. The twentieth-century practice of painting older headstones white or grey with the letters picked out in black is deplorable, both for reasons of conservation and aesthetics. It completely destroys the value of the memorial as a historical artefact and only temporarily enhances the legibility of the inscription. Modern granite memorials usually have gilded, incised lettering, applied either with gold paint or with gold leaf burnished on an adhesive ground.

Lead infill was used from early in the twentieth century, applied by hammering lead wire into the cut letters so that the letters were flush with the stone surface. Relief lead letters were also utilised (Fig. 62). A condensed sans-serif was the commonest letterform to which this technique applied.

Roman and uncio-versal lettering cut from lead was also used. Applied relief lettering of a high technical quality in brass or bronze can be seen on gravemarkers from the 1960s, more often in Germany, the USA and Canada than elsewhere.

It could be expected that the material on which an inscription is cut, or in some other way applied to the memorial, would greatly influence the letterforms. This is, indeed, usually so, but not always. A fine-grained stone, such as marble or slate, permits the mason to incise very fine detail and, providing the grain is even, to cut flowing lines and flourishes. Coarser sandstones break away much too easily to retain sharp points and corners on the letters, especially the serifs. On the other hand, soft fine-grained sandstones are much easier to cut than basalt or granite. Nevertheless, masons frequently ignored the natural attributes of the stones into which they were cutting the inscription and battled with the material to achieve the form they were attempting to create. This was probably due more to the availability of local stone than to perversity. In Scotland, for example, freestone was a material that could easily be cut in any direction without splitting, making it eminently suitable for fine letter-carving. In spite of its name, it was not stone for which masons did not have to pay, as has been suggested. It was not easy to acquire and masons usually had to make do with what they could source.

The production of gravemarkers in Europe and North America has been revolutionised in the last few decades, initially by the introduction of mechanical routers that cut lettering of predetermined styles. This was superseded by shot-blasting through computer-cut rubberised stencils, where a fine jet of water laced with an abrasive powder, usually silicon carbide, is sprayed at high pressure onto the stone. More recently, computer-controlled water jet and laser cutters can carve or cut virtually any shape or letterform. While the ancient handcraft survives and flourishes as a specialist art form, most inscriptions on gravestones are now produced by one or other of these mechanical methods. Lettering incised by shot-blasting or laser engraving can easily be identified by the lack of the characteristic traditional V-shaped cut (Fig. 108). Although the techniques are very cost-effective, compared with handcrafted work, they are rarely used creatively. Modern cemeteries and graveyards are typified by row after row of black, shiny granite memorials with lettering of little character.

Table 1—The characteristics of basic lettering styles.

Style	*Origin*	*Raised*	*Incised*	*Caps*	*Caps and lc*	*Proportions*	*Weight*	*Serif*
Uncio-versal	Pen	Yes	Yes	Yes	No	Wide	Heavy	Yes
Gothic	Pen	Yes	Yes	No	Yes	Narrow	Variable	No
Roman	Chisel/pen	Yes	Yes	Yes	Yes	Variable	Light–mid	Yes
Cursive	Chisel	Rarely	Yes	Rarely	Yes	Wide	Light–mid	No
Script	Pen	Yes	Yes	Yes	Yes	Narrow	Light	No
Italic	Chisel	Yes	Yes	Yes	Yes	Variable	Light–mid	Yes
Block	Chisel	Yes	Yes	Yes	Yes	Variable	Mid–bold	Yes
Sans-serif	Chisel	Yes	Yes	Yes	Yes	Variable	Mid–bold	No
Gothic revival	Pen	No	Yes	Yes	Yes	Variable	Light–bold	No
Ornamented	Various	Yes	Yes	Yes	Yes	Variable	Light–bold	Variable
Other	Various	Yes	Yes	Yes	Yes	Variable	Light–bold	Variable

LETTERING STYLES

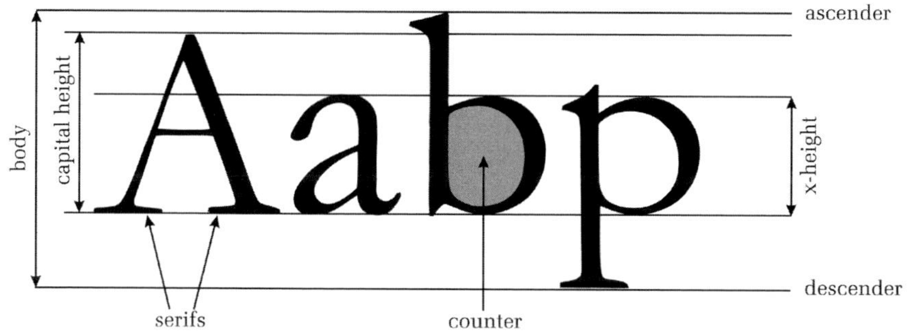

Figure 63

Fig. 63—Some terms used in the description of letters.

Before describing the various gravemarker lettering styles, some clarification of a few terms would be helpful. The words 'majuscules' and 'minuscules' refer to capitals or upper-case and small or lower-case letters respectively. The word 'capital' is a general alphabetic term. 'Lower-case', on the other hand, is typographic, although, mixing epithets to some extent, it is more practical to use these terms. Serifs are the swollen terminations of the letter strokes. Ascenders are the parts of lower-case letters that rise above the x-height, as in 'b', 'd' and 'l'. Descenders are the parts that drop below, as in 'g', 'j', 'p' and 'q' (Fig. 63). Light, medium and bold are analogous to the various weights of letters in typography. Similarly, condensed, medium and wide refer to the widths of the letters in proportion to the height and are the same as typographic condensed (narrow), medium (regular or normal) and extended. The term 'false relief' is often used for inscriptions where the background has been cut away, leaving the lettering standing proud. The use of the word 'false' in this context is rather strange, as the relief is indeed very real. The terms 'relief' or 'raised' are far more accurate. The opposite of relief is incised or intaglio.

I have not followed some of the taxonomic conventions used by archaeologists, or some of those used by typographic designers who traditionally have classified alphabets into 'families'. For the purposes of interpreting and understanding gravemarker lettering, some divergence from standard palaeographic practice has been adopted here. It is a distinct discipline within the field of material culture that merits its own taxonomy, although both borrowing from and contributing to other disciplines at times, especially typography and calligraphy. It has inherent characteristics that place it in a specific cultural niche. For example, the term 'Lombardic', also not favoured by several other authors but commonly used by archaeologists, has been discarded. As well as its inappropriate

Table 2—The earliest recorded dates of lettering styles.

	Scotland	*England and Wales*	*Ireland**	*Europe*	*Canada*	*USA*
Archaic roman	Before 1500	1518	Before 1500	Before 1500	—	—
Roman caps	Before 1500	Before 1500	Before 1500	Before 1500	1720	1633
Roman caps+lc	1626	1616	1619	1694	1740	1690
Cursive	1641	1675	1722	1719	—	1736
Script	1701	1624	1749	1637	1808	1801
Italic	1649	1601	1748	1758	1740	1738
Block serif	1763	1791	1840	after 1850	1818	1828
Sans-serif	1648	1808	1650	after 1850	1798	1796
Gothic revival	1729	1638	1830	—	1796	1801
Ornamented	1709	1671	1866	1769	1804	1844

* Based on limited data

geographical connotations, it is an ambiguous epithet, as it also refers to a pre-Carolingian North Italian script to which it is unrelated.[87] This has been replaced with the more apt, if arguably rather clumsy, term 'uncio-versal' and its subdivisions uncialesque and versalesque. The term 'english letter', used extensively by Bartram for a particular version of roman capitals and lower-case, is neither apposite nor realistic when applied to similar styles from other countries.[88] Perhaps more importantly, very specific classifications based on subtle subdivisions of lettering styles are best avoided and basic groupings are more realistic. It is impractical to pigeon-hole the individuality expressed by masons in many inscriptions, especially in the seventeenth and eighteenth centuries. Knowledgeable authors like Burgess, Bartram and Gray have, to a greater or lesser degree, identified very subtle differences in inscriptional alphabet designs. The value of making distinction between very similar scripts is doubtful when applied to inscriptional forms. Variation in style, even when a skilled mason cuts the lettering, can be seen within the same inscription. This is particularly so in the case of the more rustic memorials. More generic groupings are preferred. Differences within each major class can then be defined in as much or as little detail as appropriate and necessary for the study being undertaken.

Lettering is not a static art. It evolves and changes with time and space. It is a product of personality, culture, skill and tradition. It interacts with the medium through which it is expressed and with the environment to which it is exposed. Before the later industrial period and the current age of 'high tech', the choice of lettering and its use was much simpler. Masons and other inscription-carvers knew one or, at most, a very few basic lettering styles, and they interpreted them as they thought fit. From the nineteenth century matters changed dramatically. The wide range of faces produced by the type-founders and adopted by the masons effectively ended the cultural traditions that had gone before. Starting in the early 1970s, the endless flow of new digital typefaces, combined with the technology that can reproduce the typographic letterforms in stone and other materials, rendered the simple classifications of earlier styles even less appropriate. A classification of gravemarker lettering styles must be applicable to inscriptions in any medium or material, from different geographical regions and from different historical periods, including the present. It must be sufficiently robust that it can accommodate a range of variation within each style. Inscriptions in newer gravemarkers with lettering that is, in effect, typographic is best classified as such and does not come within the scope of this book. That is not to suggest that there is no scope for typographic studies of contemporary gravemarkers.

There will always be difficulties when we try to fit lettering styles into discrete groups but it is a necessary evil and the only practical approach if some sort of objective analysis of form is to be undertaken. Ten basic groups of gravemarker lettering styles can be recognised. The lettering on most inscriptions will fit into one or other of these, although there

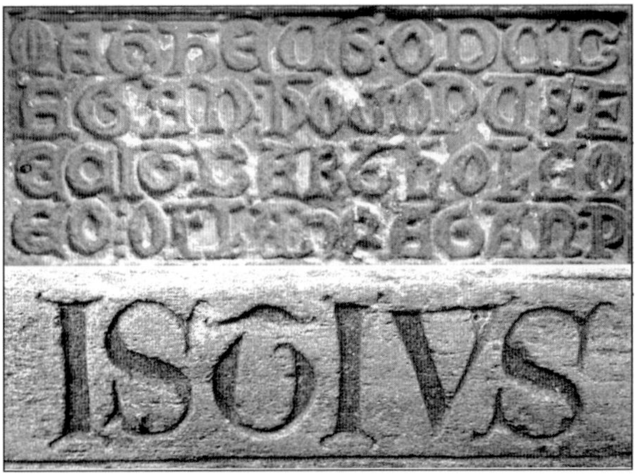

Figure 64

Fig. 64—Uncio-versal. Above: uncialesque, Devenish Island, Co. Fermanagh, Ireland (mid-fifteenth century); below: versalesque, Ardchattan, Argyll, Scotland (probably twelfth–thirteenth century).

will be forms that are intermediate between two styles. Inevitably, some inscriptional forms will not fit within any of the main groups or even the transitional forms between them and it is best to classify these as 'other', supplementing this with additional descriptive epithets as necessary (Tables 1 and 2).

Uncio-versal (Fig. 64)

The lettering on gravemarkers and memorial crosses of the Early Christian period to the late Middle Ages has been cited probably more than that of any other period by archaeologists, historians and palaeographers researching inscriptional forms. The inscriptions are usually noted as part of a single stylistic tradition, albeit with a degree of variation. In reality, the influences of two distinct manuscript forms can be seen clearly in these inscriptions. One is the uncial and its variants. The other is the versal form with distinctive linear serifs, narrowing of verticals and bulging curves. When these were adapted and carved in stone or wood they acquired distinct attributes. For a short time in the immediate post-medieval years there is some evidence of forms transitional to roman. The principal features of the letters derive from pen scripts but in some versions the translation to an inscriptional form has given the style a much heavier character. Other styles, such as those found on some early British and Irish graveslabs, are almost linear. This is an entirely capital letterform with no distinct lower-case. On crosses and many other Celtic artefacts the lettering is in relief rather than incised.

Gray suggested that it was more appropriate to refer to the form as the 'Gothic capital'. This term goes back at least to the eighteenth century

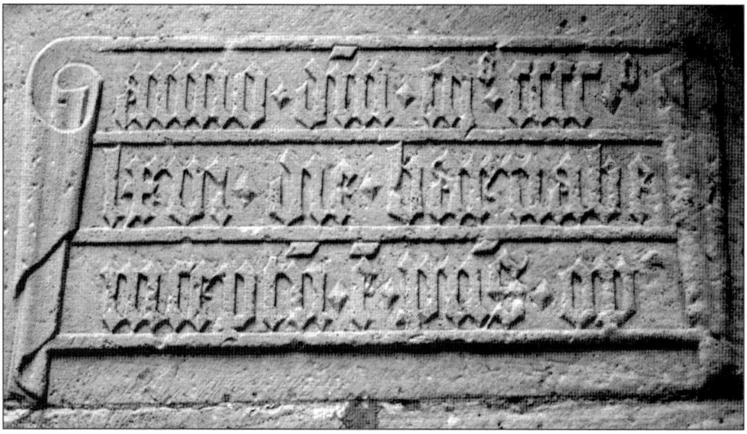

Figure 65

Fig. 65—Medieval gothic, Eschwege, Hessen, Germany (1466).

and was used by Thomas Astle in 1784. It could be somewhat misleading when the usual perception of gothic lettering is the black letter. Stanley Morrison suggested uncialesque. A more suitable term is uncio-versal, which effectively covers the range of the style. The terms 'uncialesque' and 'versalesque' can then be used according to the letters' proximity to uncial and versal respectively.[89]

Uncio-versals were revived in a modified form early in the nineteenth century and were often used until the middle of the twentieth century for lettering cut on marble memorials with lead inserts.

Gothic (Fig. 65)

Most inscriptions in the easily recognised gothic form, whether they be incised or relief, are in a style analogous to textura or 'black letter', seen as richly textural masonry inscriptions. The rotunda form appears to have been shunned by medieval masons. The bold, very condensed gothic form is eminently suited to inscriptional treatments and was probably a relatively easy style to cut, but it is often difficult for the modern eye to read. This is exacerbated by the common use of contractions. It was always incised as a mixed-case form, although the height of the capital was often made the same height as the lower-case. The form does not have serifs as such. These are replaced by angular terminations to the vertical lines. Other than slight variation in weight and proportions, inscribed gothic lettering is remarkably uniform in style. Slight variation in the forms of some letters is mainly expressed as more florid terminations to the characters. The use of points between words and sentences is fairly common.

Fig. 66—Roman. Above: roman capitals, Corcomroe Abbey, Co. Clare, Ireland (1775); below: roman capitals and lower-case, Darton, Yorkshire, England (1772).

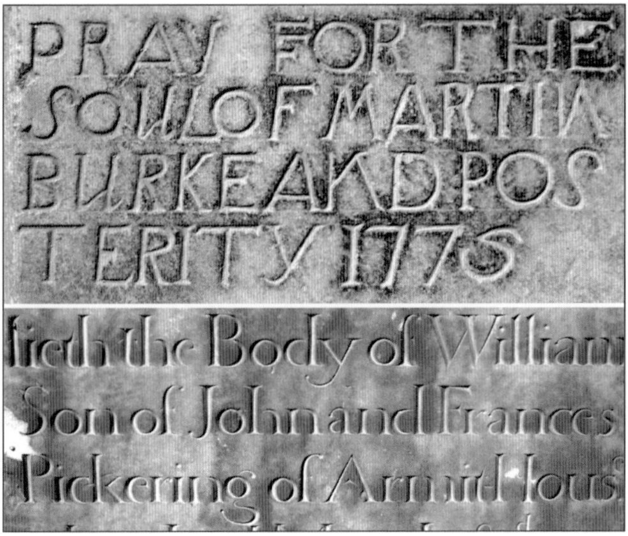

Figure 66

Roman (Fig. 66)

The principal features of roman lettering (written 'roman' rather than 'Roman') are capitals with proportions based more or less on the classical models, with narrow B, E, F, P and R, and wide C, D, G, H, M, N, O and W, terminal serifs and variation in the width of the lines from which the letters are constructed. The verticals are usually thicker than the horizontals. The extent to which these attributes are expressed varies greatly. Sometimes letters exhibit little or no variation in line width. The fishtail-shaped serifs vary in size and shape. Sometimes there is a droop or even V-shape or nick in the terminal horizontal of the serif. Occasionally, we find forms that are clearly roman but have barely discernible serifs. Ligatures were common in roman capital inscriptions between the sixteenth and eighteenth centuries. Roman capitals were interpreted in many ways, sometimes with skill and sometimes with honest naïve flair. The ability of roman lettering to withstand such variation in treatment yet retain its basic character makes it one of the most interesting forms used on gravemarkers. Two other lettering styles have serifs, uncio-versals and block serif. Uncio-versals cannot be confused with roman except in its transitional form, but lettering in which the serifs are fine horizontal lines, similar to and often based on the typeface Bodoni, could be considered block serif with the serif thickness greatly reduced. Conversely, very bold roman lettering may have thick serifs that may be difficult to distinguish from that form. Such anomalies are discussed in the section on recording and analysis.

Several main subgroups of roman inscriptions, some entirely in capitals and others in capitals and lower-case, can be recognised. Inscriptions entirely in lower-case are known but this is probably due to an omission on the part of the masons. It is not unusual to find inscriptions in which

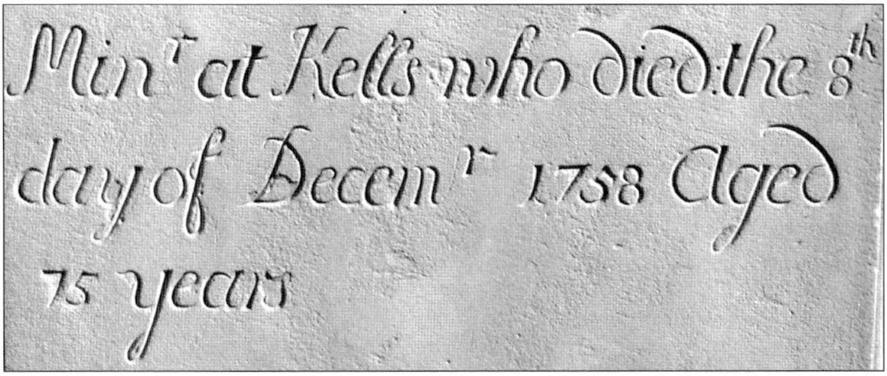

Figure 67

Fig. 67—Cursive lettering, St Michael's Church, Dumfries, Dumfriesshire, Scotland (1758).

capitals and lower-case are mixed in words and sentences. The earliest 'archaic' or 'primitive' forms are crude and heavy in weight, with lettering in relief rather than incised. Sometimes a horizontal line separated each line of lettering, and ligatures were used extensively and creatively. Serifs are indistinct and usually reduced to swellings at the ends of strokes. Point separators between words were used. There is a gradual transition from late forms of uncio-versal to this form, and from it to the more advanced roman styles. There are two main groups of advanced romans, those based on 'old style' attributes with the thicker parts of the letter strokes significantly rotated anticlockwise, and those that are 'modern' with the thicks on the verticals, greater contrast between the thick and thin strokes and with a tendency towards crisp, narrow serifs. This latter form, in its embryonic stage, was called the 'english letter' by Bartram, the term being adopted from the extensive discourse on the 'English vernacular letter' by Mosely.[90] Quite distinct from the mainstream developments of roman in much of Europe, relief lettering on seventeenth-century gravemarkers in German Oldenburgerland and the Friesian Islands constitutes a remarkable development of 'modern' attributes at a very early date, including the use of a strong vertical stress in some forms and sloping of the letters in others. The extent of variation in these roman forms, resulting from the ingenuity of early masons, craftsmen and other letter-cutters, makes it difficult to place many roman lettering styles into discrete categories.

Cursive (Fig. 67)

The distinction between cursive inscriptional lettering that derives from the roman form and script styles that emulate or are strongly influenced

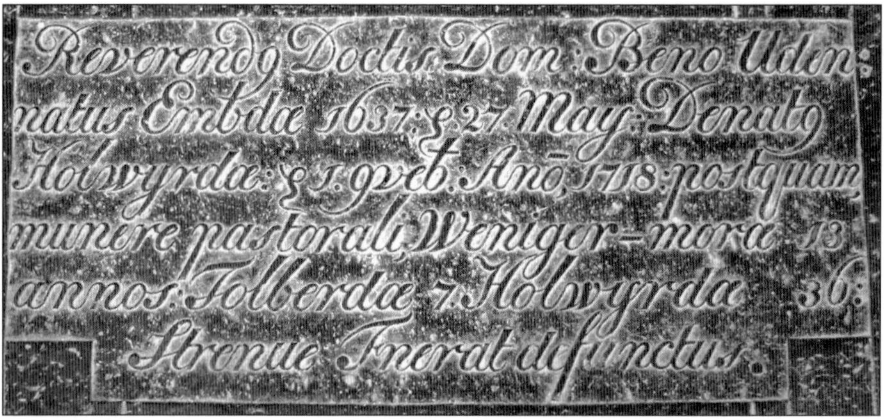

Figure 68

Fig. 68—Script lettering, Holwierde, Groningen Province, Netherlands (1718).

by pen calligraphy has been detailed at some length.[91] Its form differs in a number of key attributes from italic, with which it can be confused. Italic capitals are sloped versions of the roman style and the lower-case letters retain their serifs. Cursive capitals are more florid and the lower-case letters, rather than having serifs, begin and end with a curved line. It has also been shown that there is a clear evolution from roman to a fully developed cursive form before the lettering of the penman was evident. It is therefore appropriate and practical to distinguish between cursive and script.

Cursive lettering is often monolinear, with little or no variation in the line thickness, and always lacks serifs. The letters tend to be separate and do not run into each other. The round letters are frequently circular or nearly so. It is usually incised, although some relief forms were cut. Other than gravemarkers where only initial letters are used, cursive inscriptions are in capitals and lower-case, with a few exceptions. The weight of the letters is usually fairly bold. Cursive lettering is sometimes flourished but much less so and in a more restrained form than script.

Script (Fig. 68)

Script lettering emulates copperplate writing of the penmen and copybooks of the late eighteenth and nineteenth centuries. It is almost always incised. It has cursive, flowing lines in both the lower-case and capitals, with each letter running into the next. The inscriptions are often extensively flourished. These are sometimes illustrative and in the form of figures, animals or plants. Some inscriptions are entirely in capitals that are sometimes so florid that they are almost illegible. Thick and thin lines

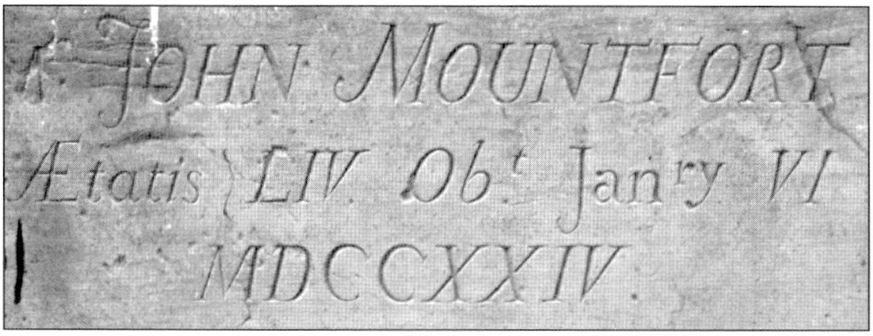

Figure 69

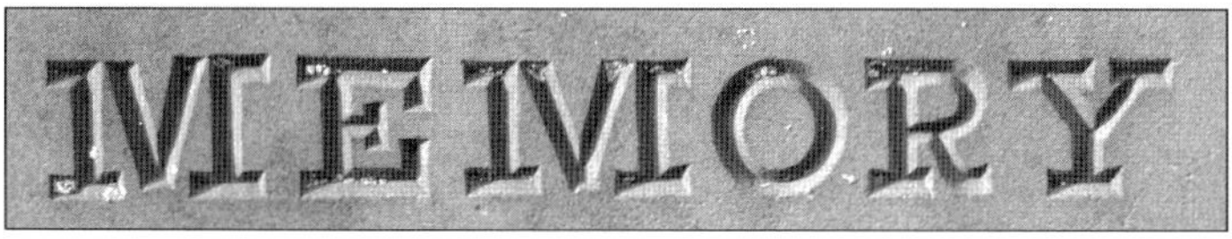

Figure 70

Fig. 69—Italic lettering, Copp's Hill Burial Ground, Boston, Massachusetts, USA (1724).

Fig. 70—Block serif lettering, Sweetheart Abbey, Dumfriesshire, Scotland (1843).

copy what would be made if the script had been written with a flexible nib and not a chisel. Letters are usually narrower than tall and very light in weight. In its purest form there are no serifs, although they are present in some lettering transitional between script and italic.

Italic (Fig. 69)

It is useful, if simplistic and a little inaccurate, to describe italic as sloped roman. Typographically, these are often two quite different forms. An italic typeface is usually designed to complement the upright roman version of the font and the basic forms can differ markedly from it. Inscriptions on gravemarkers in a roman-based sloped style are derived from both italic and sloped roman. It is simpler to refer to them all as italic. It is occasionally difficult to distinguish italic from script, but the initial letter can usually be used to determine the style to which it belongs.

Gravemarker lettering is not often cut exclusively in italic capitals. When it is, it is usually used alongside roman, either as the introductory words of the inscription or as emphasis. Italic capitals and lower-case are more common as introductory text or for a concluding epitaph. The variation in style is similar to that found in roman forms. Flourished italic initials are common.

Block serif (Fig. 70)

Several styles very closely related to roman were used on gravemarkers, including what would typographically be described as block serif, slab

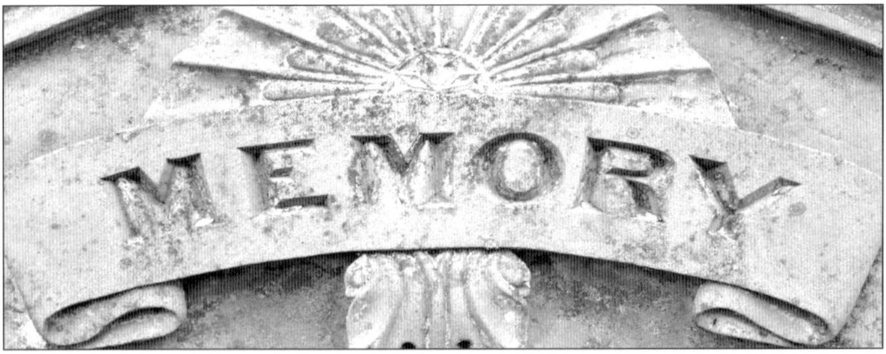

Figure 71

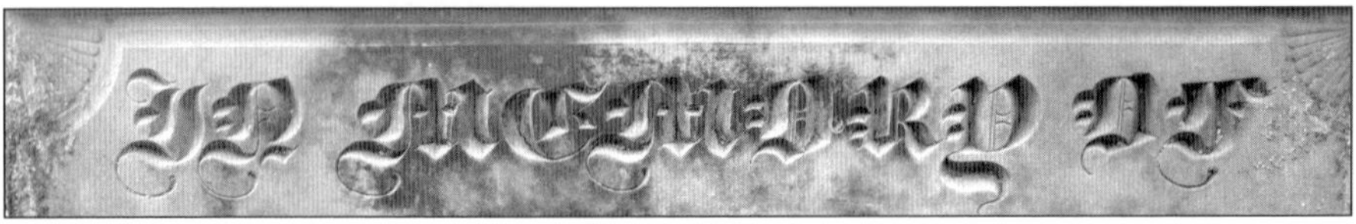

Figure 72

serif or egyptian. These are basically roman forms, sometimes monolinear, round to very wide in proportion and often bold in weight. Frequently, block serif lettering was in relief rather than incised. The serifs, which can be square or bracketed, are prominent and have significant depth. The styles are best grouped together as block serif.

There are gravemarkers inscribed solely in the less extreme forms. Block serif was more often used in the introductory words of the inscription, in either capitals or capitals and lower-case, and used especially for words such as SACRED or MEMORY.

Sans-serif (Fig. 71)

As the name suggests, sans-serif lettering entirely lacks serifs. The letterforms are simple, sometimes even geometric, contrasting with the proportional interpretations of roman styles. It is often used as relief lettering and in a condensed style of relatively bold weight. Although lower-case was used, most sans-serif inscriptions are in capitals.

Sans-serif inscriptions were often deeply cut and frequently used with other styles, including script and gothic. In the twentieth century the lettering often had lead inserts. Many monumental masons, who were responsible for the supply of headstones used in British cemeteries and graveyards at that time, trained their apprentices to cut a rather geometric and characterless sans-serif form. It was a fairly easy style to learn and made few creative demands. It can still be seen on many of the shot-blasted or router-cut headstones today. While lettering resembling sans-serif forms can be found as early as 1648, it is really a style of the very late eighteenth, nineteenth and, especially, twentieth centuries. The way that light strikes

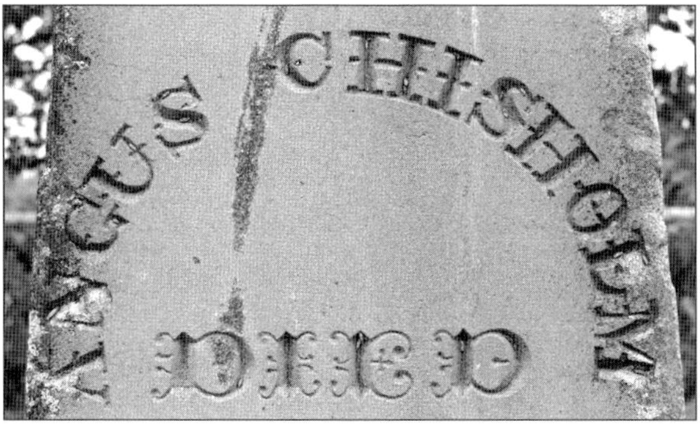

Figure 73

Fig. 71—Sans-serif lettering, Annan Cemetery, Dumfriesshire, Scotland (1832).

Fig. 72—Gothic revival lettering, Half Morton Churchyard, Dumfriesshire, Scotland (1840).

Fig. 73—Ornamented lettering, New Glasgow, Nova Scotia, Canada (1829).

the end of the V-cut lines of the incised sans-serif letters sometimes creates the appearance of a terminal serif. Nevertheless, the relative simplicity of the letterform, often reinforced by a tendency towards a geometric basis for shape and proportion, makes it quite unmistakable. The constructivist mannerisms of this style contrast strongly with the very subtle aesthetics of the classical roman.

Gothic revival (Fig. 72)

Gothic lettering, which was previously seen in medieval times, was once again used at the end of the eighteenth century, often in a highly decorative way with many flourishes. It was usually used for the words IN MEMORY OF, or its equivalent, at the top of the headstone, together with sans-serif, block serif or, more rarely, script forms. Interestingly, we do not see the equivalent emphasis in *Heir Ruhet* on German or Pennsylvanian German headstones. Revival gothic was usually incised and with extensive flourishing, inspired by writing manuals and copybooks.

German and immigrant German gravemarkers in the USA and Canada revived the earlier Fraktur tradition in inscriptions, using gothic for the entire text in the late seventeenth century and throughout the nineteenth century.

Ornamented (Fig. 73)

Ornamented is a useful classification for any of the above styles that have been enhanced by some sort of decorative treatment such as shadow,

Fig. 74—Unclassifiable lettering, Ruthwell, Dumfriesshire, Scotland (1709).

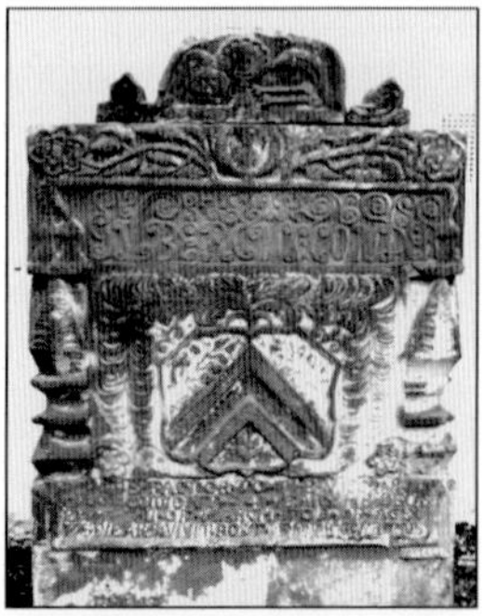

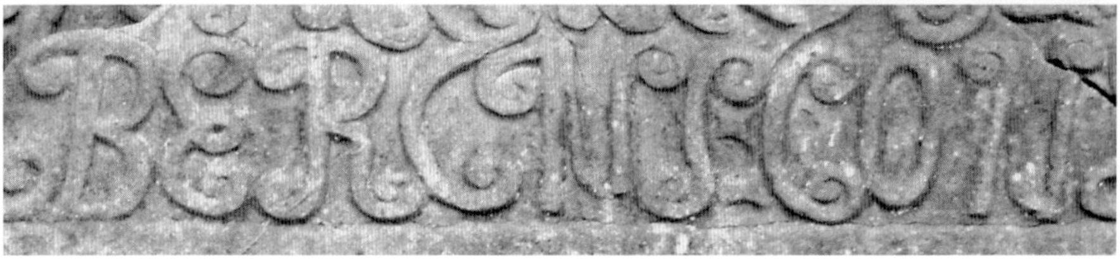

Figure 74

outline or texturing. Flourished letters should not be included as, strictly speaking, the flourishes are usually not part of the individual letterform.

Other (Fig. 74)

Occasionally an inscription will be encountered in a lettering style that cannot be placed in one of the above categories or is an eccentric letterform, the origin of which can only be guessed.

GRAVEMARKER LETTERING CHRONOLOGY

General trends

Anyone who walks through a burial ground with memorials that cover a span of several centuries cannot fail to notice the variation in the design of the gravemarkers erected at different times. Closer examination will show that the inscriptional lettering styles over the years vary just as much, reflecting changing fashions, skills and tastes. The variation sometimes corresponds with that seen in manuscript written forms and in lettering on other artefacts, but often diverges considerably from it. The history of inscriptional lettering is one of alternating stability, revival and experiment. It is punctuated with periods of banality and richness. It is complicated by considerable asynchronous geographical differences in traditions and customs, and its study is impaired by the differential rates of artefact survival. Having said that, the materials used for funerary memorials, predominantly stone, are more durable than most and, arguably, provide us with an unparalleled corpus of research material.

Commemorative practice and funerary memorials pre-date classical antiquity. The significant period in gravemarker lettering history really starts at the beginning of the ninth century with the Carolingian Renaissance. While not disregarding the importance of the earlier roman inscriptional forms, from this time onwards the complexity of funerary lettering art increases, and studies of the consequent diversity of inscriptional forms contribute much to our understanding of material culture. We see the perpetuation of earlier styles, but these are often largely overtaken by new developments that sometimes recycle attributes from them.

The ninth-century Carolingian capital, which incorporated many roman elements, is different from the classical form, less open and less ordered. In southern Italy some inscriptions have the round G, uncial E, M, H and

Fig. 75—Some Romanesque capitals.

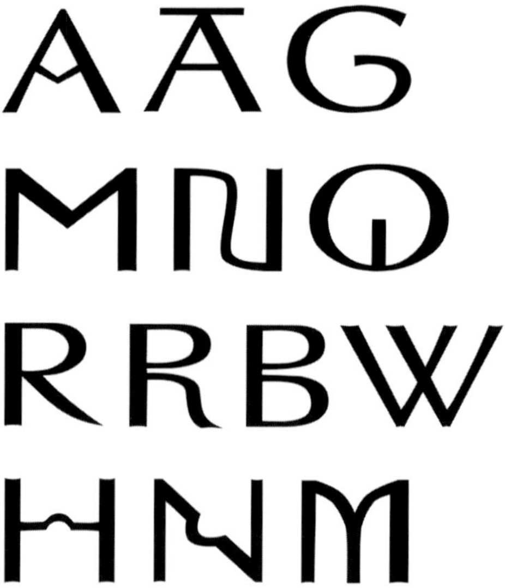

Figure 75

U. The Q with an internal tail was also used, although this can be seen rarely in Roman inscriptions. This short Carolingian period terminated abruptly at the end of the ninth century. Sometime before that, the Vikings from the north, the Magyars from the east and the Moors in the south of Europe had brought their own cultures and traditions and more or less imposed them on their conquered peoples. Alien non-Latin alphabets were introduced to western and southern Europe—runes by the Vikings and Arabic by the Moors. Northumbria and Ireland were the first to feel the effects of the Norse invasions. At one point, a Viking king ruled from Dublin. The Danish conquest of England was halted by King Alfred in AD 878. The recovery from the effects of this colonisation began in the mid-tenth century and continued until the mid-eleventh. The shape of things to come can be seen in an inscription on the church of St-Genis-des-Fountaines at Roussilon in France. The condensed and very stylised forms are probably influenced by Mozarabic manuscripts. Mozarabs were Christians who were permitted to practice their religion under the Moors. This relationship between manuscript and inscriptional forms throughout the Middle Ages is rare, each interpreting current styles independently, although Higgitt suggested a possible connection between book script and inscriptions in medieval England.[92] Anglo-Saxon inscriptions of this period used the A with a top crossbar and R with a straight, pointed leg. At the same time in the Italian Ottonian Empire, the uncial D, E, U and M were incorporated in inscriptions. They also adopted capital A with a broken crossbar (that is, in the form of a V) and Q with an internal leg that Gray considered to be non-roman.[93]

The Romanesque period revived classical traditions, yet at the Church of San Martine at Lucca (AD 1111) and in the cathedrals of Modena (AD 1063) and Pisa we see the uncial forms in the Q, G, E and M, as well as the A with a top crossbar and/or a broken horizontal and M with a short central V. In a dedication at Moissac, Spain (AD 1063), the capital M has a short V and a line projection downwards from it, a form that can be found in Scotland in the eighteenth century and in Connecticut (Norwichtown) in the nineteenth. Gray believed that this attribute may have come from Greek mosaics. A characteristic of Romanesque inscriptions is the extensive use of ligatures. This was not uncommon before but reached a frenzy in the eleventh century, with scribes and masons constructing numerous, and often unusual, letter combinations. Other forms that recur in later post-medieval gravemarker inscriptions include the H and N with a nick in the cross-stroke (Fig. 75).

The end of the Romanesque and the beginning of the medieval gothic period marks an increase in the number of extant graveslabs and the beginnings of the use of monumental brasses in churches. From the thirteenth to the early sixteenth century, gothic textura and uncio-versals were the predominant inscriptional forms on both these artefact types. There is usually little distinction between capitals and lower-case in gothic textura memorial lettering. The 't' and 'p' usually extend above and below the x-height of the letters, and words are separated by dots. In Italy, although gothic forms were used, the roman models still hung on and were revived in the fifteenth century with a modified style that was almost sans-serif. This is an elegant letterform with roman proportions and subtle thicks and thins. After about 1470 it was abandoned and the 'correct' roman forms once more dominated, especially on more formal memorials. Further north, inscriptional lettering was far more experimental and we find a significant divergence in European cultures. In central and western Europe the letter-carvers appear to have turned to the Romanesque for inspiration. Even in Germany, especially in Hessen, inscriptions on buildings and early gravemarkers are versalesque, not gothic. Versalesque was also the source for the transitional forms to archaic roman that became common on graveslabs towards the end of the sixteenth century.

The seventeenth century saw the beginnings of what could be seen as the consolidation of a discrete cultural focus—gravemarker inscriptional lettering. As we have seen, lettering on funerary memorials of the first 1,500 years or so of the Christian era played an important part in the history of material culture. But it is from the seventeenth century onwards that inscriptions on funerary artefacts become some of the most abundant accessible sources of palaeographic information and make some of the most important contributions to our understanding of material culture.

A time of change—Roman lettering from archaic to incised

In Italy, Spain and eastern France, roman inscriptions throughout the Middle Ages and the Renaissance were intaglio (incised). The relief archaic roman form was the first and most commonly used early post-medieval

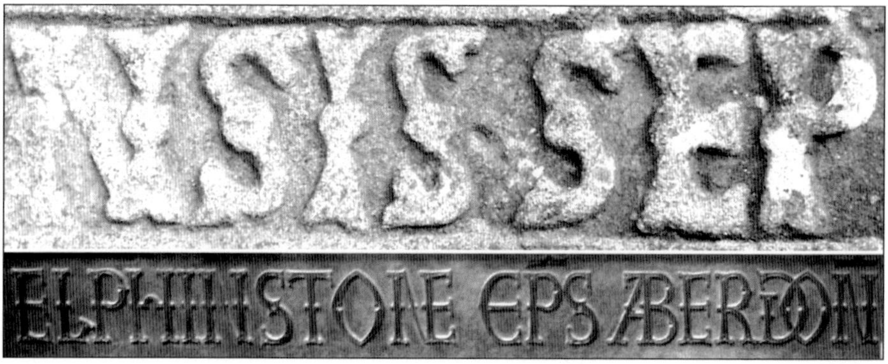

Figure 76

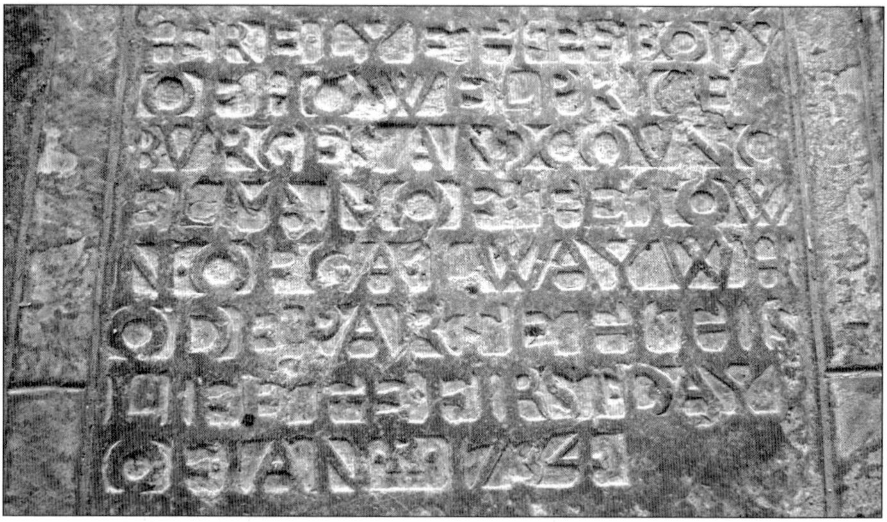

Figure 77

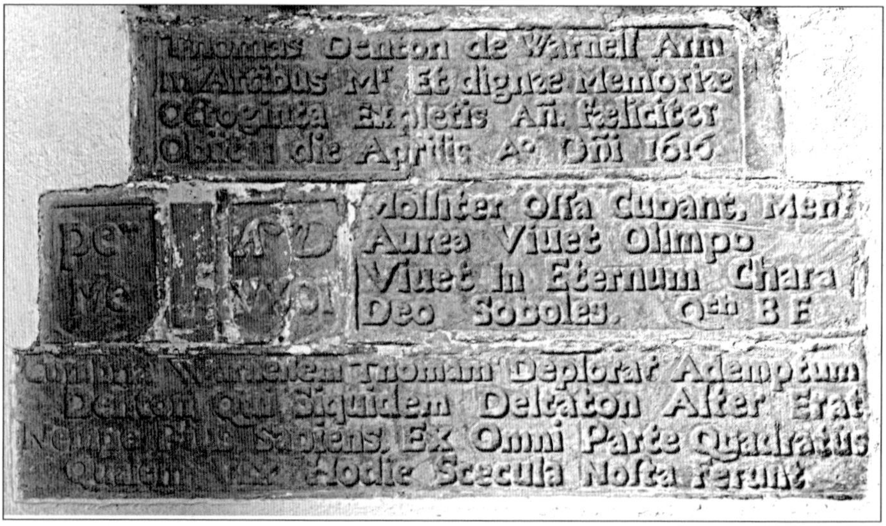

Figure 78

Inscribed in remembrance

Fig. 76—Roman capitals with versalesque elements. Note the tapering lines, the dot in the centre of the verticals and the form of the serifs. Above: graveslab, the Howff Burial Ground, Dundee, Scotland (1577); below: the Elphinstone tomb, King's College Chapel, Aberdeen, Aberdeenshire, Scotland (1519).

Fig. 77—Raised roman, St Nicholas' Church, Galway, Co. Galway, Ireland (1734).

Fig. 78—Raised archaic roman capitals and lower-case lettering on a mural memorial, Sebergham, Cumbria, England (1616).

inscriptional style on gravemarkers in western Britain, Ireland and much of western Europe. Incised roman was still chosen for many formal interior memorials. Relief archaic roman was rarely used after about 1650, although it evolved into other forms in Britain, Ireland and the rest of central and northern Europe.

Archaic roman capitals are proportionally slightly taller than wide. Some letters are occasionally equal to or wider than the height, including H and W. The thick lines forming the letters retain the entices of the versal form but there is frequently evidence of rudimentary serifs. In these early inscriptions, we see variants of the capitals A, B, E, M, R and W that can be classified as 'archaic' or 'advanced'. Archaic attributes can be identified in a modified form to the present day as revivals. The form of A with the broken horizontal bar is most often found on early tombstones. Another archaic form has a line across the top of the letter. The capitals B and R with the curved parts of the letters separated at the vertical and the E with a short central horizontal are predominantly early forms. The archaic forms of M with the central V not reaching the baseline, the W comprising two Vs and the straight-legged R are found far more frequently in inscriptions before the eighteenth century than afterwards. In relief archaic roman inscriptions, A, B, E, M, R and W are usually of the early form already described. The N is often mirrored, as are some other letters from time to time. The numeral 8 is often formed of two contiguous circles. Ligatures are common, especially TH, HE, THE and HN. Dots separating words are round or square. In an interesting variant of archaic roman there are round dots or points in the centre of many of the verticals and horizontals of the letters. There are several examples of this form on graveslabs in the Church of St Nicholas, Galway, Ireland (1566), the Howff Burial Ground, Dundee, Scotland, and in bronze on the Elphinstone tomb in King's

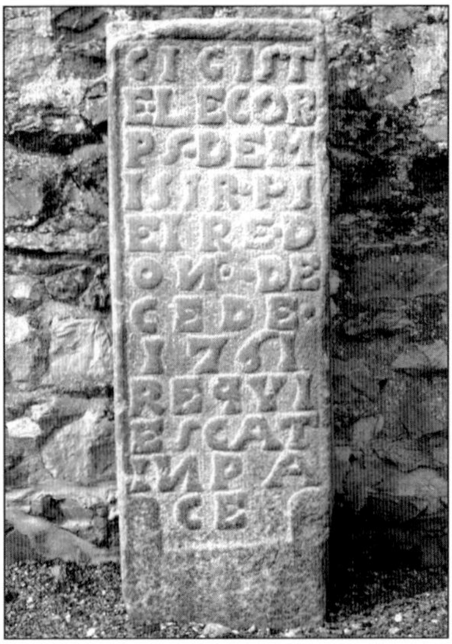

Figure 79

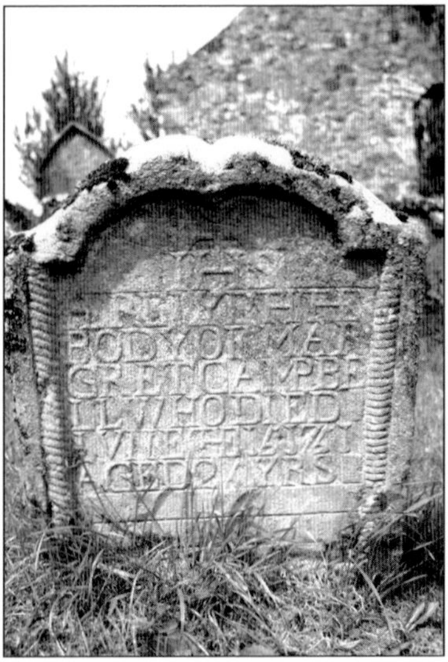

Figure 80

College Chapel, Aberdeen, Scotland (1519) (Fig. 76). This characteristic can also be found in some versal forms and may represent evidence of a transition between the two styles. While relief archaic roman inscriptions are most often found on graveslabs, they were occasionally cut on vertical headstones in Britain and Ireland. The earliest inscriptions in archaic roman date from before 1500, but most are from the end of the sixteenth and into the seventeenth centuries. In the early multi-line layout, they appear sporadically up to the early nineteenth century (Fig. 77). A style that is virtually indistinguishable from it was used for the initials of the deceased and date on many headstones. Headstones with early eighteenth-century archaic roman inscriptions in both capitals and lower-case can be found in the Irish counties of Sligo and Roscommon. There is a good example at Sebergham, Cumbria, dated 1616 (Fig. 78).

Three quite different forms of relief roman inscriptional styles may or may not have evolved from the extreme, heavy archaic form. The first of these is a wide, bold roman seen on graveslabs in Britain, Ireland and parts of western Europe, especially north Brittany and Normandy. This form has quite distinct, but usually rather crude, fully developed serifs (Fig. 79). It is a purely inscriptional form that varies little and does not appear to be related to any contemporary typeface. A lighter version was used on graveslabs and headstones in Ulster throughout the eighteenth century (Fig. 80). Related to it, but questionably distinct, is the lettering found on graveslabs, *stèles tabulaires* and discoid gravemarkers in the Basque Region of southern France (Fig. 81). There are many interpretations of this form that vary in width, weight, serif formation and in the design of some of the letters. Some letters, such as the O, are sometimes carved very much smaller than the rest. Although also seen in British, Irish and Breton inscriptions, this stylistic interpretation reaches its climax in Basque culture, so much so

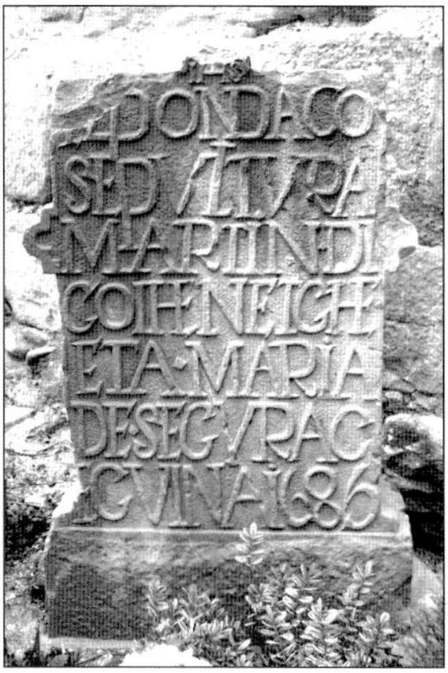

Figure 81

Fig. 79—Raised roman, Caulnes, Brittany, France (1761).

Fig. 80—Raised roman capitals, Kildress, Co. Tyrone, Ireland (1751).

Fig. 81—*Stèle tabulaire* with Basque lettering, Ainhoa, Pyrénées Atlantique, France (1686).

Fig. 82—The Basque typeface Koldako.

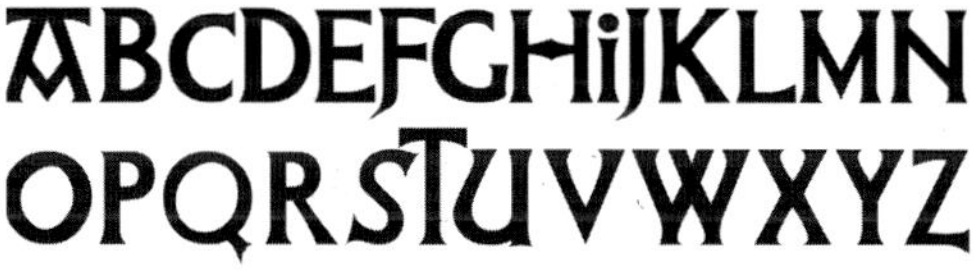

Figure 82

that the variant has been referred to as 'Basque lettering'. Early inscriptional Basque lettering is no more than one of many subtle regional inscriptional versions of early relief roman. Several of the individual characteristics of some letters have been adapted and exaggerated for modern use. These include A with both broken crossbar and apical horizontal line, capital I with a dot above, small capital O, upturned curved leg of the R, the use of V for U and the curvilinear enhancement of some letters. These recent adaptations can be seen throughout the Basque Region on signs and in twentieth-century typography, but several, including the dotted capital I and upturn on the leg of R, also occur in texts on lintels in vernacular architecture in Germany. The use of this so-called Basque alphabet has been encouraged by organisations, including Lauburu in France, to embed and raise the profile of Basque culture (Fig. 82). This lettering is being used very effectively on modern Basque discoid gravemarkers in the region.

A third very different form is found commonly on graveslabs and headstones in the Dutch province of Groningen and in north Germany, especially in Oldenburgerland and the Friesian Islands (Fig. 83). Although this relief roman style was cut as early as the middle of the sixteenth century and lasted until the nineteenth century, when it was largely superseded in Germany by gothic Fraktur, it is a fully developed roman with serifs, quite unlike the archaic form. It is characterised by the very strong vertical stress, emphasised by the contrast between thick and thin lines. Some inscriptions, including mid-sixteenth-century examples in Groningen Province, slope to the right but, strictly speaking, are not italic. Serifs range from small and distinct to large and conspicuous. The initial capitals are usually the same height as the rest of the lettering, although they are sometimes in a script form. The W is formed of two Vs, and both it and the Λ are often inclined. The earlier headstone inscriptions in this

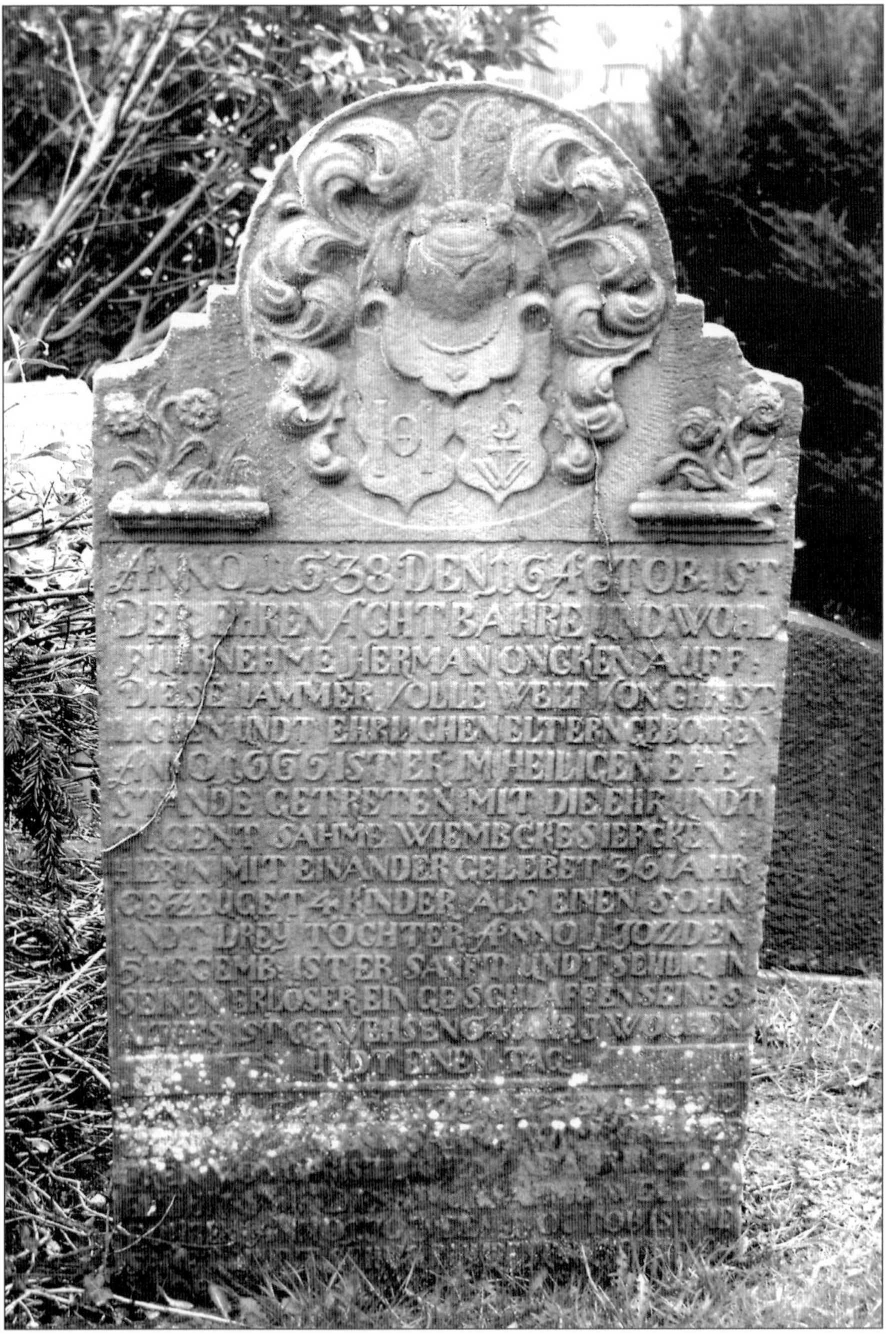

Figure 83

Fig. 83—Headstone with raised roman lettering, Sande, Oldenburgerland, Germany (1638).

Table 3—A comparison of raised roman lettering on headstones in Oldenburgerland and Ireland.

	German	Irish
Date	Early 17th to 19th century	Early 19th century
Proportions	Very condensed to medium	Moderately wide
Stress	Strongly vertical	Strongly vertical
Contrast between thicks and thins	Marked	Marked
Serifs	Bracketed, small to large	Bracketed, small
Initial capitals	Uniform height, or script	Larger than text
E and F central line	Short	Short
R leg	Curved	Curved
U	With right vertical	U rounded
M	Almost reaching baseline	Almost reaching baseline
A	Vertical or sloped	Vertical
W	Vertical or sloped	Vertical

Table 3

part of Germany are close to archaic roman in style and there are a few examples of transitional forms, although the north German style probably did not evolve from it. Runge suggests that the design was influenced by Claude Garamond's typeface 'Antiqua', but the resemblance is superficial.[94] Indeed, it is much more akin to typefaces called 'modern', not to be seen until Didot's font of 1784. Masons in County Cork, south County Limerick and south County Tipperary, Ireland, cut a very similar form to these German inscriptions at the beginning of the nineteenth century. This remarkable coincidence is all the more striking as the headstones are not unlike each other in basic concept, with an illustrated pediment and inscriptional panel below. The similarities include almost identical basic forms, the very strong vertical stress and marked line-width contrast (Table 3). There appears to be no evidence of contact between masons in the two countries.

By the middle of the seventeenth century the dominant relief roman was largely superseded by intaglio forms. Masons, and type-designers somewhat later, realised that the traditional forms could be varied.[95] In consequence, as well as general stylistic temporal and geographical trends, there were important changes in the more subtle elements of letters. The masons' interpretation of the details of a letterform, for example height to width proportion, line thickness or capital to lower-case height ratio, perhaps tells us more about current local culture than the selection of the basic style itself (Fig. 84). Trends in these less obvious changes are best interpreted and understood through statistical analysis. At various times there were alternative versions of some letters, including some that are archaic in character. The use of one form in preference to another increases and decreases both geographically and over time. The archaic and advanced forms of a letter can sometimes be seen in the same inscription,

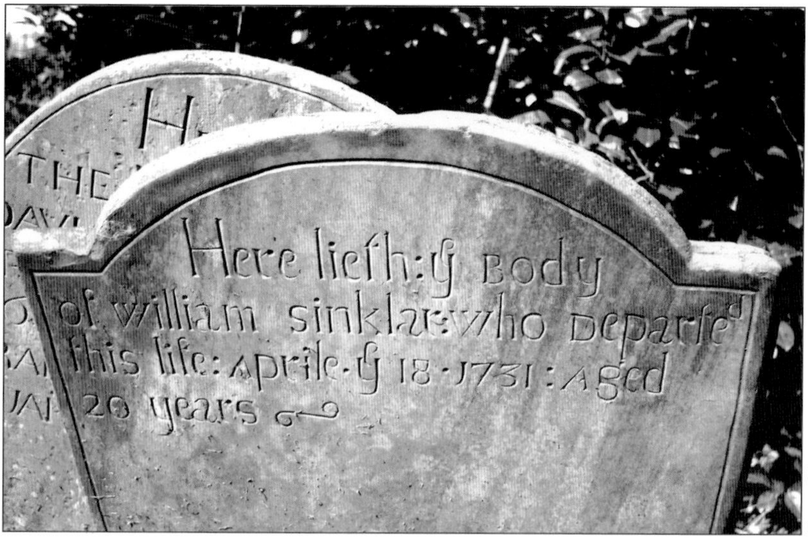

Figure 84

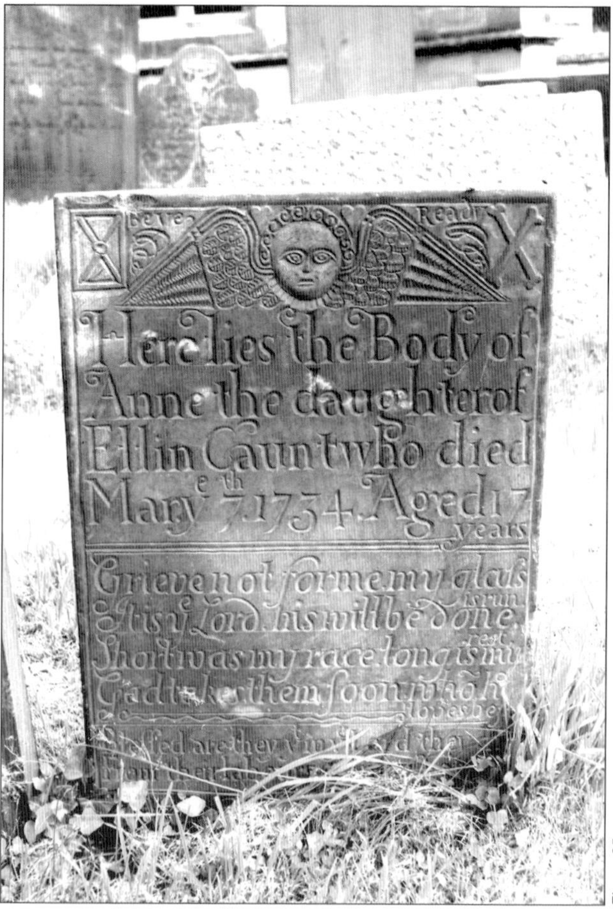

Figure 85

Fig. 84—Incised roman capitals, Grey Abbey, Co. Down, Ireland (1731).

Fig. 85—Skilfully cut vernacular headstone, Hickling, Nottinghamshire, England (1734).

as at Kilbirnie, Ayrshire, Scotland (1727), where the early and later forms of A are present. There are also geographical differences in the frequency of use of these forms. As with the archaic form, ligatures and mirrored letters are common in intaglio inscriptions.

In Britain, the early forms of A, B, E, M, R and W occur with decreasing frequency up to the nineteenth century, although some can be seen in inscriptions even today. In Ireland and the USA, archaic forms of A and W continue to be relatively common well into the nineteenth century. In the seventeenth century, and occasionally in the sixteenth to eighteenth centuries, the capital letters I and J were interchangeable in English-language and Latin inscriptions, most often in roman but sometimes in other styles. This can make it difficult to determine the letter when only the initials of the deceased are cut in the tombstone. Usually, but not invariably, the J is distinguished by the vertical of the letter having a short horizontal line through the middle. This is sometimes shortened to a dot.

The consequence of the increase in demand for funerary memorials, and for headstones in particular, was the appearance of numerous vernacular markers. Although formal memorials were still erected to commemorate the rich and famous, many more were made by less-skilled masons, craftsmen and untrained individuals. The range of gravemarkers resulting from the need to erect a permanent memorial, or even a temporary one in the case of wooden gravemarkers, is more than matched by the range of inscriptional lettering that has been incised on them. In Europe and North America, many elaborate gravemarkers of the seventeenth and eighteenth centuries with skilfully cut lettering can be classed as vernacular (Fig. 85). No strict line of demarcation exists between those cut by the amateur and those cut by the professional. There is a continuum from one to the other. If necessary, it is better to recognise the distinction between vernacular and commercial memorials made by Little, already cited. The rapid takeover of incised classical roman as the dominant style, beginning in the seventeenth century, coincided with this rise in popularity of the headstone as a memorial. It is also the period when we see some of the most ingenious and inventive treatments of inscriptional lettering and layout.

Although inscriptions in roman capitals and lower-case, rather than all capitals, can be found as early as 1616, 1619 in Ireland and 1626 in Scotland, it was not until the end of that century that they become much more popular on headstones and graveslabs. They were, however, employed extensively by master masons on formal mixed-case inscriptions. After a short period when cursive and script became much more widely used, especially in Scotland, roman capitals and lower-case were once again very commonly utilised and became the dominant form for the main text of gravemarker inscriptions by the end of the eighteenth century. In basic form the eighteenth-century roman differed little from that used 100 years earlier, other than differences in the proportions of capitals in relation to the lower-case letters (Fig. 86). Some conventions had gradually

Fig. 86—Roman capitals and lower-case, Simsbury, Connecticut, USA (1731).

Fig. 87—Mason's guidelines on headstone, Kirkconnel Churchyard, Dumfriesshire, Scotland (1786).

Fig. 88—Roman capitals on exterior brass plate, Witherslack, Cumbria, England (1700).

Fig. 89—Headstone, Cherryville Burial Ground, Pennsylvania, USA (1762).

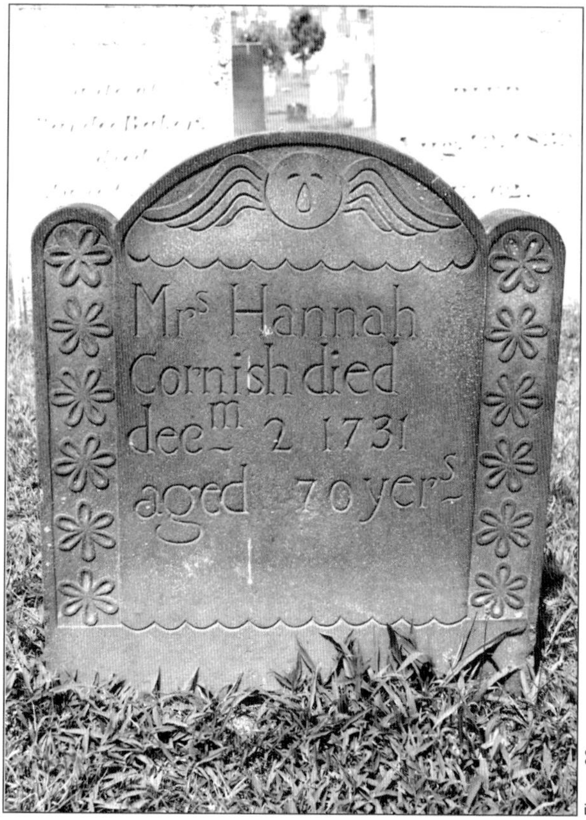

Figure 86

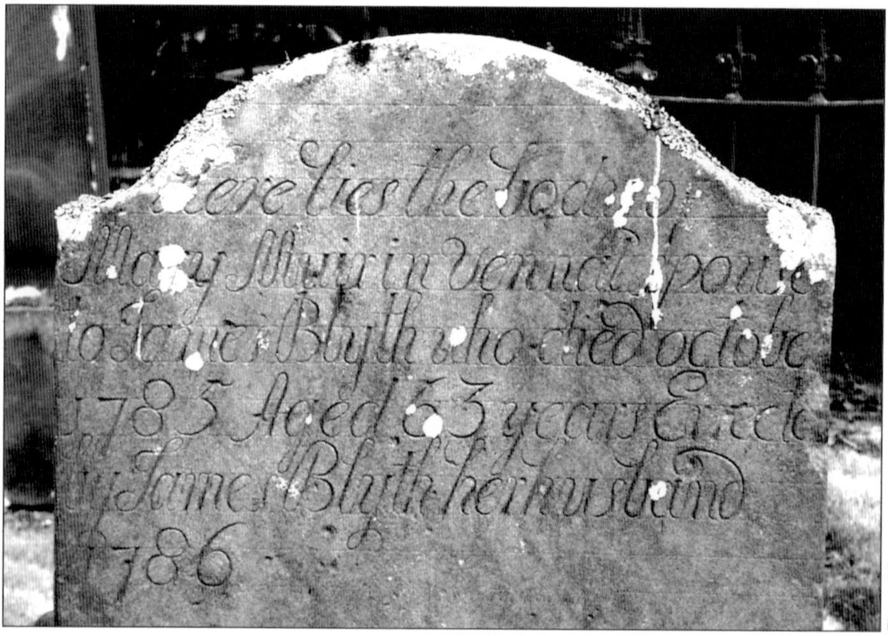

Figure 87

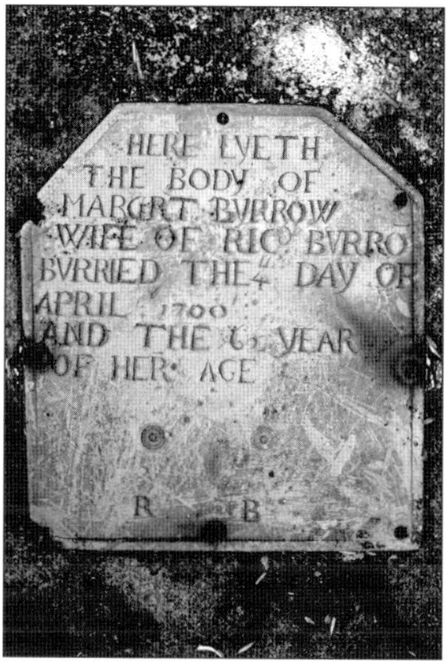

Figure 88

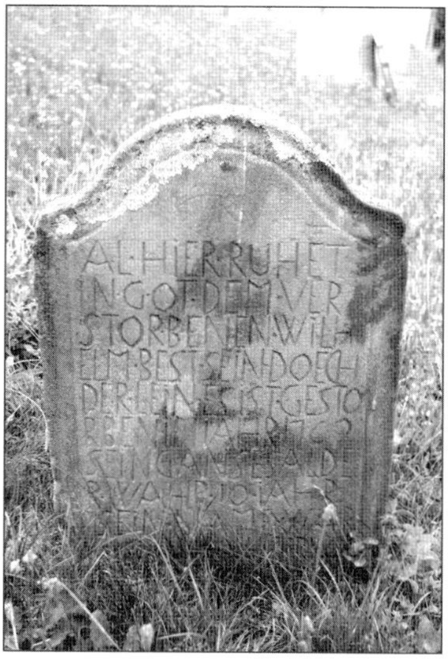

Figure 89

evolved in the design of the roman form. For instance, it seemed to be good practice to make the height of the capital exactly twice the height of the lower-case letters. Although the mason did not always achieve this, construction lines scratched on some gravestones indicate that this was the aim (Fig. 87). It also appeared to be 'correct' to make the capital and lower-case O perfect circles. In less well-incised inscriptions, the serifs may be very small, poorly formed or missing altogether. Some have little discernible variation in weight.

Capitals of a similar roman style to those on headstones had been used on the earliest exterior brass plates in England from the very end of the sixteenth century and throughout much of the seventeenth (Fig. 88). The roman capitals of early seventeenth-century plates tend to be bold in weight and wide in proportions. Later romans, including those with lower-case, were lighter, more condensed and generally more elegant. Roman capitals and lower-case became increasing common in the eighteenth century. Many engraved brass plates have lettering that is 'Modern' in style, with exaggerated thicks and thins, vertical emphasis and hairline serifs, pre-dating these attributes on stone inscriptions and typefaces by some considerable time.

The development and evolution of German sensitivity to good letterform is apparent in their roman seventeenth- and eighteenth-century gravemarker inscriptions, both in their homeland, in Pennsylvania and in parts of Nova Scotia to which they introduced their culture and traditions. We see elegant proportions and a much better understanding of line and space than is typical in most British, Irish and other American gravemarker lettering (Fig. 89). Even the few surviving wooden graveboards of the last quarter of the eighteenth century, with many ligatures and extensive use of the archaic form of A, demonstrate a rare finery in the construction of

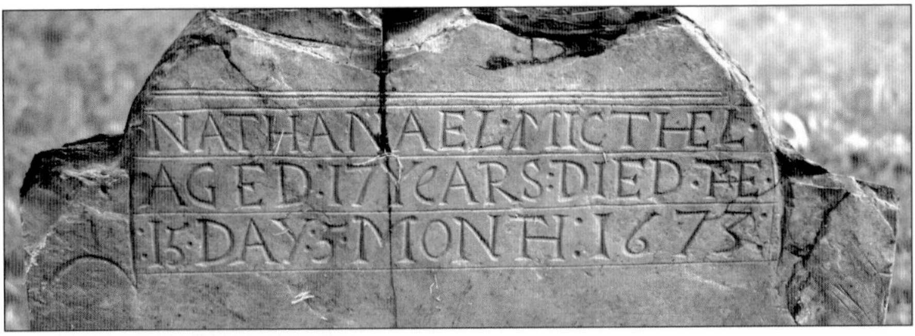

Figure 90

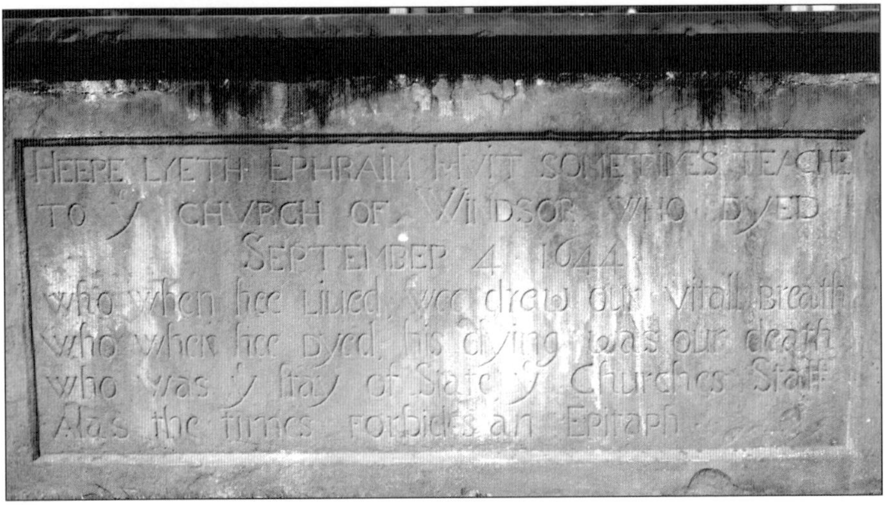

Figure 91

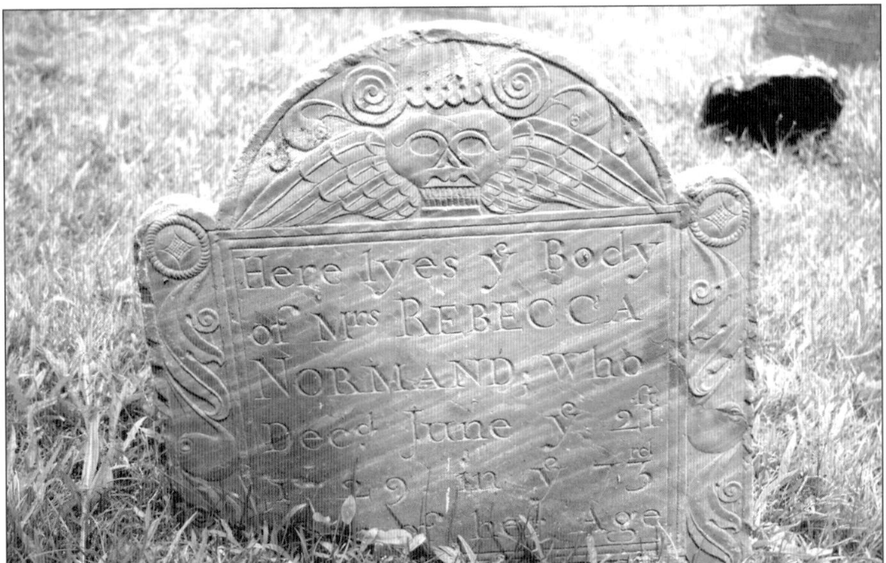

Figure 92

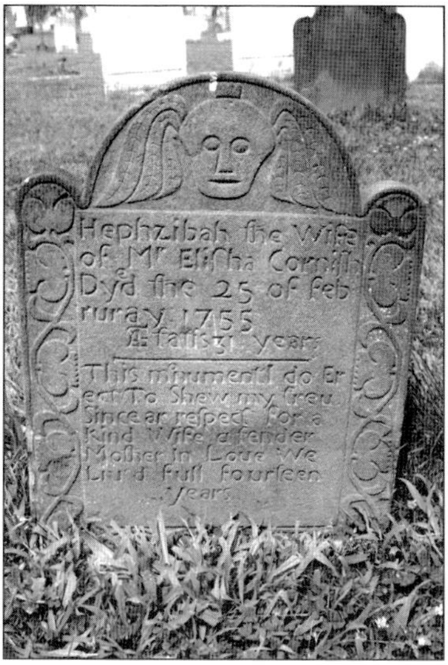

Figure 93

Fig. 90—Early New England gravemarker, Cambridge, Massachusetts, USA (1673).

Fig. 91—Inscription on box tomb, Windsor, Connecticut, USA (1644).

Fig. 92—New England headstone, Marblehead, Massachusetts, USA (1729).

Fig. 93—Roman lettering with cursive characteristics, Simsbury, Connecticut, USA (1755).

the letters. In much of Germany in the eighteenth century there was a reversion to the less-elegant Fraktur forms that had been simmering below the surface for some time, except in Oldenburgerland and Friesland, where the distinctive forms of relief roman capitals evolved and continued to be used up to the twentieth century.

The beginning of the seventeenth century also marks the advent of gravemarker inscriptions in the USA. Most of the earliest inscriptions in the USA were roman but naïve, mostly lacking serifs, frequently with ligatures and often with a horizontal between the text lines (Fig. 90). One of the earliest examples of gravemarker lettering was clearly cut by a skilled and creative mason.[96] The roman inscription dated 1644 on a box tomb at Windsor, Connecticut, is extremely accomplished, mixing capitals and lower-case (Fig. 91). It uses a form of H with a nick in the horizontal line and archaic forms of M, W and U. The initial letters are larger than the rest of the text and the Y has a long, curved tail. Some headstones in the same burial ground show similar attributes and may have been cut by the same mason. Many of the New England inscriptions on slate are very similar to each other in style and are based loosely on a standard roman form, even when cut in different stone, either all capitals or capitals and lower-case (Fig. 92). Script occasionally occurs with roman but rarely on its own. Individuality is not lacking, however, in the interpretation of roman form. In Simsbury, Connecticut, for example, there is roman lettering with cursive characteristics (Fig. 93). In New York State, the eighteenth-century roman developed rather distinctive long ascenders and descenders and very conspicuous fishtail serifs (Fig. 94). Many inscriptions in the old burial grounds of Trinity and St Paul's Chapel, New York City, are of this form.

The late eighteenth century was a time of change. Type-founders and

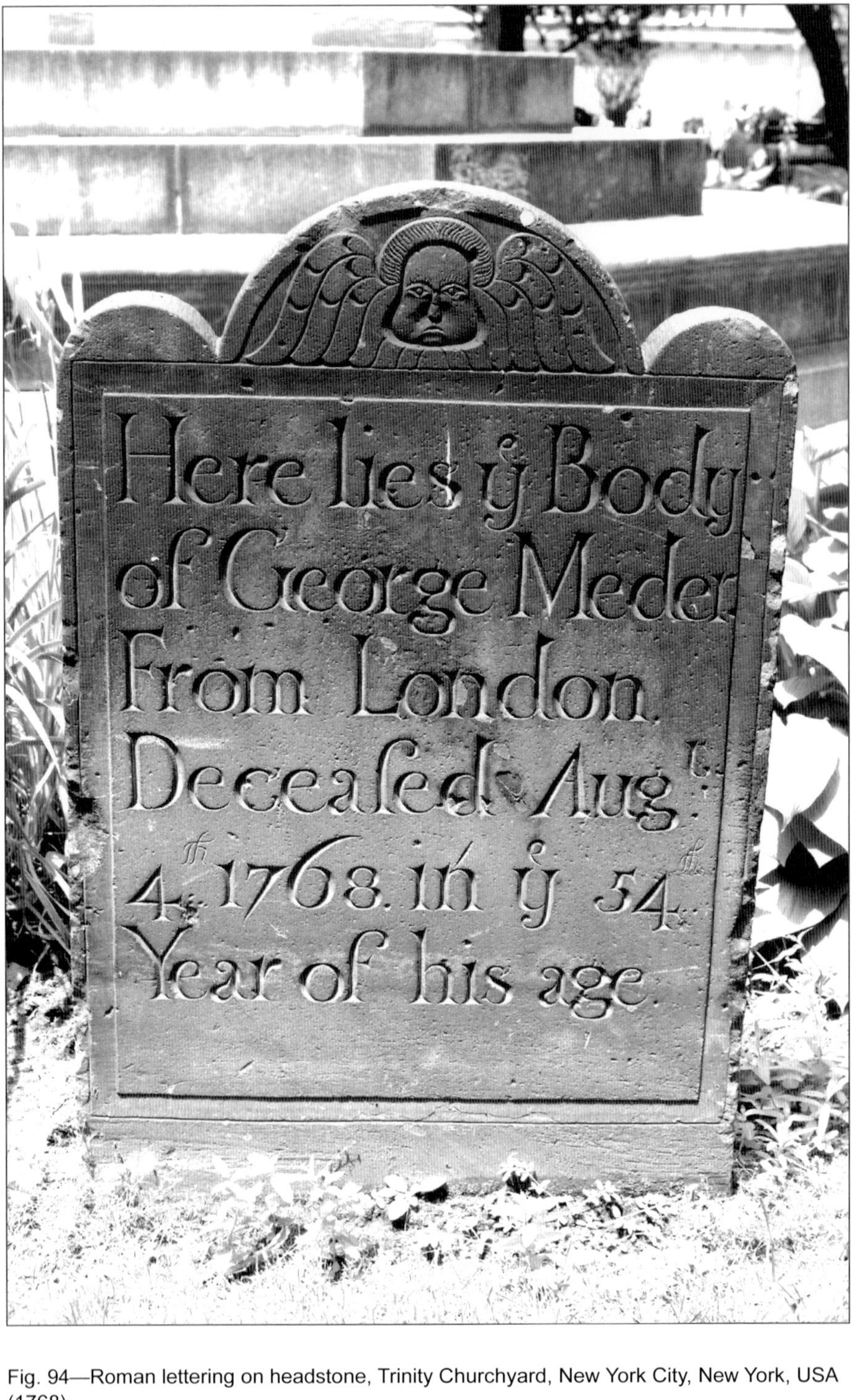

Figure 94

Fig. 94—Roman lettering on headstone, Trinity Churchyard, New York City, New York, USA (1768).

Inscribed in remembrance

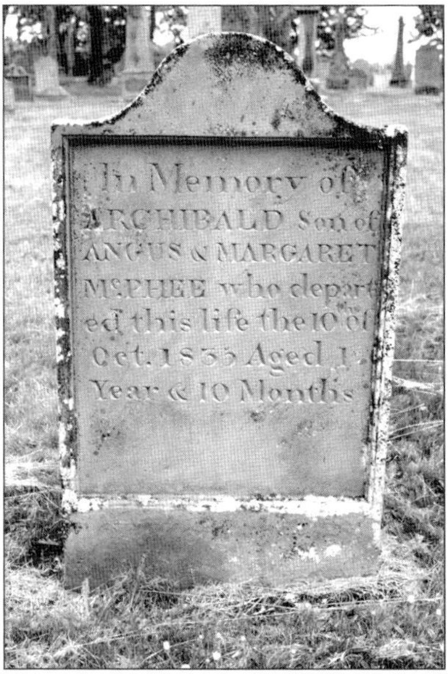

Figure 95

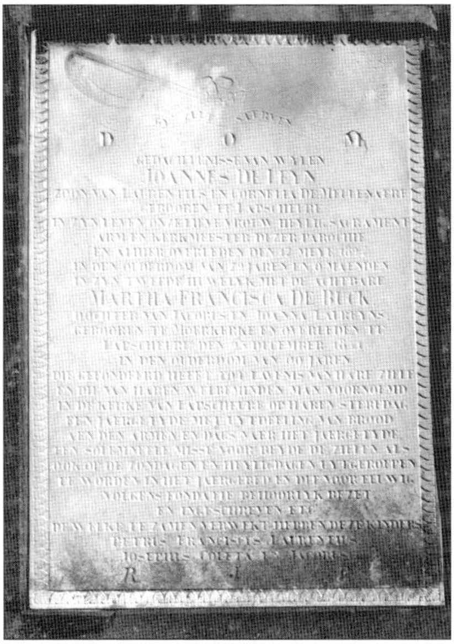

Figure 96

Fig. 95—Lettering in the so-called 'english letter', Laurel Hill, Nova Scotia, Canada (1835).

Fig. 96—Wall memorial, Lapscheure, Belgium (1841).

their fonts were making their mark on the choice of lettering for use on gravemarkers. The typeface 'Baskerville' was probably the basis for a more robust roman with bracketed serifs that came to be known as the 'English vernacular letter'. Although widely accepted, it is an unfortunate term for a letterform that was used extensively on gravemarkers in other parts of Europe and North America (Fig. 95).[97] By the end of the eighteenth century, typeface design, including roman in all its manifestations, was the greatest influence on gravemarker inscriptions. In Britain, Canada and the USA, and to a much lesser extent in Ireland, headstones with mixed-style inscriptions predominated, the lettering very much based on currently fashionable type forms. In Germany more traditional approaches were adopted. Elsewhere in continental Europe the lettering used on gravemarker inscriptions was much more restrained (Fig. 96).

Some styles that were to become the mainstay of the memorial masons' repertoire by the beginning of the nineteenth century first appear on gravemarkers at a remarkably early date. In England there is an italic in an inscription of 1624 and script on a headstone of 1675. True sans-serifs with non-roman proportions were cut in 1648 in Scotland and 1650 in Ireland. Even gothic revival lettering appears on an English headstone of 1638. It is thought that block serif, an extreme development of roman, and the 'Modern' style appeared on stone before type. Although lettering close to block and sans-serif forms appears in the seventeenth century in Britain and Europe, together with cursive, script and italic, they are really much later innovations.

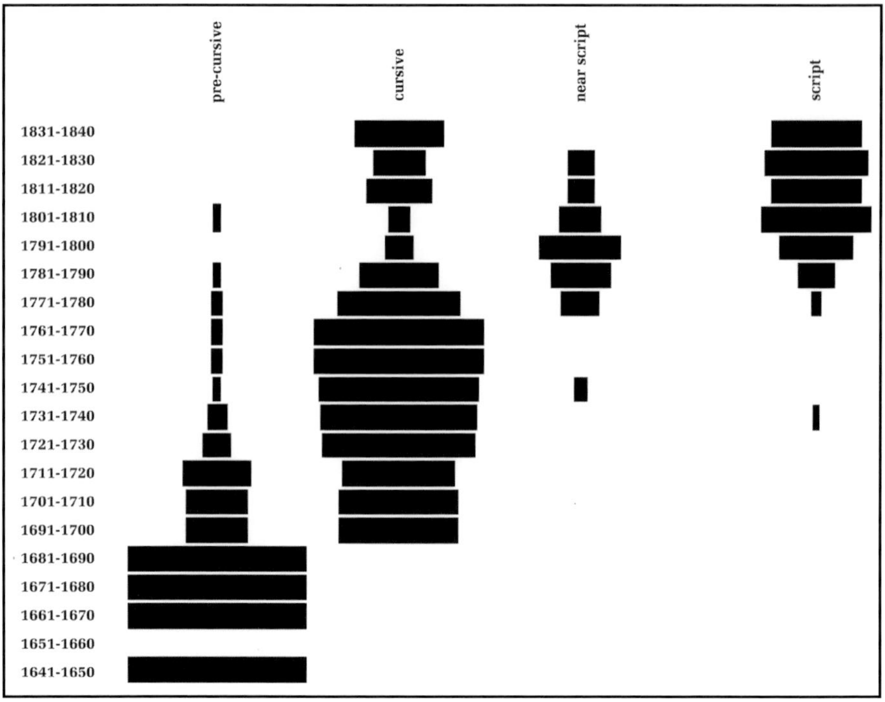

Figure 97

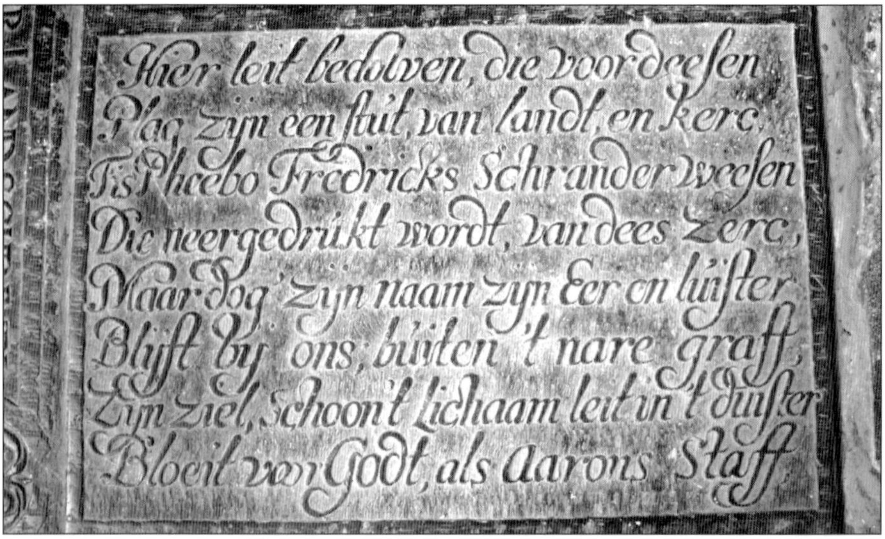

Figure 98

Fig. 97—The development of script forms from 1641 to 1840 based on a four-group classification. The width of the bars represents the frequency of the style.

Fig. 98—Variant of cursive inscription on graveslab, Noordbroek, North Holland Province, Netherlands. Although the basic forms in this inscription are cursive, the individual letters are joined with a fine line as in script (1695).

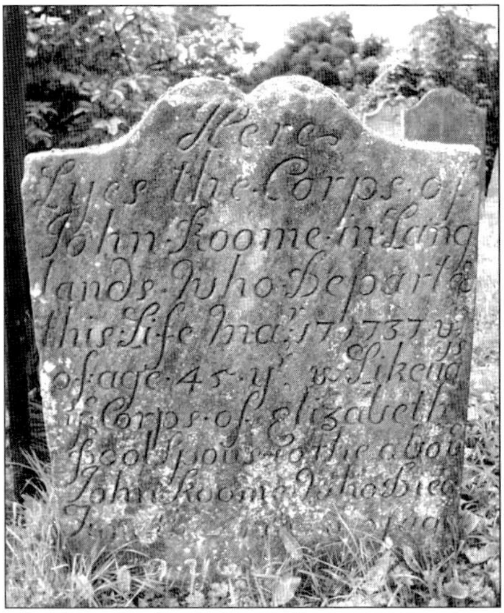

Figure 99

Fig. 99—Fully developed cursive, Dornock Churchyard, Dumfriesshire, Scotland (1737).

Informality and the copybook—the development of script forms

Towards the end of the seventeenth century, when roman inscriptional lettering was predominant, a new form began to appear in western European inscriptions. This is a lettering style that can be generically classified as cursive. It is reasonable to support the widely accepted view that the contributing influences to the development of this cursive form were writing or calligraphy, and the masons' attempts to emulate the penmanship of writing masters such as Cocker and the Bickhams. There is good evidence, however, that the development of cursive lettering on gravemarkers was an evolutionary process, initially quite independent of writing styles, and that pen forms were copied only several decades after the establishment of a cursive tradition. By classifying inscriptional forms into various groups, from 'pre-script' that show only some slight traces of cursiveness to 'pen' forms that have clear characteristics of writing, such as the use of 'looped' ascenders or descenders, the continuous joining of letters and the thicks and thins of pen strokes, it can be demonstrated that there was a slow and gradual change from one form to the other (Fig. 97).[98]

Cursive inscriptions are not endemic to Scotland, but they are found more commonly on gravemarkers there than anywhere else. Variants of cursive can be seen in some English, Irish, French, Belgian, Dutch and Scandinavian inscriptions, including headstones and formal graveslabs within churches (Fig. 98). Gray wrongly considered this form to be peculiarly English.[99] An analysis of Scottish inscriptions reveals some key dates. Letterforms with cursive characteristics were identified on tombstones as early as 1644. This is a hybrid form between roman and script at Brechin Cathedral Churchyard, Angus. The earliest fully developed cursive did not appear until the very beginning of the eighteenth

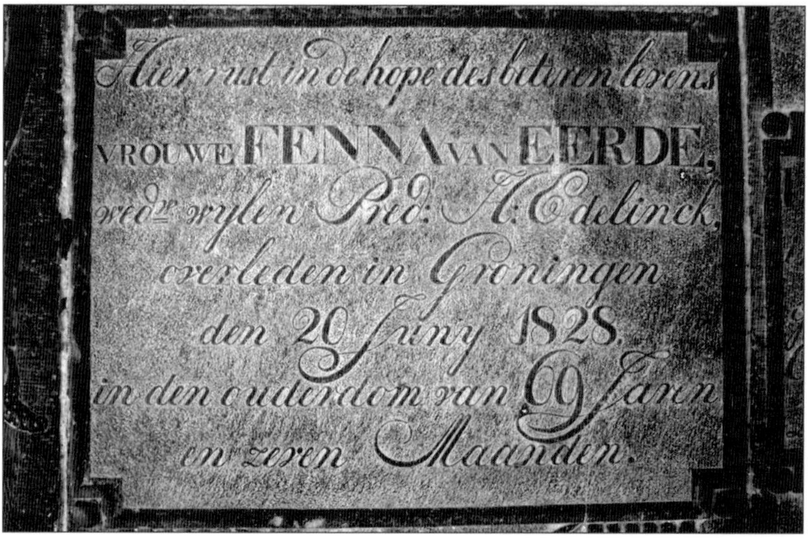

Figure 100

century. Cursive lettering not showing the influence of pen-written forms was commonly used in the middle of the eighteenth century. The first use of true pen forms was between 1741 and 1750, reaching its peak in the early nineteenth century.

The initial hints of cursiveness in the early examples of this form can be seen in some lower-case letters, especially ‘e’ and ‘r’, and a general rounding of letters that, in the roman style, are classical in construction. The slope in these early primitive and hybrid forms is only a little off the vertical. Later developments in the direction of script are evident in the extended curvature of the descenders, lower-case ‘a’, ‘b’ and ‘f’ and the form of capitals (Fig. 99). When true script evolved, the slope was significantly greater and new forms of lower-case ‘w’ and ‘s’ appear. The final change to forms based on pen-written specimens is clearly identified by the variation in line thickness that parallels the pressures of a pen on paper, resulting in the distinctive thicks and thins. The influence of the pen is also evident in scripts where letters are linked by fine lines as in writing (Fig. 100). Initially only some letters were joined, but later the lettering is continuous. Not only did the lettering itself emulate penmanship in the later inscriptions; decorative flourishes around words such as IN MEMORY OF or the deceased’s name became frequent in pen-script forms and also in gothic, in which the pen influence was often equally evident. In some examples the decoration is virtually identical to that illustrated in the eighteenth-century copybooks (Fig. 101). Both cursive and script forms are relatively uncommon in Ireland and Germany. They are also rather rare in the USA and Canada, except on Scots-Irish gravemarkers.

Many of the inscriptions in stone in script lettering from about the middle of the eighteenth century were not cut as deeply as contemporary roman forms and, through the ravages of time, these memorials have

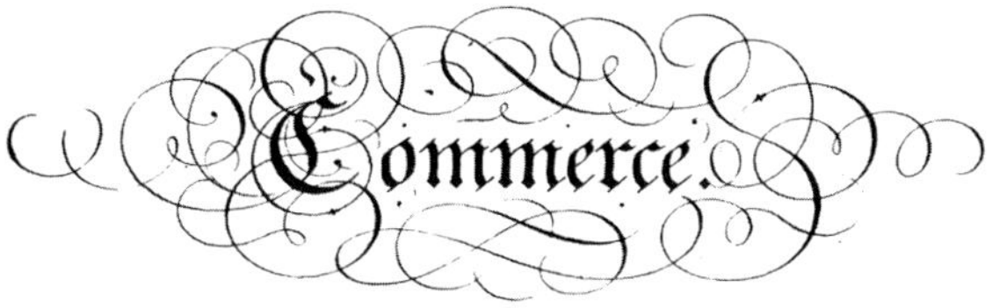

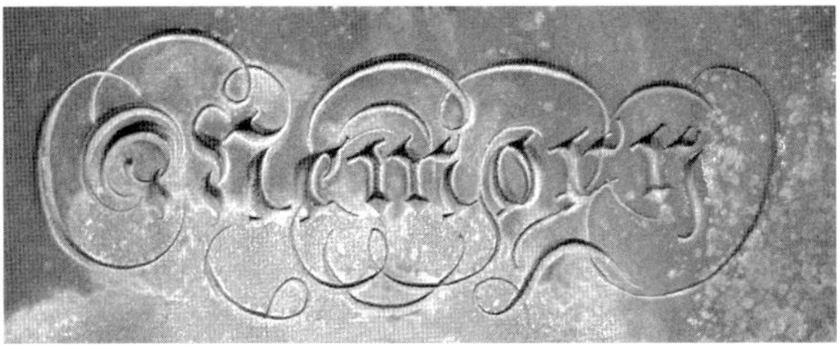

Figure 101

Fig. 100—Script lettering on graveslab, Holwierde, Groningen Province, Netherlands (1828).

Fig. 101—Writing from Bickham and Bickham's *The universal penman* and similar lettering on a headstone at St Mary's Church, Dumfries, Dumfriesshire, Scotland (1830).

become some of the most difficult to read. A thinner flowing line in these later inscriptions required a much shallower cut, and the cutting of curvilinear shapes to greater depth was probably more difficult. However, relief cursive and script lettering was used on hard slate graveslabs in the Netherlands.

Further evidence that the cursive forms were distinct from later scripts and that they were not attempts to emulate written forms can be seen in small, funerary brass plate engraving in England. Two basic styles of non-roman lettering were used on both internal and external small brasses of the seventeenth to nineteenth centuries, with considerable variation within each and some overlap in form. The simpler style is little removed from a very cursive italic but with distinctive flourishes on the capitals, ascenders and descenders and exaggerated thickening and thinning of the lines (Fig. 102). The more commonly used form is far more elaborate, resembling a delicate pen-written script, with extensive and exuberant flourishes (Fig. 103). The more elaborate style pre-dates the simpler form by about 50 years, appearing first in the 1670s, although the simpler form was used more frequently up to the early 1700s. Engraved lettering on precious metal artefacts similarly diverges from the trend seen in stone and small brass plate inscriptions. There is no evidence of a gradual development of the cursive to the script forms, as happened in the case of gravestones. After the almost exclusive use of roman capitals up to the end of the seventeenth century, engravers followed two quite different approaches to their craft: one was an emulation of pen script but with strong suggestions of italic attributes, while the other was a cursive style that was quite independent in its concept and similar to the cursive on gravemarkers.

It took more than 100 years for there to be any identifiable influence of the pen on gravemarker lettering, following the gradual change from roman

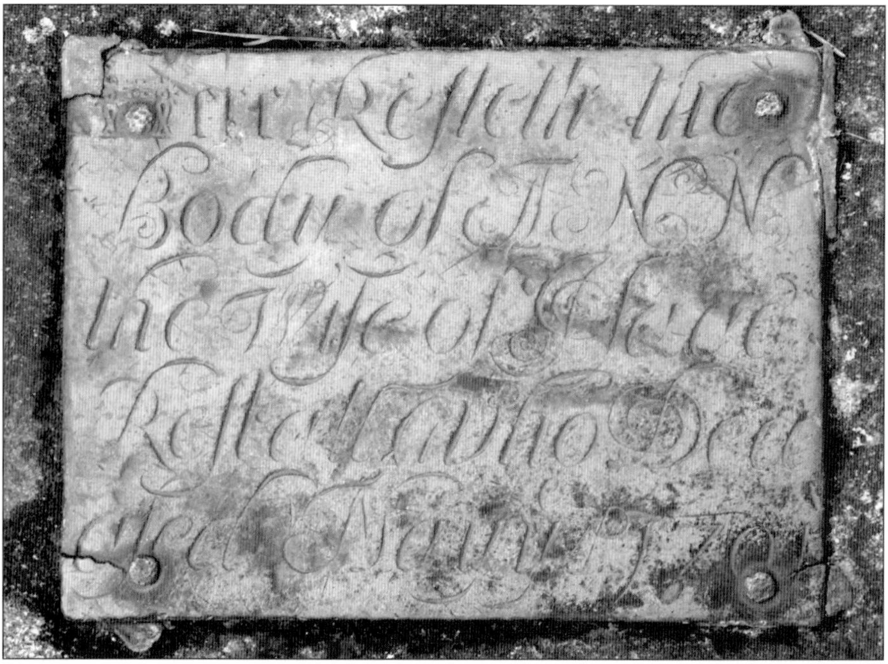

Figure 102

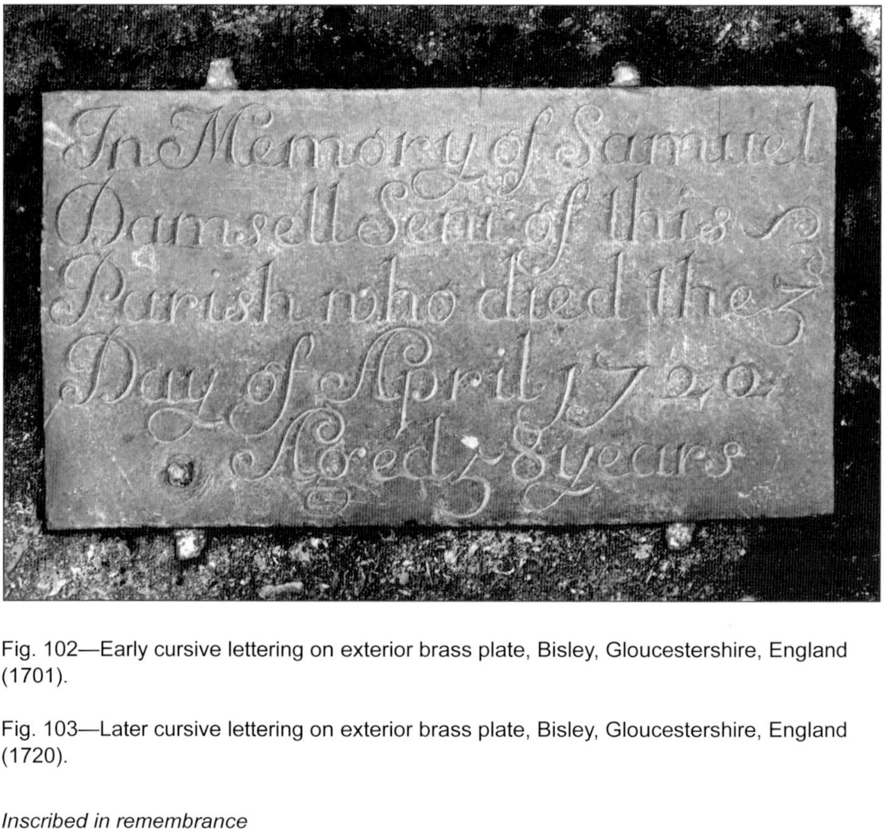

Figure 103

Fig. 102—Early cursive lettering on exterior brass plate, Bisley, Gloucestershire, England (1701).

Fig. 103—Later cursive lettering on exterior brass plate, Bisley, Gloucestershire, England (1720).

Inscribed in remembrance

forms that started in the 1640s. This suggests that the initiation of cursive inscriptions was not an attempt to copy written forms. Why the masons began to make their inscriptions more cursive, a pattern of development that took place throughout western Europe, is difficult to say. While roman lettering, especially capitals, gives an impression of formality, cursiveness tends to indicate informality, freedom and a more personal touch. Perhaps the use of sloping forms and more curved shapes was simply a reaction against that austerity of the roman forms. The similarity of some of the characteristics of the earlier cursive forms to written forms is probably coincidental. This would have been recognised by the masons who then looked to copybooks and handwriting for inscriptional sources. Among the most likely to have been used are Edward Cocker's *The pens transcendencie; or, faire writings labyrinth* (1657), John Ayres' *A tutor to penmanship* (London, 1698) and George and John Bickham's *The universal penman* (London, 1741). The fact that none of the commonly used 'secretary' styles of the later part of the seventeenth and first half of the eighteenth centuries are to be found on British gravemarkers of that period further supports this hypothesis. It would appear that cursiveness in gravemarker lettering, and possibly that on other artefacts, was simply a desire to introduce less formal attributes to the inscriptions. The script forms on stone gravemarkers and engraved brass plates that are quite clearly based on pen forms and that were probably copied directly from contemporary handwriting manuals have quite a different history and origin, even if, on occasion, some similarities between the two were recognised and some letters copied or enhanced by the engravers and masons.

Decadence, banality and opportunity—the nineteenth and twentieth centuries

The nineteenth century is often referred to as the 'Golden Age' of cemetery commemoration. If that time is to be judged by its excesses of vanity expressed through memorials that exude sentimentality and by its vivid representation of the class distinctions that pervaded Victorian society, so be it. Arguably, as a period in which we can celebrate the letter-cutter's art in Britain, the USA and Canada, the title is unwarranted. The embryos of the styles and uses of lettering on British, Irish and ex-patriot Canadian and Australian Victorian memorials can be found on headstones towards the end of the eighteenth century and the early part of the nineteenth century. The increased use of mechanical tools to fashion the stone made it easier to produce a high degree of finish as well as more subtle sculptural detail. The use of pattern books and type specimen sheets as lettering samples opened up the choice of lettering styles, virtually all of which were typographical, to the mason and his clients. On the other hand, creative individuality in the approach to basic lettering design was stifled and the focus was on the mixing of lettering styles, the elaboration

Fig. 104—Mixed styles on headstone, Hickling, Nottinghamshire, England (1747).

Fig. 105—Crosses at St John's Cemetery, Glantane, Co. Cork, Ireland.

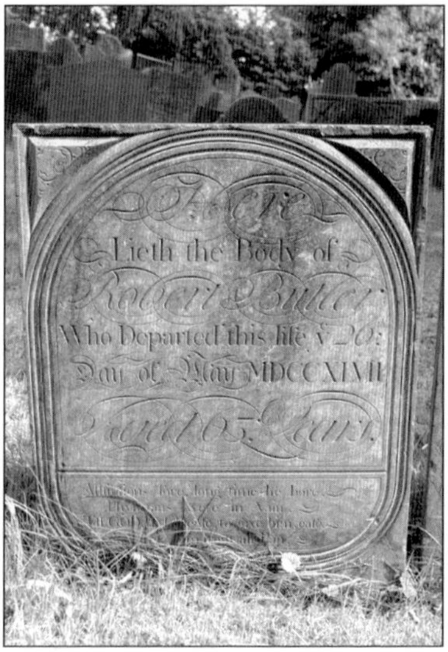

Figure 104

of flourishes and other forms of decoration (Fig. 104). As the nineteenth century progressed, most headstones and many funerary monuments were made larger, with far more attention given to the overall design of the memorial and increasingly less to the lettering than had been the case previously. The large number of Gaelic Revival memorials carved in the shape of a Celtic cross, so characteristic of many nineteenth- and twentieth-century burial grounds in Ireland, is a good illustration of one consequence of this development (Fig. 105).

A number of conventions that had been apparent on a few gravestones before became widely accepted. This included the use of either a gothic or script style for the header IN MEMORY OF, with IN and OF enclosed within the flourishes of M and Y, or SACRED TO THE MEMORY OF. Alternatively, or sometimes in addition to an elaborate header, the name of the deceased or the individual erecting the memorial was incised in a flourished gothic or script form. The remainder of the inscription was usually cut in roman capitals, roman capitals and lower-case or, at a later date, sans-serif. This heterogeneity of styles characterised the Victorian period.

The range of lettering design used for the memorials' main texts was based on contemporary fonts and ranged through the spectrum of type families, including romans, versals, scripts, gothics, sans-serifs and block serifs. In most cases, these were hardly altered from the printed form when cut on the memorial. A consequence of the utilisation of pattern books was not a reduction in the variety of lettering on memorials but an increase owing to the use of what were, in effect, revivals of historical styles. Lettering in both capitals and capitals and lower-case was used in variants that ranged from classical style to what could loosely be called block serif styles such as Egyptian, Clarendon and Bodoni, with

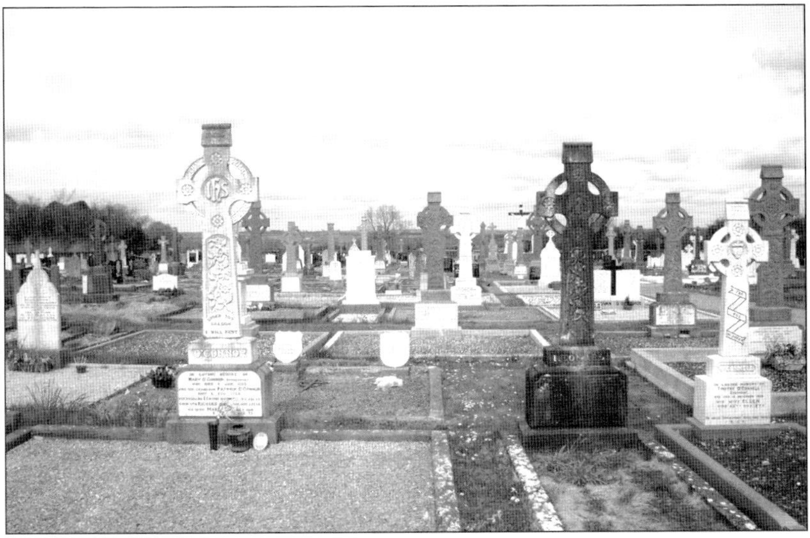

Figure 105

many intermediate forms. Roman and slab serif headers were sometimes decorated with textures. The 'new' gothic was unlike that of medieval times and had clearly distinguished capitals and lower-case, usually much wider in proportion and, consequently, much more legible, except when inappropriately used in capitals only. A new, highly decorative versal form also made its appearance (Fig. 106). Some masons appear to have been obsessed with flourishing and emulation of the penman's art in the design of the header section of the memorial inscription. Sometimes sans-serif or block serif was employed for the family name or a date on the raised margin at the top of the headstone. Frequently the letters were in relief. In the most eccentric designs, the lettering was made to appear as if it was formed from natural materials such as twigs or branches.

At the same time in Germany the traditional gothic Fraktur was used on most headstones. Memorials were often extremely elaborate, almost rococo in style or carved with detailed Crucifixion scenes. In contrast, the epitaphs and Bible excerpts, frequently of considerable length, were very restrained in design and were often cut on the reverse side of the memorial. Lettering was usually of a uniform size, with only minimal use of enlarged headers.

In the USA and Canada, the widespread use of white marble headstones in the nineteenth century was accompanied by inscriptional designs that were quite unlike those that had been used on previous stone gravemarkers. The layout on these gravemarkers usually includes iconographic representations of the willow, clasped hands, urn etc., with lettering that is exclusively typographic, industrial and almost utilitarian, in total contrast with contemporary headstone design in Britain (Fig. 107). Mixed styles, dominated by sans-serif and block serif typefaces, and recessed panels were usually employed. Inscriptions on large, architectural memorials erected

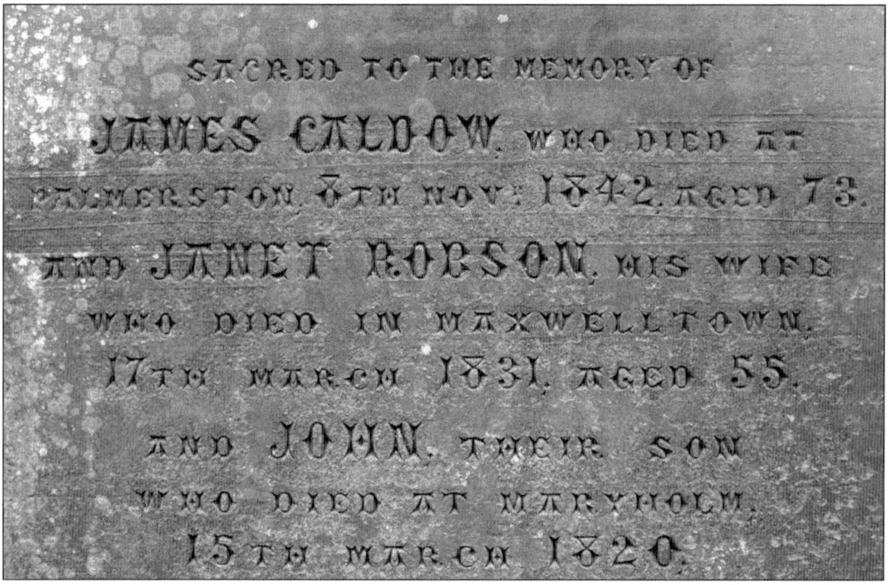

Figure 106

Fig. 106—Nineteenth-century uncio-versal on headstone, Terregles, Dumfriesshire, Scotland (1842).

Fig. 107—White marble headstone, Mountain View Cemetery, Saranac Lake, New York, USA (1862).

Fig. 108—The difference between the v-cut of hand-cut lettering (left) and shotblasting (right).

Fig. 109—Modern black marble headstones, the monotony relieved only by the presence of flowers, Annan Cemetery, Dumfriesshire, Scotland.

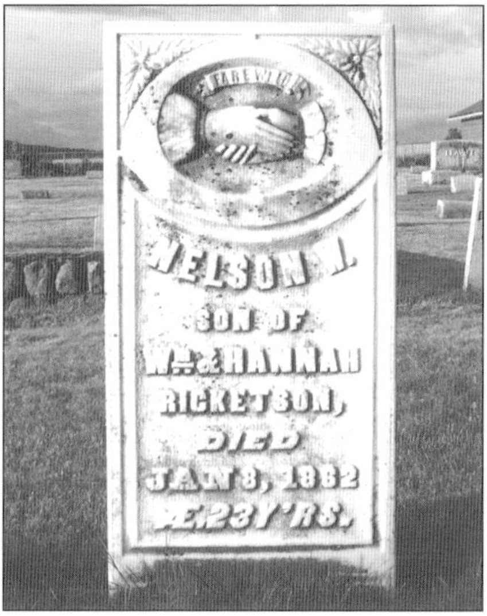

Figure 107

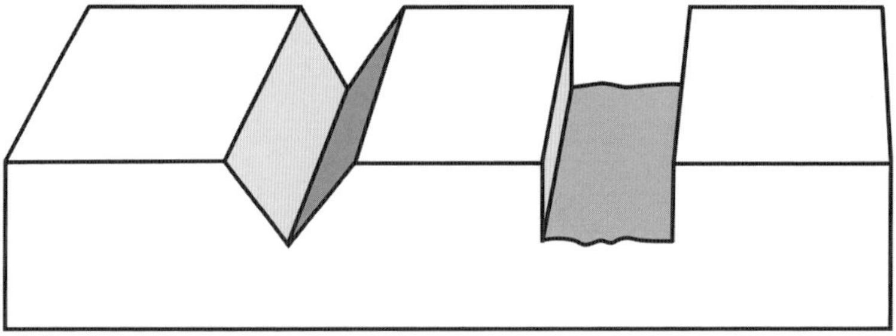

Figure 108

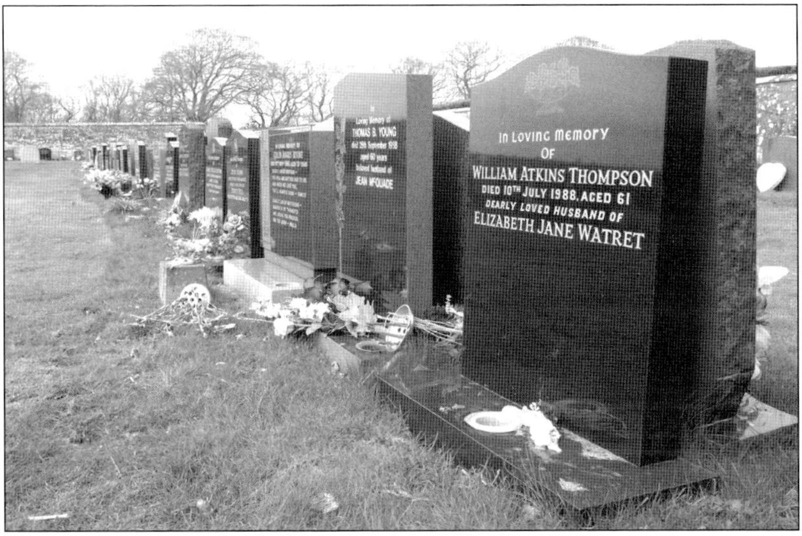

Figure 109

by wealthy Americans were usually minimal and, when more extensive, used simple lettering styles.

The excesses of the nineteenth century were greatly curtailed through the first half of the twentieth, no doubt influenced by the necessary austerity of the war years. The American Civil War between 1861 and 1865 had similarly affected gravestone design in the USA. With a few exceptions, memorials and the lettering on them were simpler, roman or sans-serif in style, and generally lacking the flourishes and extravagances of the Victorian era.

By the second half of the twentieth century a new way of purchasing graveyard or cemetery memorials had been established in Britain, a method that had been commonplace in the USA and Canada for more than 200 years. While it was still possible to commission a mason to cut a headstone to an individual design, it had become a costly business and very few were of this sort. Instead, a commercial shop-window selling approach, usually through an undertaker or monumental mason's company, became the norm. Clients could select a memorial from a range of existing designs, often made in and eventually imported from the Far East, on which standard lettering styles and images could be shot-blasted or routed from handmade or computer-controlled masters (Fig. 108). The result was predictable—the stereotype monotony that we see in many present-day cemeteries throughout the land (Fig. 109). This banality is no less evident in the lack of imagination applied to tombstone lettering design and choice. Not everyone can afford to employ a sculptor or craft letter-cutter to produce an original gravemarker, but there appears to be no reason why modern techniques such as shot-blasting and laser etching cannot be harnessed to produce creative lettering on memorials.

Fortunately, there are exceptions, rare though they may be in Britain and North America. Occasionally, the visitor to a modern cemetery can encounter a gravemarker that has been commissioned from, designed and made by a creative sculptor-craftsman. Very occasionally, lettering has been treated with sensitivity and flair and constitutes an integral part of the memorial. On such occasions we can rejoice that memorial art with its 2,000-year history is not entirely dead. Sadly, more often we have to look beyond the cemeteries for good examples of letter-cutting and, while the hard realities of costs impose restrictions on its use, there are many examples of very good and highly creative inscriptional lettering to be seen in British cities, towns and countryside.[100]

Germany has a tradition of producing notable calligraphers and type-designers, including such lettering masters as Rudolf Koch and Hermann Zapf. The understanding of good letterform that can be seen on German and German Pennsylvanian gravemarkers from the early seventeenth century is still in evidence today. A visit to a modern cemetery or monumental mason's yard in the western part of the country will be rewarded with a display of some memorials with extremely lively, creative incised lettering.[101]

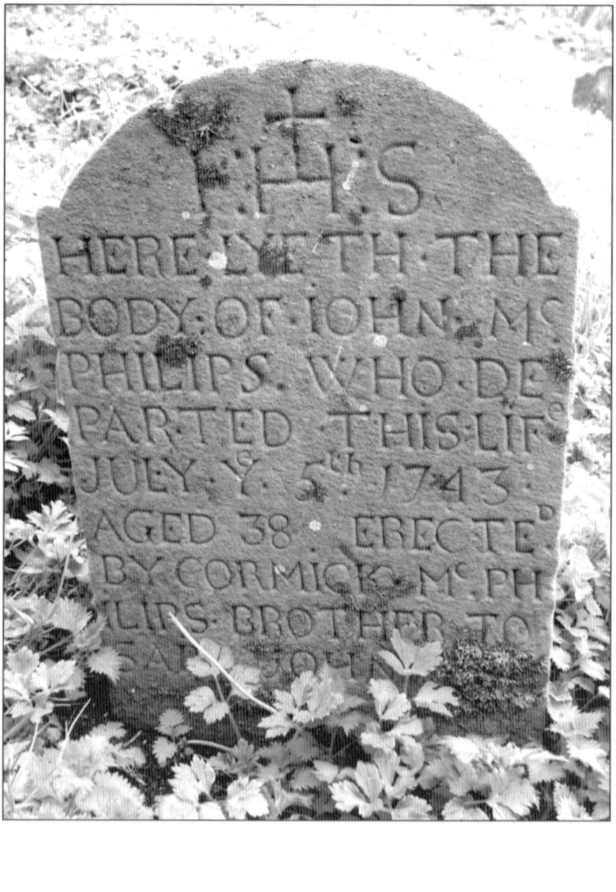

Figure 110

Fig. 110—Headstone. Note the completion of words with small letters at the end of lines. Killeevan, Co. Monaghan, Ireland (1743).

DESIGN AND INTERPRETATION

Layout

Until relatively recently, the makers of gravemarkers, memorials and monuments would not have thought of themselves as designers. The carvers of the great marble effigial European memorials of the Renaissance or the large Victorian monuments were sculptors. The masons who made seventeenth- and eighteenth-century headstones and less prestigious memorials were craftsmen. Only when pattern books were published with 'designs' for memorials do we see the use of the term. Design implies that there is some pre-planning of the object being made. With regard to gravemarker lettering, immediately we run into difficulties. While it is clear that most medieval and early post-medieval inscriptions on funerary memorials, and those from the nineteenth century onwards, were carefully planned and laid out accurately on the stone, in the seventeenth and eighteenth centuries the frequent occurrence of inscriptions in which the last few letters are compressed to fit the end of a line, or even placed above or below, is evidence that, in many instances, the inscription was not pre-drawn or painted (Fig. 110). In these cases, the mason must have simply worked from left to right, cutting the letters one by one. On superficial examination, it would be easy to conclude that the most formal inscriptions cut by skilled masons were carefully planned in advance while the more rustic were not. This view is much too simplistic. There are many formal memorials that reveal major errors of judgement, with ill-fitting lines in the layout of the text. Conversely, many rustic vernacular ones show evidence of very careful planning of the inscription's arrangement. The letters on the magnificent graveslab at Sanquhar, Dumfriesshire, Scotland, follow a systematically worked-out design, even though the individual who made it was clearly a relatively modest craftsman (Fig. 111).

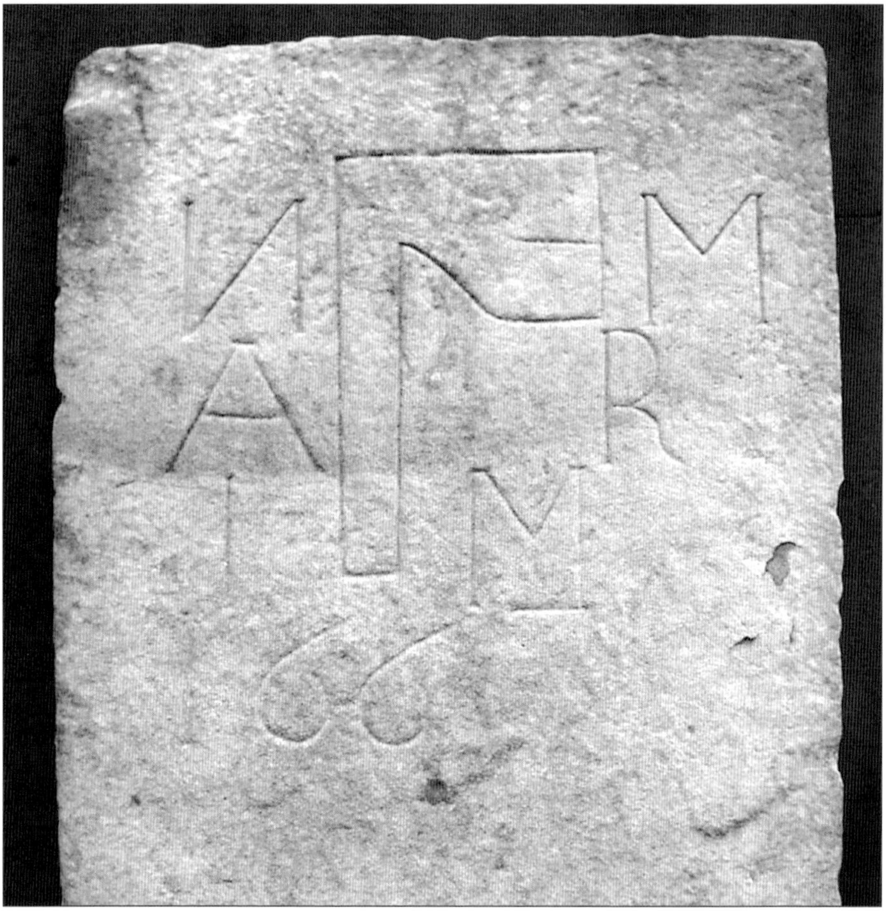

Figure 111

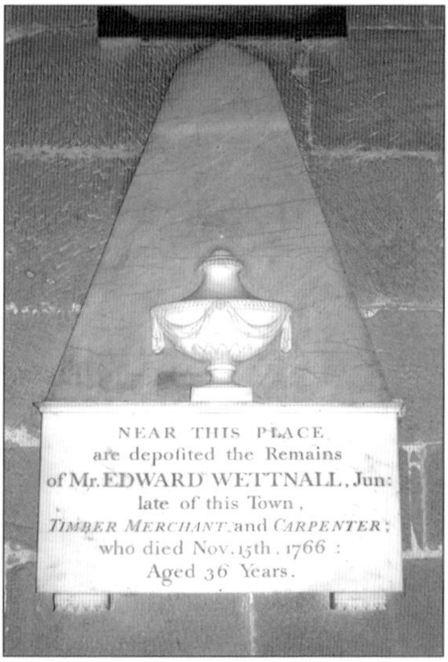

Figure 112

Fig. 111—Early graveslab with carefully planned layout, Sanquhar, Dumfriesshire, Scotland (1667).

Fig. 112—Formal memorial, Wrexham, Clwyd, Wales (1766).

Fig. 113—Graveslab with marginal inscription, the Howff Burial Ground, Dundee, Angus, Scotland (1586).

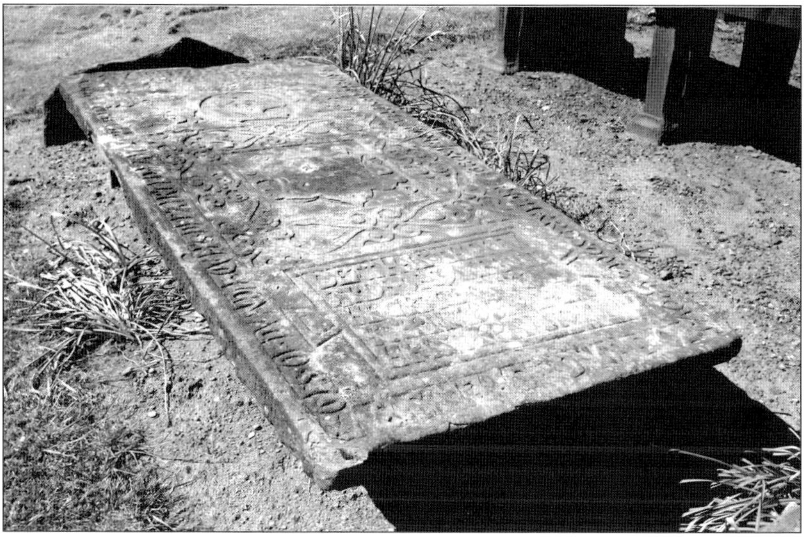

Figure 113

Marble masons of the Middle Ages and Renaissance were trained in both sculpting and letter-cutting. There were probably relatively few of these highly skilled artists/craftsmen before the great increase in demand for gravemarkers in the seventeenth century. They may have travelled some distance to undertake their work and memorials would have been ordered from outwith the locality.[102] Consequently, the selection and treatment of lettering represent the influences of the individual's apprenticeship and training rather than any local or regional differentiation owing to other factors. This would also be the case with the most formal memorials of the seventeenth to early nineteenth centuries. The sepulchral monuments in European churches and abbeys comprise an almost singular genre, demonstrating a total integration of the memorial form and the inscription. The early mural monuments, brasses and graveslabs with marginal, panelled or cartouche inscriptions apparently were considered and constructed as a single entity (Fig. 112). The formal treatment of gothic, roman, cursive or script lettering on these memorials complements the scale and grandeur of the sculpture.

The earliest text layout on graveslabs from the medieval period onwards is either an inscription running the length of the memorial, in one or more lines, or marginal, where the text begins at the top left-hand corner and proceeds clockwise (Fig. 113). Marginal inscriptions are complex and required very careful planning. Sometimes they are continued in horizontal lines through the centre of the stone. Occasionally, the text runs on to a double marginal arrangement. A slightly humorous touch is the use of a hand with a pointing finger indicating the start and direction of the text. Marginal inscriptions with small lettering were also sometimes used on monumental brasses, although most had the text in several lines below a stylised figure or figures.

Fig. 114—Headstone, Moischt, Hessen, Germany (1709).

Fig. 115—Typical New England layout, Wellfleet, Massachusetts, USA (1775).

Fig. 116—Headstone, Varel Cemetery, Oldenburgerland, Germany (1658).

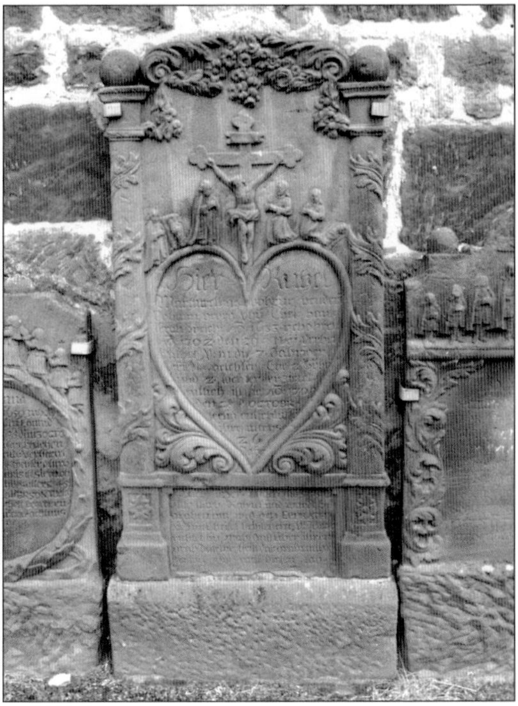

Figure 114

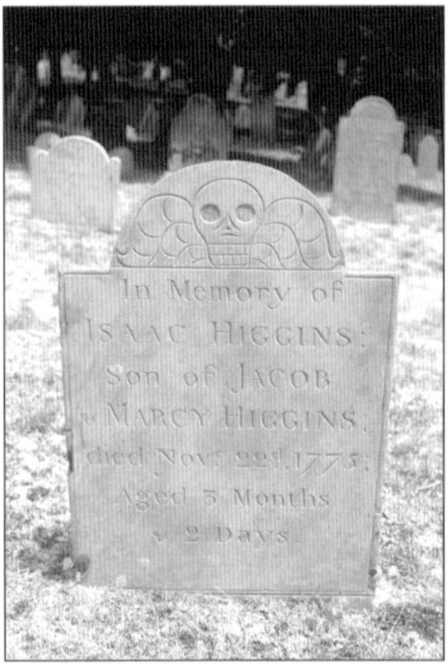

Figure 115

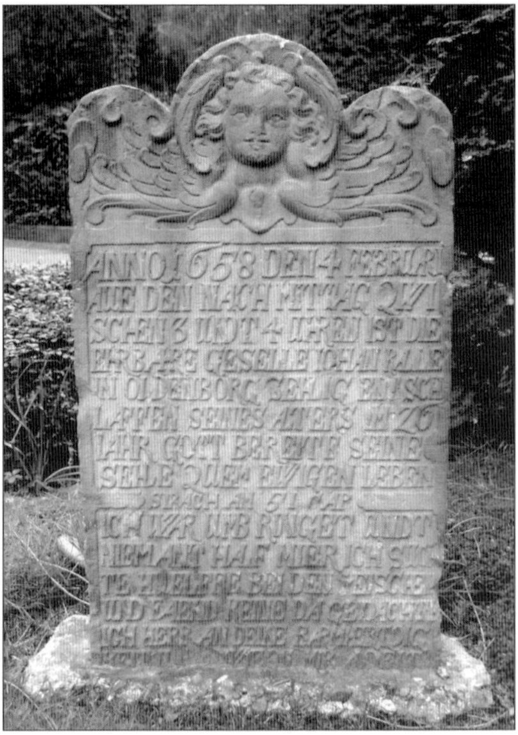

Figure 116

Following the relative homogeneity of sculptural form, both in the Middle Ages and the Renaissance, throughout much of Europe, the cultural identity of gravemarkers and the conceptual processes that contributed to their production diverge dramatically both in space and time. We see different methodologies at play, resulting from a combination of individual creativity, regional or national identity and tradition. The extent to which each of these contributed to the form of the artefact varies from place to place and throughout the period from the beginning of the seventeenth century until the present day. The increase in demand for headstones and other gravemarkers, and the consequential shortage of skilled craftsmen and money to pay for the memorials, led to a multiplicity of makers, ranging from the highly qualified mason to the naïve and unskilled individual who was capable of little more than scratching a few letters on a stone.

In Germany and some other parts of north-west Europe, masons maintained the tradition of the formal memorial to some extent, although the gravemarkers were sometimes cut with rather less skill than during the earlier period. Lettering is often small but constitutes a significant part of the memorial, arranged in a simple centred layout within a cartouche or panel. Headstones were frequently carved on both sides. The inscription is the central feature of the stone, even in the richly ornamented baroque or rococo headstones of Hessen and the north Rhineland-Palatinate and the large, pedimented headstones of Oldenburgerland and Friesland (Figs. 114 and 116). German Pennsylvanian inscriptions were treated similarly. Up until the twentieth century, headstones in Germany followed the general layout pattern of the previous 300 years.

The layout of lettering on the seventeenth- and eighteenth-century headstones of New England and New York State was simple, with lettering fitted into a blank area left on the stone by the carver. The roman lettering was occasionally embellished with cursive initial letters but, more often than not, the inscription was in simple capitals or capitals and lower-case (Fig. 115). Planning appears to have been minimal. Compared with the consideration given to the sculpting of skulls, soul effigies, cherubs and foliated borders, lettering was very much the utilitarian element of the design.

British, Irish and ex-patriot Canadian post-medieval gravemarkers before the middle of the nineteenth century are extremely diverse in form. Inscriptions range from simple initials on small memorials to extensive texts on large headstones and mural monuments, and from memorials carved solely with lettering to those on which the lettering is very much secondary to the design. In some cases the lettering is very carefully planned and laid out; in others it would appear that the carver had simply started at the top left of the headstone and worked his way through the inscription, come what may. From a palaeographic perspective, this is the period when we see great cultural diversity between districts and regions within Britain and Ireland. It is a time when there is an explosion of creativity and a flourishing of what is, in effect, folk art. Early post-

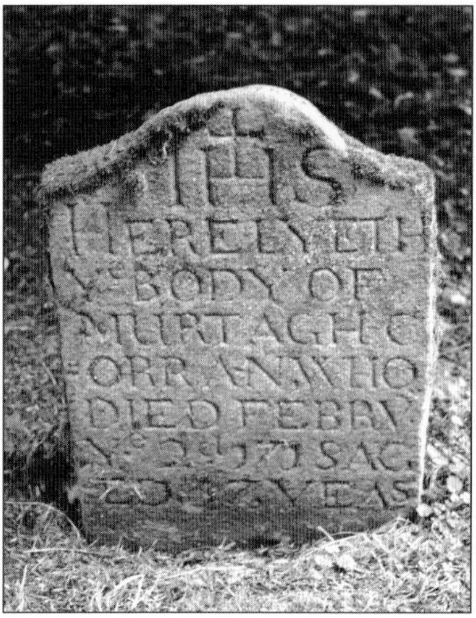

Figure 117

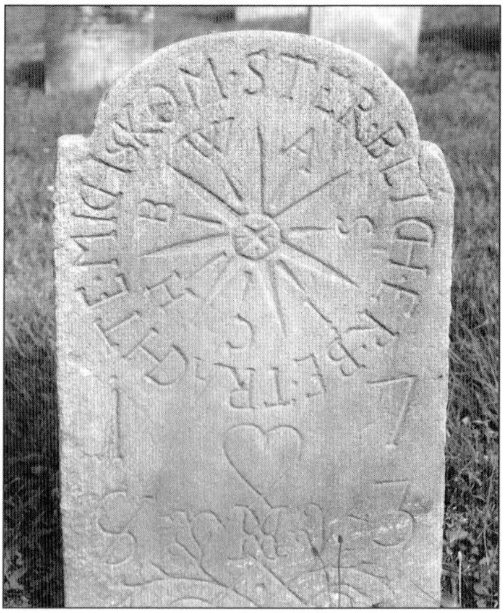

Figure 118

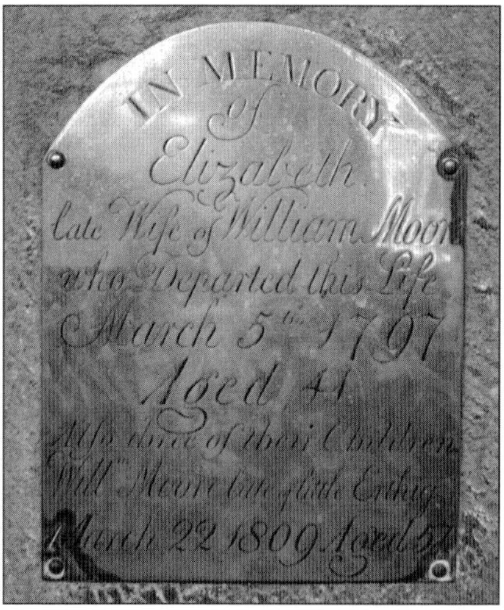

Figure 119

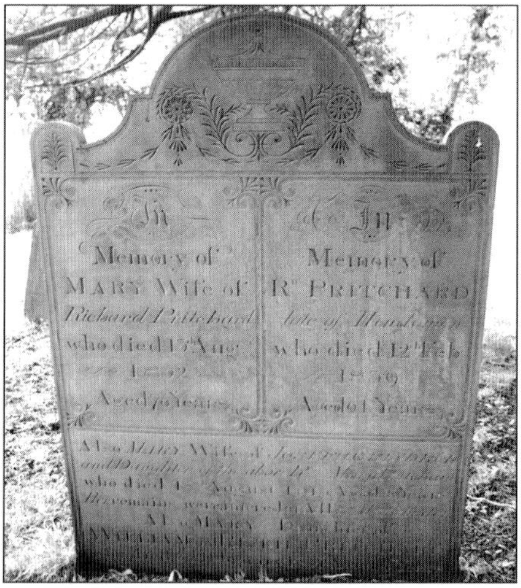

Figure 120

Fig. 117—Typical simple eighteenth-century layout, Derryvullan, Co. Fermanagh, Ireland (1718).

Fig. 118—Lettering arranged in a circle, Penryn, Pennsylvania, USA (1783).

Fig. 119—Interior small memorial brass plate, Wrexham, Clwyd, Wales (1797–1809).

Fig. 120—Two-column layout on slate headstone, Montgomery, Montgomeryshire, Wales (1852).

Fig. 121—Multi-panel layout, Varel (Lutheran Church), Oldenburgerland, Germany (1658).

Fig. 122—Successive inscriptions showing seven changes in style, Dunscore Old Graveyard, Dumfriesshire, Scotland (1670, 1726, 1747, 1778, 1803, 1830 and 1834).

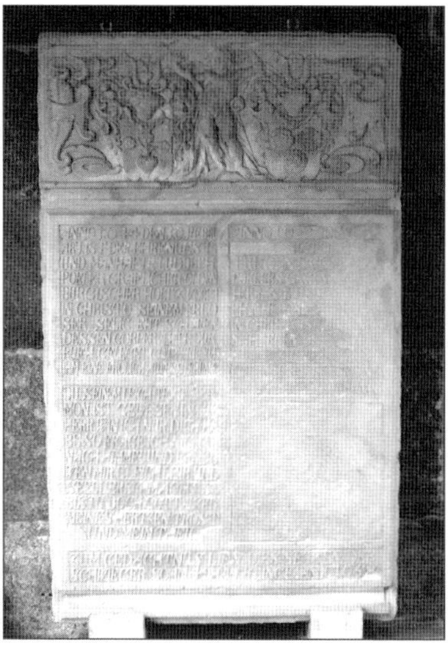

Figure 121

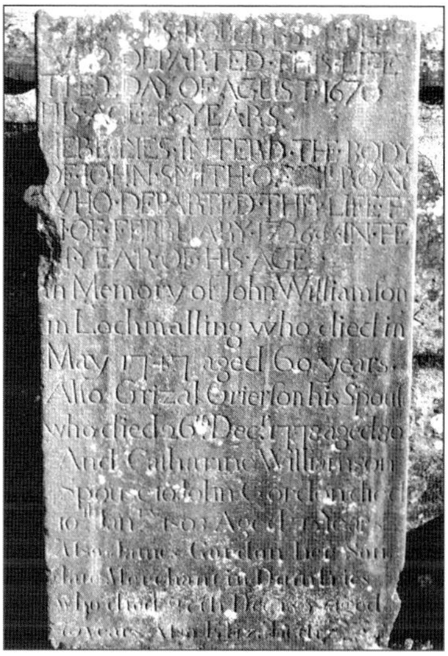

Figure 122

medieval graveslabs usually had marginal inscriptions but they were rapidly succeeded by the headstones, ledgers, table stones and chest tombs of the seventeenth and eighteenth centuries, on which the inscriptional layout is quite different. These inscribed gravemarkers are usually without ornamentation, with lettering that is either panelled or pedimented, or accompanied by iconographic or heraldic decoration. Lettering is mostly uniform in size and style, in a simple line-on-line arrangement and with occasional enlarged initials or words, often in cursive or script (Fig. 117). The simplest layout comprises single letters only, cut in the most convenient space on the stone. Occasionally, even such minimal text has been given a creative treatment. Lettering arranged in a circle or part of a circle is uncommon (Fig. 118). Some memorials have inscriptions in the tympanum or marginal texts following the curved top of the headstone. The use of the edge of a headstone is not uncommon and it was a customary practice in some British and Irish graveyards to restrict the inscription to that part of the memorial. It was more often a case of utilising every available space on the front, back, top and the two sides.

The layout on small funerary brasses was almost invariably simple, influenced only by the shapes of the plates. Most of them are rectangular, oval or heart-shaped and the lettering is centred. Early brass plate inscriptions are in roman capitals of uniform size. Later, cursive and script lettering appears, first on their own and then, at the end of the eighteenth century, used with other styles, including roman capitals, roman capitals and lower-case, script and gothic (Fig. 119).

Text on headstones and ledgers is usually arranged in a single column, but dual-column or multi-panel layouts with extensive text were frequently used on hard stone, especially slate gravemarkers in the English Midlands, Yorkshire and Wales (Fig. 120). On medieval graveslabs, the marginal

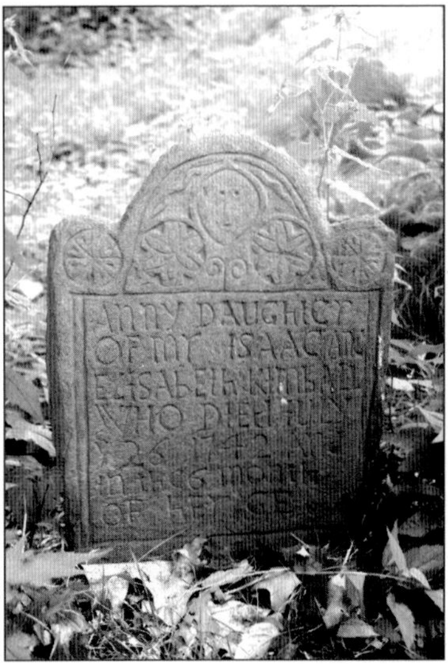

Figure 123

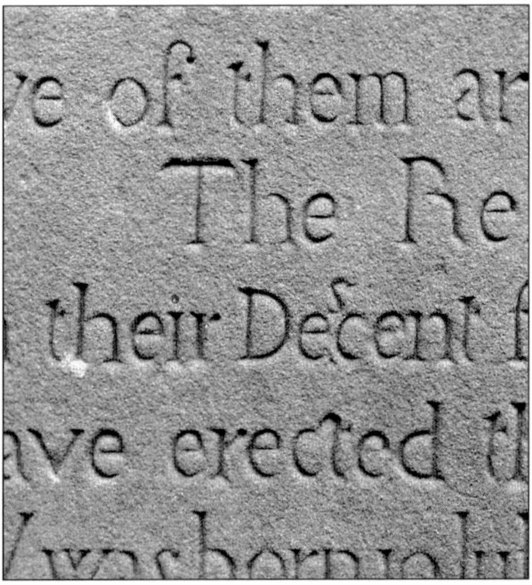

Figure 124

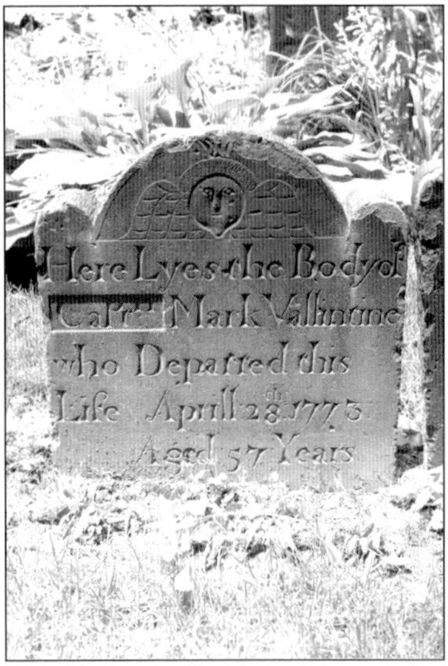

Figure 125

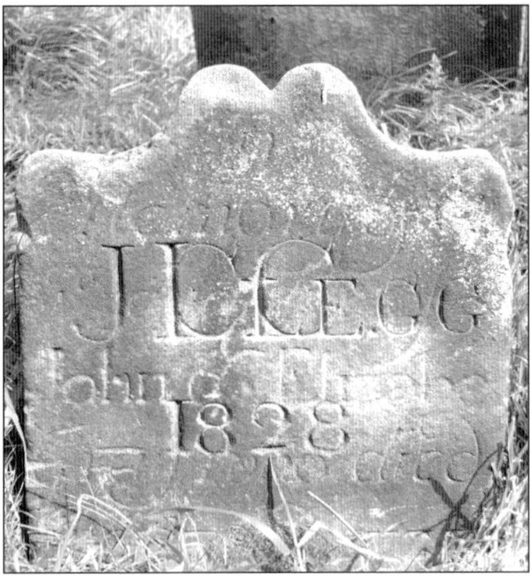

Figure 126

Fig. 123—Mixed capitals and lower-case in same inscription, Haverhill, Massachusetts, USA (1742).

Fig. 124—Correction made by adding the missing letter over the line, Tinwald Churchyard, Dumfriesshire, Scotland (1761).

Fig. 125—Correction made by the removal of a section of the stone, Trinity Churchyard, New York City, New York, USA (1773).

Fig. 126—Corrected inscription cut over original, St Mary's Churchyard, Whitby, Yorkshire, England (1828).

inscription created a central rectangular panel that was often subdivided to take initials, monograms, heraldry or an effigy. Sometimes on early gravemarkers we find inscriptions enclosed by lines or set within multiple incised panels (Fig. 121). Later, these panels were occasionally bounded by scrolls or foliated designs. When a main panel was defined, it created the opportunity to treat remaining parts of the memorial as subsections, with the pediment used for a date or surname and side columns for the initials of deceased family members.

Mixing different lettering styles in the same inscription was a trend that developed gradually over a period of 200 years from the early 1600s. In Britain and Ireland at the end of the eighteenth century gravemarkers with mixed lettering styles start to appear more frequently and become the norm in the first half of the nineteenth century. Inscriptions on large memorials have often been cut over a period of many years and show changing tastes in lettering over time (Fig. 122).

As we have seen, the fashioning of the stone, with its illustrative content, and the cutting of the inscription sometimes have been carried out by different craftsmen, especially in Scotland. This raises the question of the relationship between imagery and text. The extent to which the two were planned as a unit depended upon the type of memorial and the skill of the mason. Very formal memorials, especially mural monuments such as those in urban burial grounds, have been designed very carefully to include text and other sculpturing. Many earlier British and Irish headstones suggest, however, that lettering was considered quite separately from the rest of the stone and it is unusual to find a truly coordinated design. At best, we find inscriptions placed where a space has been left for it to fit. At worst, the lettering has been consigned to a small section at the bottom of the reverse of the memorial.

It is evident from gravemarker inscriptions in Britain, Ireland and the USA that there was a significant incidence of illiteracy amongst all but the most skilled masons and others who cut lettering. Most may well have copied their designs from other stones or samples. Without standardisation, spelling was unconventional and intuitive, resulting in the inscriptions that many find so appealing today. Many English-language inscriptions display a total lack of inhibition in the mixing of capitals and lower-case letters throughout. In some instances, such as the series of headstones at Haverhill, Massachusetts, the letter-cutters may not have been aware that there was anything unusual in their use of mixed case (Fig. 123). Nevertheless, the use of mixed case in some inscriptions must have been a deliberate choice of the letter-cutter, who was demonstrating both flair and creativity in the design of the text.

When the mason made some sort of inscriptional error by omitting a letter, he sometimes simply cut the missing character above the text line (Fig. 124). If, however, the wrong letter or word was cut and the mason, or someone else, later recognised the error, it was not a matter of simply erasing the mistake. Several solutions were employed. The method least

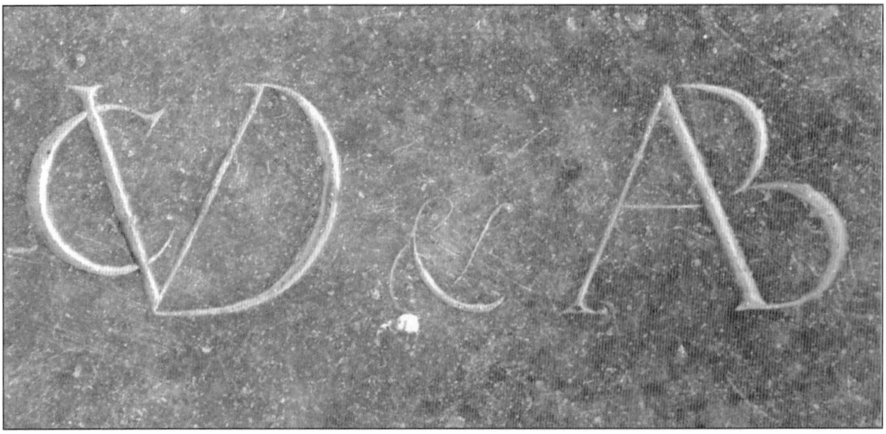

Fig. 127—Two monograms, Oude Kerk, Amsterdam, Netherlands (seventeenth century).

Fig. 128—Ligatured numerals, Dundrennan, Stewartry of Kirkcudbright, Scotland (1685).

used was to cut a deletion line through the offending letter or word. More often, a rectangular section was removed from the stone and the correct inscription cut in the recess (Fig. 125). There are headstones of the seventeenth to nineteenth centuries with anything from a single letter to a complete section removed and recut. Occasionally, the mason simply cut the correction over the original inscription (Fig. 126).

Ligatures and flourishes

Monograms are groups of interwoven letters, incorporating a person's initials (Fig. 127). They can often be found on tombstone memorials as established family emblems. The grouping of two or more letters together in the form of a single alphanumeric character or ligature is quite a different matter, with a different purpose and very different history. The ligature is an ancient device that can be traced back to the earliest literate civilisations. Its use goes back to the earliest days of our alphabet and even before. The Romans occasionally used ligatures in their incised capital inscription. The use of ligatured AE in Latin was integral to the written language, but other letter combinations were employed as a feature of the inscriptional design.

Ligatures were widely used in gothic textura inscriptions. The straight verticals of the letterform made it easy to combine letters, although their use exacerbates legibility problems inherent in the style. The earliest ligatures on post-medieval gravemarkers date from the very beginning of the sixteenth century and become increasingly common and widespread throughout the next 200 years, with a peak in their use in the middle of the seventeenth century in Britain and sometime later in Ireland and the USA.

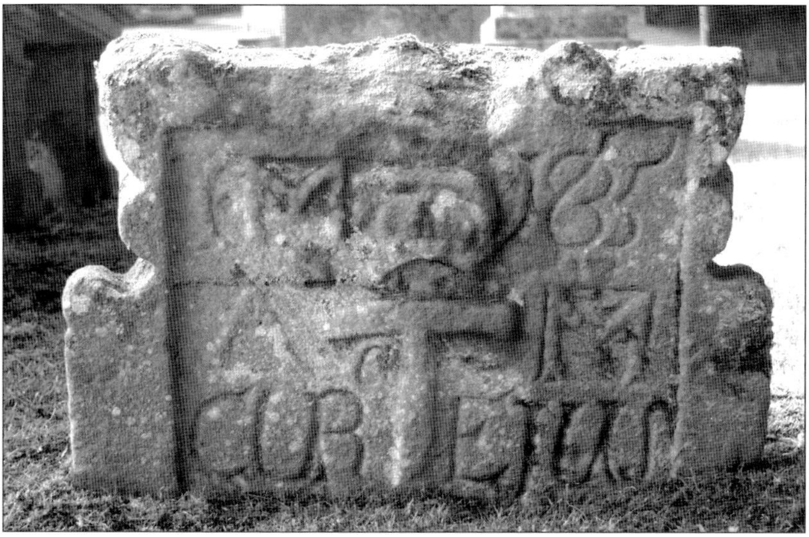

Figure 128

In the seventeenth and eighteenth centuries they were most frequently used in roman-style inscriptions and, much less commonly, in cursive texts. Ligatures of lower-case letters or capitals combined with lower-case letters are very rare indeed. Why this should be, at a time when inscriptions in roman capitals and lower-case were predominant, could be explained by the much greater difficulty of combining the shapes of lower-case letters. Ligatured numerals are also very rare (Fig. 128).[103]

Many more letter combinations constructed as ligatures have been found on Scottish gravemarkers than anywhere else. More than 70 have been recorded.[104] Many of the letter combinations would have been easy for the mason to contrive, but some inscriptions exhibit ingenuity in the way the letters have been put together. A magnificent headstone of 1720 in Annan Old Cemetery, Dumfriesshire, includes several creatively cut ligatures in relief archaic roman style, including VE and MB in NOVEMBER, with a curious interjection of a P in the MB, as well as several others throughout the inscription (Fig. 50). A fragment in Dunning Churchyard, Perthshire, dated 1745 combines AL and WH in an interesting way, and a beautiful headstone of the same date in Monikie Churchyard, Angus, ligatures OUN. By far the most common ligature in Scotland, as well as in much of Europe and the USA, is HE. This is twice as common as THE. The combinations ME, TH, ND and NE occur frequently, and others increasingly less so. An analysis of the frequency of the occurrence of individual or groups of letterform attributes in Scotland reveals some interesting patterns in the distribution. The use of ligatures was dramatically more common in the far north of the country than in the south. As well as these general trends, detailed analysis can show more local patterns, even within what is, apparently, the same cultural region. In south-west Scotland, ligatures were used significantly more in the south of Dumfriesshire than elsewhere in

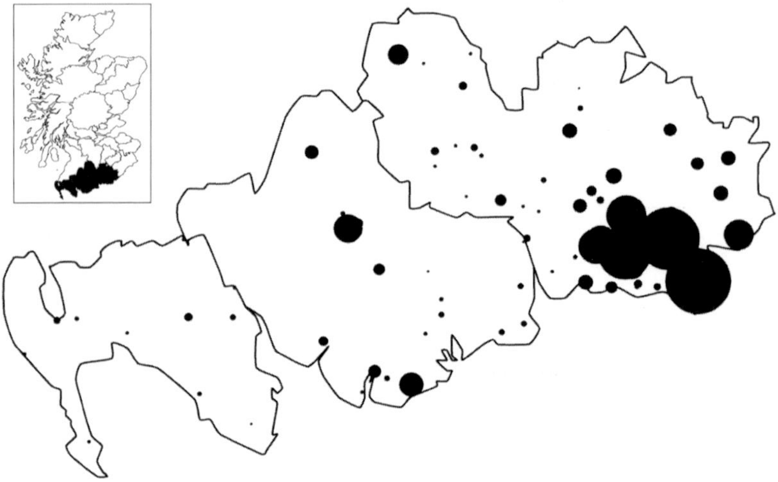

Figure 129

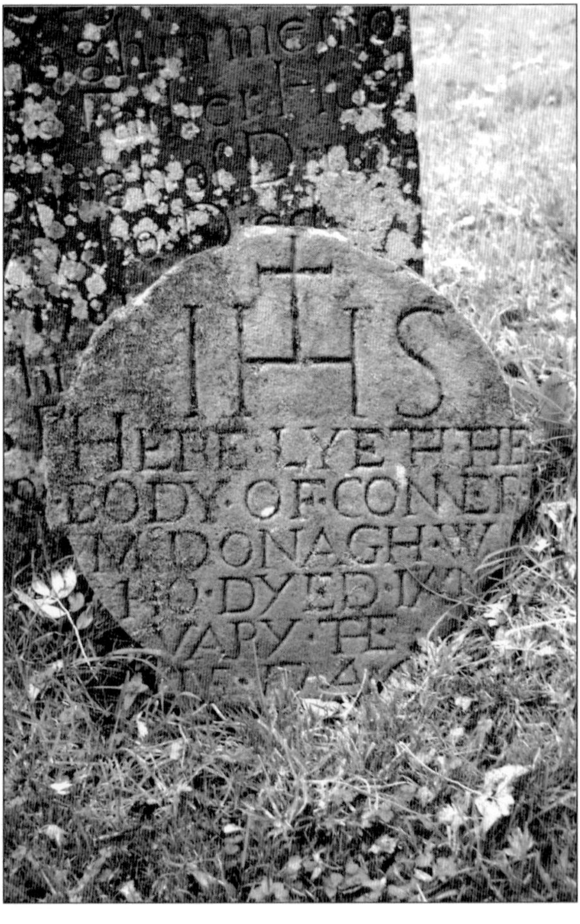

Figure 130

Fig. 129—The relative frequency of ligatures in south-west Scotland.

Fig. 130—Ligatures on discoid headstone. Note the ligatures TH, THE and NNE, Galloon, Co. Fermanagh, Ireland (1741).

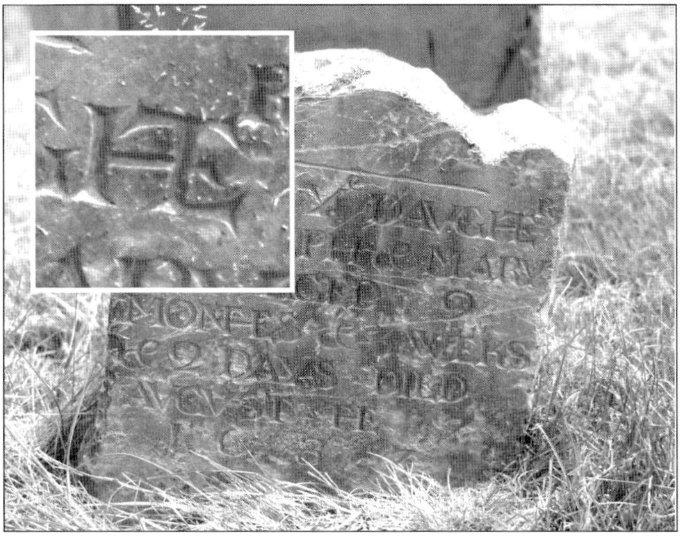

Figure 131

Fig. 131—The rare ligature HTE, Roxbury, Massachusetts, USA (1687).

the county, the Stewartry of Kirkcudbright or Wigtownshire (Fig. 129).[105]

Ligatures are much less common in England and Wales. In spite of their widespread and frequent use on Irish discoid gravestones, perhaps surprisingly, combinations other than HE, TH and THE are extremely rare but include TE, AN, NE, NN, NNE, MB and ME. The ligature THE is the most common, followed by TH, with HE used least often (Fig. 130).[106] Ligatures are much more common in the north but are also found in the counties of Cork, Wicklow and Sligo.

In Hessen, Germany, the ligatures HE, NN, HR and ND were frequently used, with HE and ND by far the most common. Some other ligatures, including AB, ME, MB and HL, have not been found elsewhere in the country. In the far north of Germany ligatures are rare.

Curiously, ligatures are extremely rare on German Pennsylvanian headstones, with only NE having been recorded, but they are frequent in the non-German southern part of the state, predominantly in the form of HR and ME. In New York State and Connecticut many inscriptions are in capitals and lower-case, so fewer ligatures occur. Roman capitals were used more than any other style in Massachusetts, and HE and TH are common. The use of the archaic character thorn (written as y) with e, representing 'the', reduces the frequency of ligatured THE, although it was still used.[107] The unusual ligature HTE in the word DAUGHTER at Boston Copp's Hill, King's Chapel and Roxbury has not been seen elsewhere (Fig. 131). Very few all-capital inscriptions were cut in Canada and ligatures have not been found on any headstone.

It appears to have been a convention to incorporate many ligatures in inscriptions on early graveslabs in archaic roman, but this practice was not universal. Even with the abundance of relief archaic roman inscriptions in the north of France, ligatures are rare and only HE has been

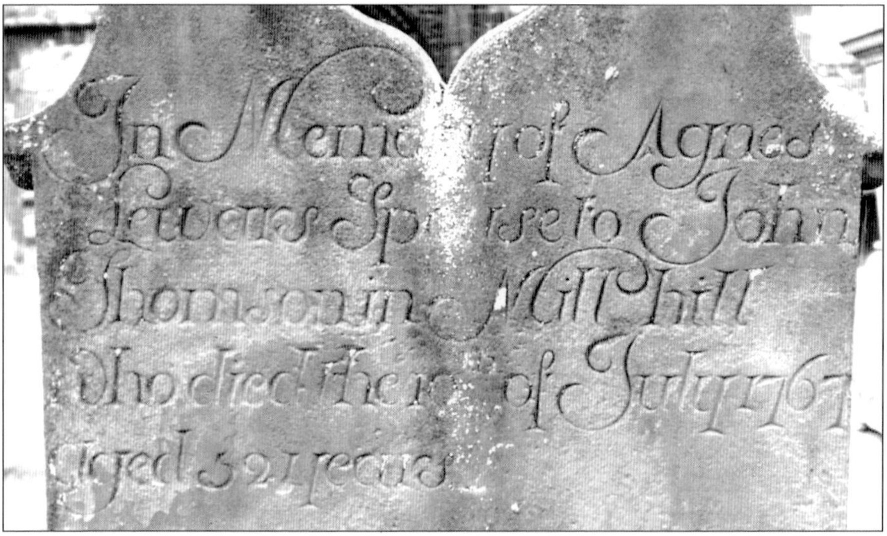

Figure 132

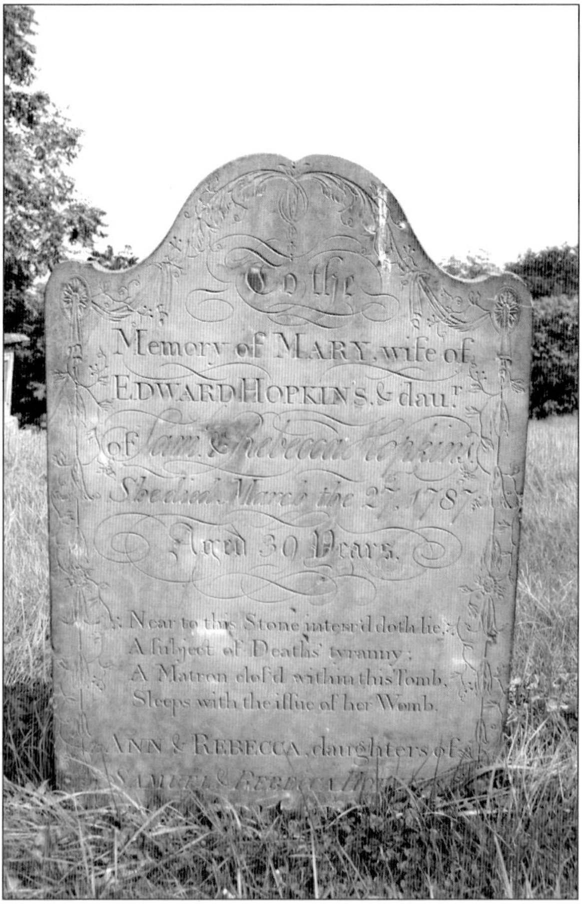

Figure 133

Fig. 132—Flourished initial letters, Sweetheart Abbey, Dumfriesshire, Scotland (1767).

Fig. 133—Fully developed flourishes on headstone, Nether Broughton, Nottinghamshire, England (1787).

Inscribed in remembrance

noted. On the other hand, they occur commonly on inscriptions in the Basque provinces of Labourd and Basse Navarre, but not in Soule. Sixteen forms have been found on Basque gravemarkers, including DE with the E interjected in the D. This ligature, which occurs in three different forms, has been erroneously claimed to be uniquely Basque. It occurs in Roman inscriptions. Furthermore, the word DE does not occur in Euskara, the Basque language, and the inscriptions on Basque discoid headstones and graveslabs on which it is used are in French.

The adoption of ligature use may well have been a consequence of several factors, some of which are not the most obvious. A ligature clearly is a space-saving device. It is not difficult to find inscriptions in which it would appear that the mason has used ligatures to be more economical with space for the lettering on the stone. Nor is it hard to find cases where the mason has used a ligature to ensure that a line of lettering would fit and where the only alternative would be to split the word. Masons appear to have been wholly unconcerned about carrying over a letter or two to the next line, splitting a word where we would consider it bad practice. Some were used as acceptable combinations much more frequently than others. All this suggests that their use was an established custom. It is very likely that the employment of ligatures was a convention handed down over the years and applied for traditional and aesthetic reasons, even if in many instances it would also serve the purpose of solving a layout problem.

With some important exceptions, inscriptional flourishing was very much a British and Irish tradition, adopted by Canadian and some other New World immigrants. Nineteenth-century headstone design in these countries is characterised by the use of linear embellishments made by extending one or more of the elements of a letter or letters, usually initial or terminal characters but also the ascenders and descenders of lower-case letters, to form often complex loops and curves (Fig. 132). Flourishing was also used to fill space when a line of lettering was short. Formal roman lettering, whether capitals or lower-case, is not amenable to enhancements of this nature. Flourishing is most often applied to script and gothic, and in regions where these were not the predominant lettering styles, including most of continental Europe and the USA, flourishes are uncommon or absent. Script is uncommon on North American nineteenth-century 'white stone' memorials. Even in German gothic texts letters are rarely flourished and, when present, they are usually restricted to short extensions of the initial letters. The earliest flourishes are very restrained and comprise a very simple augmentation to an initial letter. In its extreme form, flourishing can dominate an inscription to the extent that the lettering becomes secondary and almost illegible. By the nineteenth century in Britain and Ireland all but the most modest headstones had some degree of flourishing to the lettering. In Victorian times masons appeared to vie for supremacy in their skill in cutting flourishes of the most florid nature (Fig. 133).

Some early gravemarkers in Oldenburgerland exhibit an entirely different approach to flourishing inscriptional lettering. Every capital throughout the entire inscriptions on some headstones at Bockhorn, Varel and Wiarden is flourished. The effect is all the more dramatic because the lettering is in relief rather than incised (Fig. 134).

The designs and models for flourishes on lettering of the late eighteenth century onwards owe much to the embellishments of the penmen, illustrated as specimens in their copybooks. The thickening and thinning of incised lines copy those created by varying pressure on a flexible, pointed nib. Considerable skill was demonstrated by the most accomplished masons, who cut elaborate loops, curves and flowing lines as well as figurative designs in stone that would be difficult enough to produce on paper. Similar artistry can be seen on small funerary brass plates on which the mixed-style layouts and the use of flourishes were not unlike those on their stone counterparts. The process of engraving brasses was very similar to that used by the copper-engravers who produced the intaglio printing plates for handwriting manuals and copybooks, although there is some evidence that cutting funerary brass plate lettering was considered to be a more menial task than other engraving.[108]

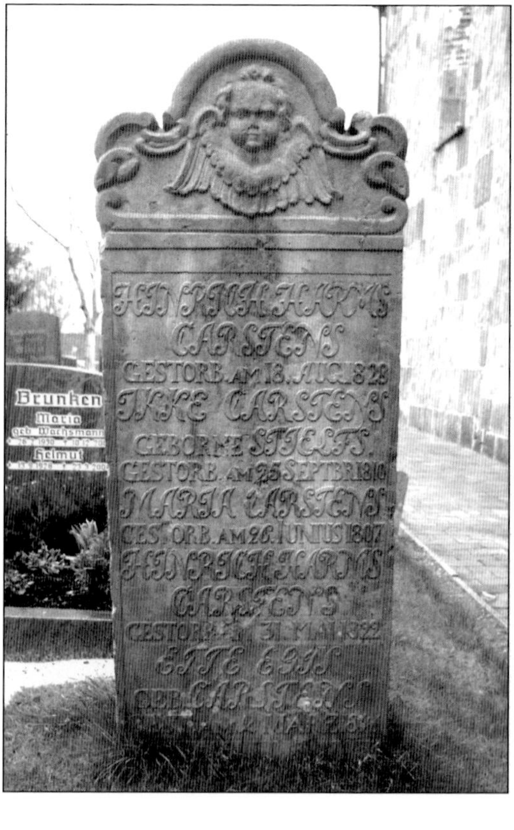

Fig. 134—Raised flourished capitals, Wiarden, Oldenburgerland, Germany (1828).

Figure 134

REGIONAL IDENTITY, INFLUENCE AND INSPIRATION

Regional identity, in the context of gravemarker inscriptions, is an overall profile assessed through analysis of the lettering used on artefacts within a defined geographical area, including the styles used, the layout of the inscription and the interpretation of the individual letterforms. Cultural identity refers to the relationship of this profile with people—population groups or communities. Cultural identity is not static; it changes through time. An analysis of gravemarker lettering of the seventeenth century in a specific region will result in a quite different profile from that in the nineteenth. Also, a cultural tradition can be transplanted to a region a long way from its source. In the early nineteenth century some of the German Pennsylvanians made gravemarkers that were similar to those in their native land. German immigrants to Canada used Fraktur.

Even within relatively small regions, with marked local differences in both history and culture, there will be changes in tastes and fashion over time. Thus we see changes in the predominant gravemarker style occurring at different times in different places. The move from the preferred graveslab to the headstone as the most common tombstone memorial form occurred much later in northern Britain than in the south. Less obvious, but equally diverse, is when lettering styles and their attributes changed in different parts of Britain, Ireland, the rest of Europe, the USA and Canada. It would be much too simplistic to suggest that the development of lettering styles was a simple linear process, even in a single locality. It certainly was not. This makes the analysis of geographical trends somewhat complex. When a new lettering style became the predominant form, it did not completely replace what came before. The earlier form continued to be used, if much less frequently, and perhaps had a revival of popularity decades or even centuries later. For example, we find medieval gothic being widely used in Victorian times, albeit in a modified form. The terms 'most popular' or

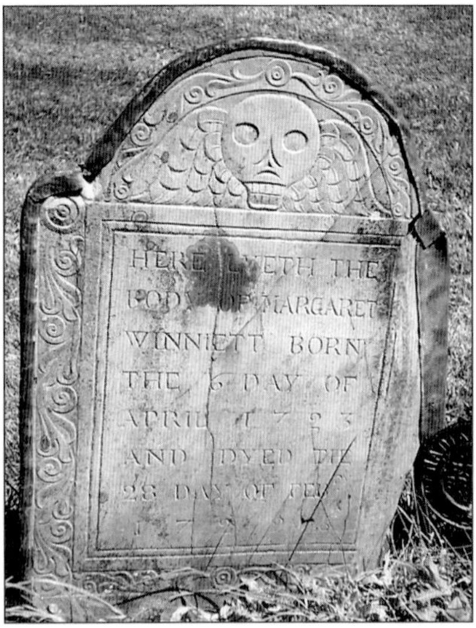

Figure 135

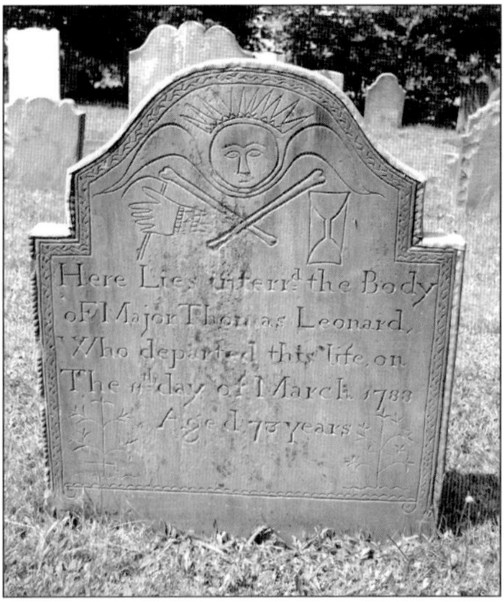

Figure 136

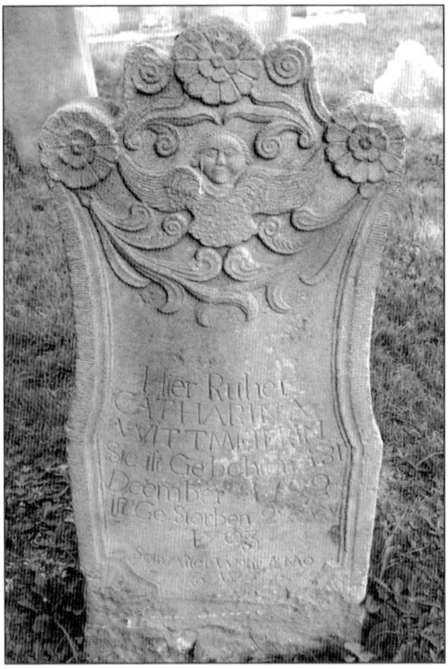

Figure 137

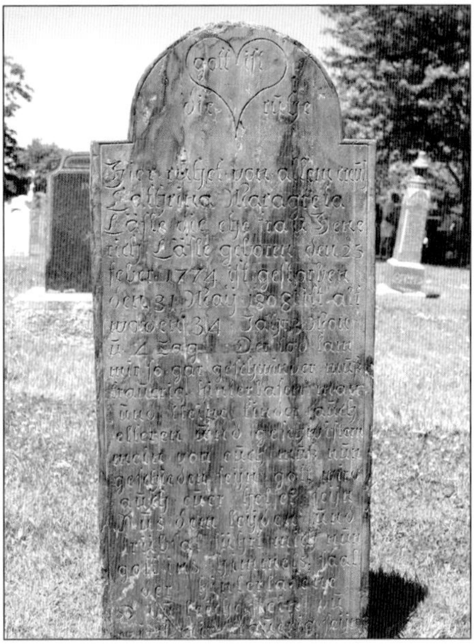

Figure 138

Fig. 135—Imported New England headstone, Annapolis Royal, Nova Scotia, Canada (1723).

Fig. 136—Distinctive Nova Scotia headstone, Wolfville, Nova Scotia, Canada (1788).

Fig. 137—German Pennsylvanian headstone, Penryn, Pennsylvania, USA (1793), similar to those in Hessen.

Fig. 138—Immigrant German headstone. Note the use of the heart symbol, Lunenburg Academy Burial Ground, Nova Scotia, Canada (1808).

Inscribed in remembrance

'predominant form' refer to a statistical assessment based on the majority of inscriptions in a single burial site, region or throughout the country.

As well as temporal differences in gravemarker design and inscriptional form, there are contemporaneous differences between districts, regions and nations. The importation of gravemarkers masks and confuses indigenous local identity. This is most evident in the case of formal memorials that were made by sculptors of high repute who exported their works far and wide, but regional identity established through research on more modest gravemarkers is not immune from the problem. Newfoundland settlers purchased headstones from England and Ireland.[109] In the eighteenth century, Boston masons supplied headstones to meet the demand for gravemarkers as far afield as Nova Scotia, and at that time many of the headstones in Virginia and North Carolina came from Massachusetts and several other north-western states.[110] Yet it could be argued that the resulting *mélange* represented the cultural identity of the people of that region, especially when we consider that individuals in the locality may have influenced the choice of design. The trade in gravestones in much of New England was so extensive and widespread that distinct local identities that can be identified through analysis in Britain and Ireland are much more difficult to establish, except, perhaps, by utilising only those that are known to be made in the vicinity. Although there was sometimes a clear contrast between the forms of native and imported artefacts, as was the case in Pennsylvania, there are instances where the imported gravemarkers and the lettering on them were the influence and inspiration for later designs. Some of the earliest gravemarkers in Nova Scotia were made in Massachusetts (Fig. 135). They may also have been inscribed there, as the roman inscriptions are similar to the contemporary ones in the area around Boston. The characteristic winged skulls and soul effigies were adopted and adapted by Canadian stonecutters. Over time, lettering style changed from roman capitals to capitals and lower-case. By the eighteenth century a distinctive local identity had developed in some parts of the province (Fig. 136).

Immigrant masons did not necessarily follow the traditions of the country from which they came. Ex-patriot Scots and Irish stone-carvers in New England developed a funerary memorial style that was entirely new. In contrast with Palatine settlers in much of Pennsylvania, German settlers elsewhere produced stones that were nothing like those in their homeland, even although they often incorporated Germanic iconography. In these situations a distinct cultural identity is evident (Figs 137 and 138).

In Ireland accomplished masons such as James Byrne, who worked primarily in the counties of Wexford and Wicklow, made at least one headstone that was erected some distance away, in south County Tipperary.[111] Compared with the USA and Canada, the making of gravemarkers outwith the local area appears to have been far more limited in Ireland, Scotland, England, Wales and, as far as we can tell,

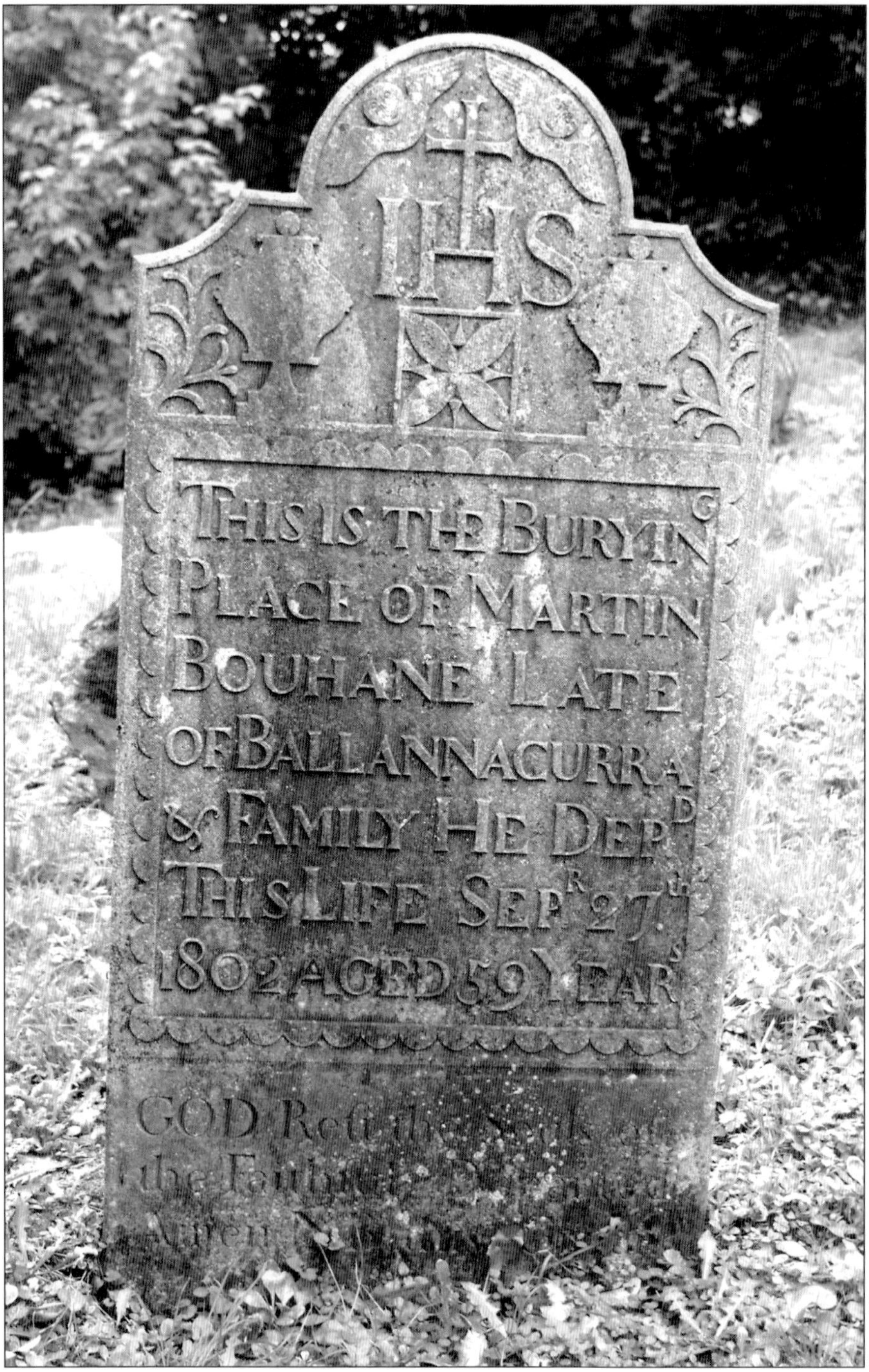

Figure 139

Fig. 139—Raised lettering on headstone, Kinsale, Co. Cork, Ireland (1802).

Inscribed in remembrance

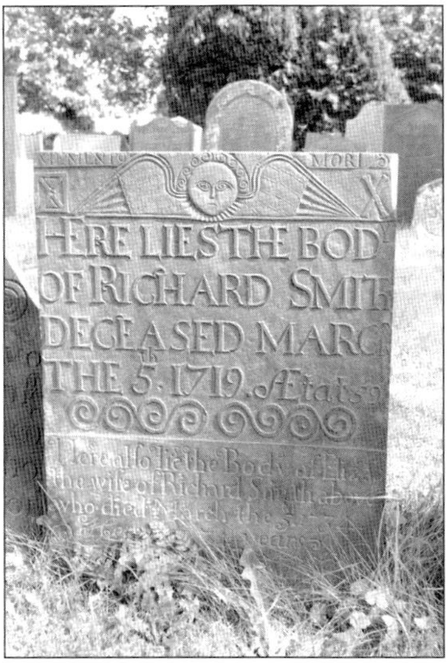

Figure 140

Fig. 140—Headstone, Hickling, Nottinghamshire, England (1719–34).

in continental Europe, at least until the early nineteenth century. The consequence of this is that distinctive identities have developed within very local areas, some of which are easy to identify without statistical analysis. The style of headstones and the roman and Fraktur lettering used for the inscriptions in the late eighteenth century in Hessen and the north Rhineland-Palatinate are quite distinct from those in Oldenburgerland and Friesland, with their relief 'modern'-style roman. A characteristic regional identity, resulting principally from lettering style, developed in the Belvoir Valley in the English counties of Leicestershire, Lincolnshire and Northamptonshire in the early eighteenth century (Fig. 140).[112]

Occasionally very similar distinctive gravemarkers or lettering characteristics are found in widely separated regions, or even countries, where there is no evidence of influential interaction. This is a phenomenon called 'convergent evolution' in zoology and botany. We see it in a distinctive form of head and shaft gravemarkers apparently found only in Bulgaria and south-west Ulster, separated by more than 2,000 km (Figs 24 and 25). Another example, which appears to be no more than coincidence, is the relief roman lettering used on headstones in some graveyards in parts of County Cork and on the gravemarkers of Oldenburgerland and Friesland. The Cork examples are nearly 100 years more recent than those from Germany (Fig. 139).

There can be little doubt that masons would have been strongly influenced by their training, and any divergence from what they learned from their master would depend on their independence, creativity and the degree to which they were prepared to break the rules of what was currently perceived as good practice. When training was minimal, the mason would probably be strongly influenced by the current local fashion and what he saw around. The letterforms would be copied either deliberately or subconsciously. This would contribute to an entrenchment of local traditions and goes a long way towards explaining why cultural identity is more strongly expressed on vernacular memorials than on more formal ones. Even when copybooks and catalogues were being used and clients were able to choose the design of the memorial, it is questionable that much thought was given to their choice of lettering. This was more likely to have been left to the mason. When Massachusetts headstones were being made for export to other states or to Canada, there is nothing to suggest that clients were offered a choice of lettering for the inscription. The opportunity for clients to select a particular lettering style for memorials appears to be very recent.

To some extent, lettering on gravemarkers followed that used on other artefacts and even in other materials. Contemporaneous glass, silver and gold engraved lettering approximates with that in stone in style, as does the lettering on coins and Scottish communion tokens. Even lettering on seventeenth- and eighteenth-century ceramics is similar in basic form to that on gravemarkers of about the same date.[113] We have already seen that typeface design was utilised extensively by masons from the end of the eighteenth century. Gothic lettering on graveslabs in the Middle Ages was similar to textura, the most commonly used script on medieval manuscripts. Even uncio-versal echoes the medieval manuscript versal and uncial styles. Other than the mutual use of roman capitals from the Renaissance until the early nineteenth century there was little correspondence between manuscript forms and the lettering of gravemarker inscriptions for a period of nearly 300 years. We do not see anything that corresponds to Renaissance italic or the secretary and court hands of legal and commercial documents.

THE RUSTIC VERNACULAR TRADITION

The word 'vernacular' is commonly used to include anything that is 'native' or 'local', whether intangible, as in the case of the spoken word, or artefact. Strictly speaking, the term should be applied solely to language or dialect. The term 'vernacular culture' is often confused with 'local culture'. Also, there are no geographical, temporal or other discrete boundaries when we attempt to apply the term to gravemarkers, and particularly to gravemarker lettering. Determining what is and what is not a vernacular funerary artefact is virtually impossible. Here I will use the term 'vernacular gravemarkers' to mean those produced on a non- or semi-commercial basis, usually—but not always—by relatively unskilled craftsmen or other individuals.

Many studies of gravestone art tend to focus on memorials created by the more skilled masons and to celebrate their aesthetic qualities.[114] Similarly, the few works that discuss tombstone lettering place strong emphasis on those that are considered to be of some artistic or creative merit and virtually ignore those by less-skilled cutters.[115] While this is perfectly legitimate in the context of art history, in so doing a resource of cultural significance is overlooked. Vernacular gravemarkers frequently display an uninhibited creative flare lacking in more formal inscriptions. It is clear that inscriptional lettering on headstones highlights the continuum from the crude scratches with a nail or similar implement on an unfashioned piece of slate or sandstone to the work of skilled craftsmen. It is easy to distinguish inscriptions that demonstrate a break from convention in the use of lettering. Whether this was due to the letter-cutter's lack of awareness of traditional principles or was a deliberate attempt to ignore them is impossible to tell. In all cases, this less-conventional lettering exhibits individuality, either in form or in the way it is used. Thus we have the use of mixed case, mirrored letters, miscalculations of line length, and the original and unusual treatment of many letterforms, all applied without inhibition

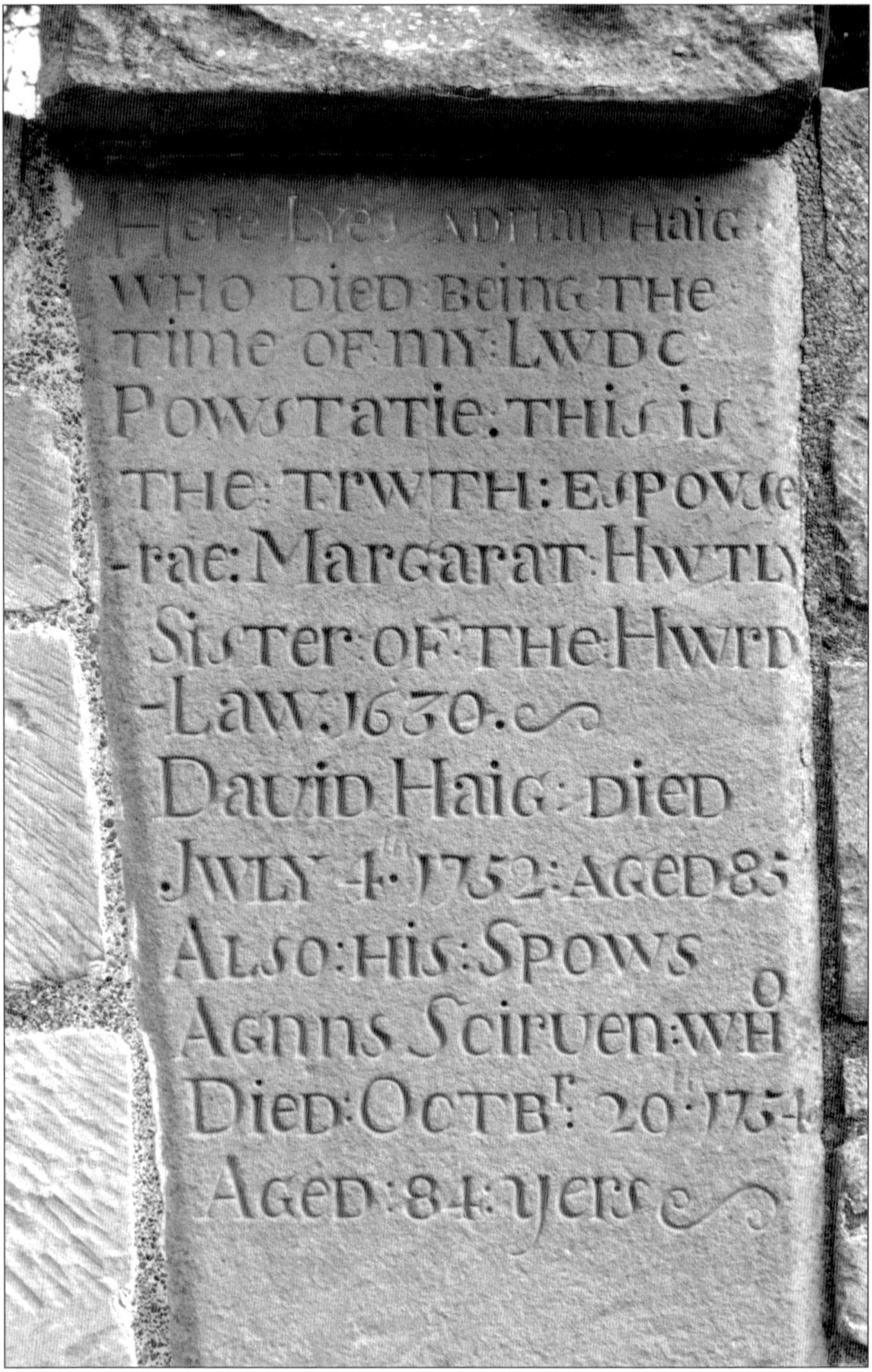

Figure 141

Fig. 141—Deliberate mixing of capitals and lower-case letters, Dryburgh Abbey, Roxburghshire, Scotland (1754).

and frequently with obvious enthusiasm. Perhaps it is not surprising that the choice of a basic lettering style and its interpretation on more formal memorials at a particular point in time and in the same district is often reflected in its application on gravemarkers made by the less-skilled and untrained individuals. It is in these vernacular or naïve inscriptions that we see the most fervent expression of creativity and inventiveness. The rules of good masonry craftsmanship and the inevitable hang-ups that these create no longer apply, through choice or ignorance. It is sometimes difficult to draw the line between the maverick mason and the self-taught letter-cutter. The headstones in the Vale of Belvoir, for example, have been made by a group of skilled though individualistic masons who produced many headstones in the first half of the eighteenth century, with styles of lettering and interpretations of letterform that are not found elsewhere.

This distinguishing feature of vernacular memorials is an abandonment of traditional 'rules' of letter formation and use. Some of it is undoubtedly a consequence of poor education, but the creative use of non-standard letterforms suggests that the individuals cutting the inscription were frequently utilising their own ideas in a very deliberate fashion. For example, the mixing of capitals and lower-case letters often appears to be planned and not just a result of literary ignorance (Fig. 141).

Furthermore, there is no clear distinction between skilled and unskilled letter-cutters. It is remarkable how well some people, apparently with no training whatsoever in the arts, can turn their hand to creative lettering. This can be seen in graffiti on the spray-painted walls of some of our larger cities, or in some of the incised graffiti on medieval and more recent buildings, which sometimes shows a remarkable understanding of letter proportions and serif formation. Identifying the differences between creativity, naivety and low levels of skill in headstone inscriptions is very difficult indeed. Whatever the genesis of vernacular tombstone lettering, we are blessed with a large number of artefacts that exhibit a vigour that tends to be stifled in more formal inscriptions. In much of Britain, Ireland, the USA and Canada, the most extreme of these uninhibited creations tend to be the minority amongst the main body of mainstream memorials. It could be argued that a high proportion of Scottish, Irish and North American headstones of the seventeenth and eighteenth centuries are vernacular and represent a rural craft, with all the idiosyncrasies that this displays. We may never know what went through the minds of the individuals who carved lettering on these vernacular memorials, in particular to what extent the individuality of their creations was deliberate or planned. Nor can we be sure of the extent to which the work of trained masons, with which they may or may not have been familiar, exerted an influence on their output. By studying inscriptions on gravestones in discrete geographical areas and by making comparisons between them within such distinct cultures as those of Scotland and New England, it can be shown that vernacular tombstone lettering reflects a local culture more than that on formal memorials.[116] The local letter-cutters, whoever they were, were not tied by craft skills embedded through teaching or apprenticeship and were free to express themselves through their work (Figs 142–5). Consequently, vernacular tombstone lettering can be used as an important indicator of cultural diversity, alongside the well-researched areas such as the visual arts and crafts, architecture and language.

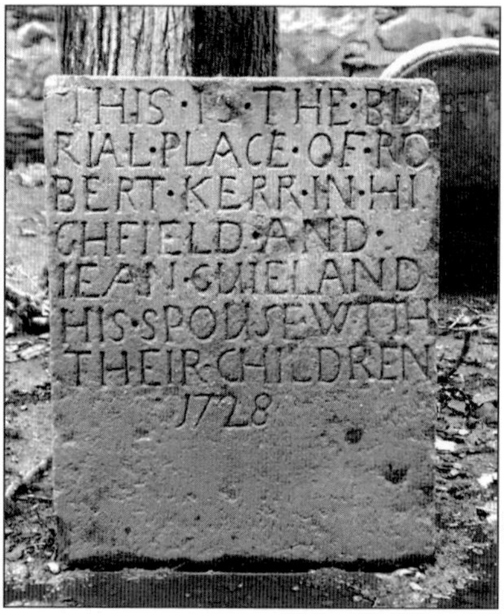

Figure 142

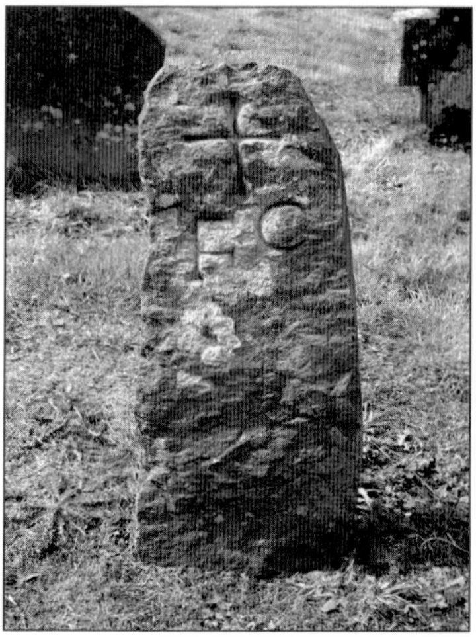

Figure 143

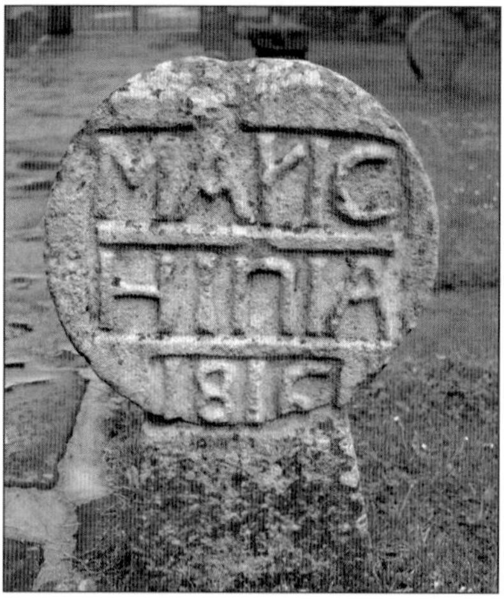

Figure 144

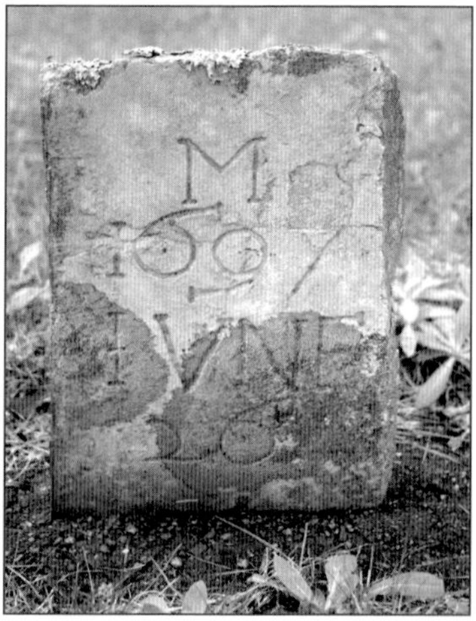

Figure 145

Fig. 142—Vernacular headstone, Dalry, Ayrshire, Scotland (1728).

Fig. 143—Vernacular gravemarker, Drumsnat, Co. Monaghan, Ireland (possibly early nineteenth century).

Fig. 144—Vernacular discoid gravemarker, Etxalar, Pyrénées Atlantique, France (1816).

Fig. 145—Vernacular gravemarker, Wrentham, Massachusetts, USA (1697).

RECORDING AND ANALYSIS

How to record

Before any research work is undertaken on gravemarker lettering it is imperative that the aim of the project is clear. The requirements for research that simply lead to the development of an archive are quite different from those where the aim is to undertake detailed analysis and interpretation. Although there are some extensive gravemarker image collections in existence in the form of archives or publications, it is unlikely that they will be adequate in either case for a detailed study of gravemarker lettering.[117] Almost invariably, the images or drawings will not have been taken with any focus on palaeography or letterform. They will not provide the material for anything other than very superficial research. Archives and publications are extremely useful as guides to burial grounds and help to identify places where research could be fruitful. A first-hand survey will almost certainly have to be made if anything original is to be contributed to our knowledge of lettering on these artefacts.

Drawing has its place in archaeology, but in palaeography it is of very limited use and, arguably, can result in false interpretation. Drawn plans of burial sites can be useful and, for some studies, essential. Drawings of inscriptions have inherent drawbacks, even (or especially) if made from rubbings, as is often done in spite of the potential damage to the gravestones by this procedure. An accurate drawing of incised or relief lettering on a gravemarker will represent only what the inscription is like at that point in time. If that is all that is required, then there is no problem. An example of the sort of difficulty that arises is when a very eroded incised roman appears heavier (bolder) than one that has survived in a better state, even though they may have been identical when cut. From a palaeographic perspective, the freshly cut original form of the letters should be interpreted and recorded. Until very recently, there was a valid argument that photography was neither practical nor the best recording method for detailed research on some aspects of funerary artefacts. The costs of large-scale, data-intensive surveys, for example, would be prohibitive in most instances. With the advent of digital photography and the availability of high-resolution cameras at very modest prices, there can be little doubt that digital imaging is the most effective, reliable, practical and economical procedure for recording gravemarker lettering. A high-resolution image will record the degree of erosion, which can be assessed at the data entry stage of the research. Objective and accurate interpretation of the original form requires some knowledge and skill, which can be acquired with practice. Misjudgements in recording lettering attributes by this method will be far fewer than the potential errors resulting from the drawn record.

Digital images for later analysis do not have to be made at an extremely high resolution, unless later enlargement of detail is likely. A resolution of about three or four megapixels will be adequate and will constrain file sizes. If it is likely that the images could be used for publication, a higher resolution will be required. Compression will reduce the size of the files even more. Most compression methods, including JPEG, used in most digital cameras, result in loss of image quality. This will not be a problem when the images are for record purposes. The best image quality is from a camera's 'raw' format. This also provides greater flexibility in later image-processing. If the storage capacity of the cards used in the camera and the computer's hard disk is sufficient, the 'raw' format can be used but is usually unnecessary for gravemarker imagery.

Weather can have a profound effect on photographic recording in the open, not just because of the discomfort of working in the cold or rain but also because of variable light conditions. Provided there is sufficient illumination, digital images taken in dull weather, with or without later enhancement, can be perfectly satisfactory. They are often better than those taken in a strong cross-light that over-emphasises the texture of the stone and masks the clarity of the inscription. The best conditions are when there is diffused light falling at an angle of about 45 degrees to the plane of the gravemarker surface. If a headstone is aligned in the traditional Christian manner, with the head to the west and feet to the east, the best time to photograph the inscription will be mid-morning in the northern hemisphere, when the inscription is on the east-facing plane, as is usual. The use of a reflector can improve photographs taken at other times. The most difficult situation is when the sun is behind the stone, especially late in the day, shining directly towards the camera. Photographing inscriptions within dark church buildings can also be a problem. In places with poor illumination, a very high sensitivity (ISO) setting and long exposure with camera support can be used, but may result in unacceptable degradation of digital images. Alternatively, a flash unit positioned to shine at 45 degrees to the memorial will produce good results, provided that the coverage is adequate. Similarly, a flash unit can be used to improve the photography of exterior memorials. Never use a flash pointing straight at the inscription, as this will completely flatten the three-dimensional form of the letters. If several burial sites are being surveyed in the one day, ensure that the images for each burial site will be easily identified when it comes to downloading to computer. Record the image numbers carefully, use separate camera cards, or take a much simpler approach and photograph the burial site sign or church board at the end of the series of images so that this can be used to identify the batch later.

Sometimes it is useful to make a note of the actual text of the inscription. There are some established conventions used to record transcriptions of inscribed text. These are listed below.

<table>
<tr><th>Transcription</th><th>Format</th><th>Representing</th></tr>
<tr><td>ABCD</td><td>Roman capitals</td><td>Legible characters</td></tr>
<tr><td>GHIJ</td><td>Italic</td><td>Damaged legible characters</td></tr>
<tr><td>[KLMN]</td><td>Italic in brackets</td><td>Reading uncertain</td></tr>
<tr><td>—</td><td>Horizontal dash</td><td>Uncertain number of missing characters at beginning or end of text</td></tr>
<tr><td>[—]</td><td>Horizontal dash in brackets</td><td>Uncertain number of missing characters within text</td></tr>
<tr><td>[.]</td><td>Full stop within brackets</td><td>Single missing or illegible character</td></tr>
<tr><td>[...]</td><td>Full stops within brackets</td><td>Missing or illegible characters, one dot for each character</td></tr>
<tr><td>:</td><td>Punctuation within text</td><td>Punctuation mark within text</td></tr>
<tr><td>$\overline{\text{OP}}$</td><td>Line over two or more characters</td><td>Ligatures</td></tr>
<tr><td>|</td><td>Vertical line</td><td>Line breaks</td></tr>
<tr><td>||</td><td>Two vertical lines</td><td>Text interrupted by ornament or other feature</td></tr>
</table>

The following is a sample transcription of the inscription on the gravemarker illustrated in Fig. 27.

$\overline{\text{HE}}$RE:LIET|H:T$\overline{\text{HE}}$:B|ODY:O|F:IO$\overline{\text{HN}}$|:O:DO|$\overline{\text{NE}}$LLY: |
WHO:DEPA|RTED.THIS.|LIFE.FEB|ERY:Y|[E]—

What to record

Think very carefully about the sort of analysis that could be made and, until the full recording and analytical procedures are established through trials, record at least twice as much as you think will be needed. Photograph the whole memorial and details of the lettering as well as the overall inscription. If a good photographic record is made, it should not be necessary to prepare a pro-forma record sheet. It may be desirable to make a detailed record of measurements, including the dimensions of the memorial and the height of the lettering. A measuring scale can be placed and photographed alongside the gravemarker. Caution should be observed when recording the height of a headstone as it is usually difficult or impossible to determine how much of the stone is below ground. It may also be useful to draw a site plan, if one is not already available, and to note the material from which the memorials are made, together with any other textual details that cannot later be gleaned from the photographs, depending on the nature of the study. Some researchers may find it best to record some of this information directly to a laptop computer on site. If the aim of the survey is to establish or enhance an image archive, all that is required is to select, post-process, organise and catalogue the photographs, then add them to an image database. It is more likely that some sort of analysis is to be undertaken. Very little research is undertaken today without the involvement of computers and analytical software. Computer analysis, if used correctly, is more objective than human estimate and opinion. Providing that the correct safeguards are in place, the output from statistical tests is reliable, even if its interpretation is not necessarily so and may be subject to bias. Data entry for computer analysis can be a tedious chore. Keeping things simple is the best way to ease the task.

Any number of characteristics or attributes (statistical variables) can be assigned and recorded. These fall into two categories, qualitative and quantitative. Objective analysis of gravemarker lettering is likely to be primarily quantitative, everything being capable of treatment as numbers. Measurement can be on a continuous scale, e.g. the dimensions of the memorial or the height of the lower-case letters, or discontinuous, scored as counts or incidence (presence or absence) of an attribute, e.g. lettering style or the presence of ligatures. It is best to select a large number of attributes in the first instance. This is important as scores can later be amalgamated but not increased. Also, in the initial stages it cannot be known which attributes are contributing most to the study. Only a few may be used in the final analysis.

Several difficulties arise with data entry. The date of each inscription should be identified. Almost all dates on memorials should be considered as estimates. Memorials were not necessarily made in the year of the burial. Some were erected and dated in anticipation (pre-dating), while others were placed on the grave many years afterwards (post-dating). Fortunately, it is often easy to recognise an anachronistic inscription, but not always, and caution should be exercised. Gravemarkers may have several distinct inscriptions with different dates. Each of these should be treated separately, as should distinct sections of the inscription, for example the introduction (e.g. IN MEMORY OF) or epitaph, if they are in a different style. The use of more than one style in the same inscription should not be confused with memorials that have several inscriptions cut on different dates. Another problem is variability of lettering style within the one text—even different styles used in the same word or sentence. In such cases the recorder should decide whether they are to be recorded separately as different styles or whether the style of the majority of the letters should be assessed. As long as consistency is maintained and the same procedure is carried out throughout the data-recording, it should not affect the outcome.

The actual attributes that need to be recorded will vary according to the limits of the study and the regional boundaries within which the record is to be made. Masons were human and few inscriptions will retain absolute consistency in form. There is little point in attempting to identify and record very subtle differences in some attributes. For example, in older inscriptions there may be considerable differences in the proportions, serif formation or line width between letters in the same word or text. Relatively broad categories are preferred, and any differences in detail can be noted in some other way. The following are some suggestions that can contribute to the palaeographic profile of a group of gravemarkers or burial sites (Fig. 146).

Style

The style of letter can be recorded under one of the main groups—gothic, uncio-versal, roman, italic, cursive, script, sans-serif, block serif or decorated. Always include a variable 'other' for lettering that does not fit within any of the main groups. Record whether the inscription has been cut in one or several styles.

Case

Capital or capitals and lower-case.

Inscriptional method

Relief (raised) or incised (intaglio). Included here could be painted and inlaid.

Ligatures

Record the presence or absence of ligatures. If they are present, it may be worth recording the actual ligatures.

Letter proportion

The proportion of lettering is best recorded as a ratio—narrower, equal to or wider than the height of the lower-case.

Fig. 146—Some suggested attributes that can be used in statistical analysis (top to bottom): case, cut, ligatures, proportion, weight, capital height and serif form.

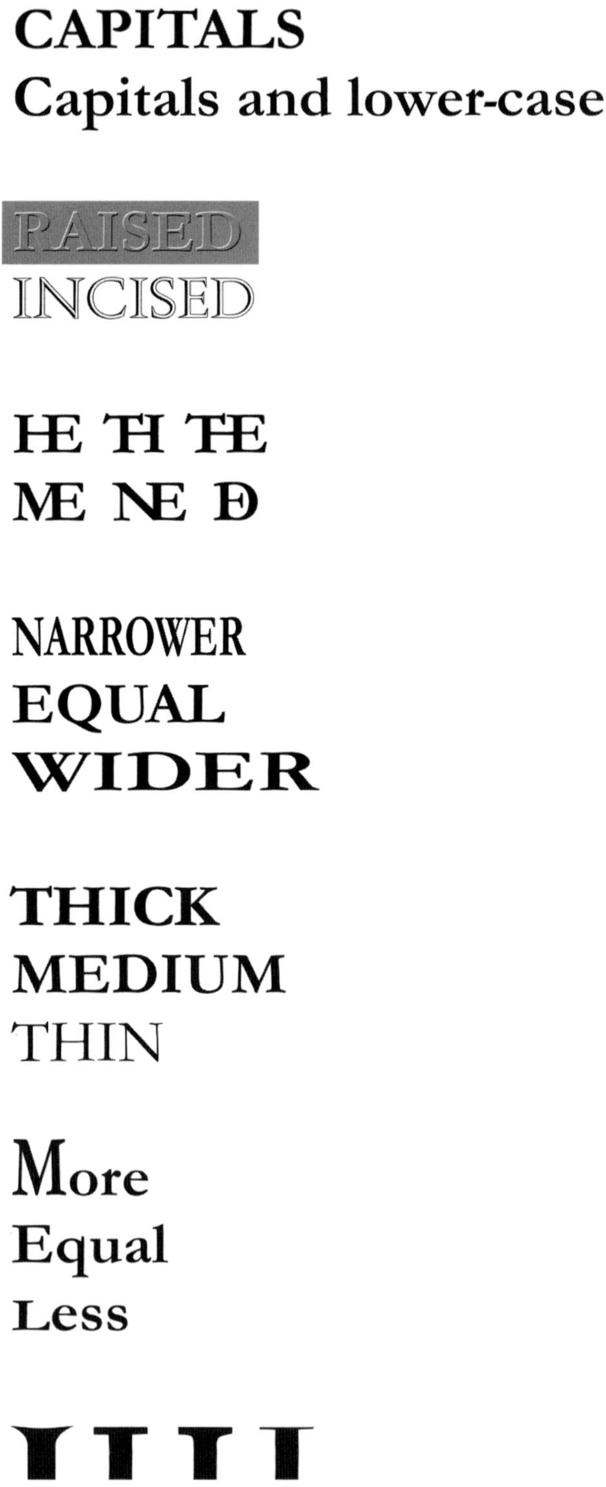

Figure 146

Weight
Record lettering as thick, medium or thin. This is analogous to the typographic terms bold, medium and light. The assessment will be somewhat subjective but will be acceptable if done consistently.

Capitals
It is useful to note the height of the capital letters as a proportion—less than, equal to or greater than the height of the lower-case lettering.

Distinctive letterforms
Record some of the distinctive forms of letters, if these are present, e.g. the archaic forms of A, B, E, M, R and W.

Serifs
In more detailed studies of roman lettering, it may be necessary to record the formation of the serif—classical 'fishtail', block, linear or bracketed—provided that the serif form does not place the lettering in another style.

Cut
Depth of cut is difficult to record and would have to be done on site. As it is influenced by the degree of weathering, it may not be practical, except in the case of very recent inscriptions.

Statistical analysis

This is not a statistics manual. Anyone who wants a detailed guide to statistical analysis should consult one of the many books on the subject.[118] Fortunately, with some basic computer skill and relatively little knowledge or experience of statistics, it is possible to perform many basic routines using computer software, including spreadsheets and some databases. For more advanced work there are dedicated statistical packages such as *SPSS*, *Statistica* and *Statgraphics*.[119] The aim here is to introduce some basic and a few more advanced analytical procedures that can contribute to an understanding of the cultural diversity of gravemarker lettering. Statistical analysis of gravemarkers, beyond simple counts and frequencies, is utilised surprisingly little, even though it is used extensively in archaeology, where procedures are well advanced. A good example of the value of relatively simple statistical procedures in gravemarker research is the work of Stone, who made a detailed study of gravestones in Long Island, New York. Another is the statistical analysis of New England gravemarkers and other artefacts by Deetz.[120] Univariate statistics utilise one variable only. Bivariate methods analyse two variables simultaneously. More than two variables are analysed using multivariate techniques. Multivariate analysis of gravemarker design is conspicuous by its absence.

When a researcher studies human, animal or plant populations, it is

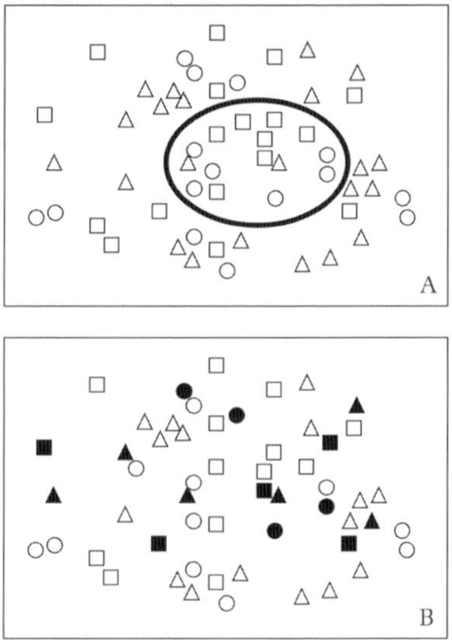

Fig. 147—Sampling models from 55 hypothetical burial sites of three types. A: random sampling (within the ellipse), B: purposive sampling representative of burial ground types (solid shapes).

Figure 147

almost always impossible to record information from every individual. Sampling is the only practical solution. On the other hand, gravemarker lettering studies can usually utilise a comprehensive record of a burial site, in which every gravemarker inscription can be included. If the study is of a region that has many burial grounds and it is impractical to survey them all, the recorded data sets then become a sample of the entire area from which the profile of the region is extrapolated. A sample must be both sufficiently large and representative so that there is some confidence that it reflects the nature of the entire group. Samples can be random or purposive. Random samples of burial grounds may not be representative of gravemarkers when the burial sites can range from large urban cemeteries to small, deserted rural graveyards. A bias towards one or other could be introduced unintentionally. If the historical, locational, demographic and possibly ethnic profile of the study area is to be represented, some sort of structured sampling is necessary. In the example illustrated (Fig. 147), circles, squares and triangles represent three burial site profiles that differ in terms of location (urban/rural), demography and period (date range of gravemarkers), and comprise respectively fifteen, eighteen and 22 of each type, being 27.3%, 32.7% and 40% of the total. In the first model (A) a random sample of fifteen sites is enclosed within the ellipse. Randomisation has greatly under-represented the third type, with only two of the 55 sites selected, even although they comprise 40% of the total. In the second model (B), four, five and six of each type have been selected. This is much more representative of the total number of sites. Sampling in this way can compromise objectivity. In some situations it may be more appropriate to treat each group of burial site types as a distinct entity, then comparisons can be made between them.

One point to remember is that, no matter how large the sample, if the

Table 4—Frequency table with eight variables (columns) and 25 sites (rows).

Site	*Attributes*							
	Mixed	*Gothic*	*Roman*	*Italic*	*Script*	*Sans*	*Block*	*Other*
1	0.236	0.066	0.724	0.039	0.092	0.053	0.026	0
2	0.216	0.026	0.802	0.043	0.043	0.078	0.009	0
3	0.068	0.017	0.915	0	0.034	0.034	0	0
4	0.750	0.250	0.500	0	0	0	0.250	0
5	0.587	0.238	0.540	0.063	0.095	0.048	0.032	0
6	0.354	0.021	0.771	0.104	0	0.042	0.062	0
7	0.590	0.224	0.522	0.067	0.007	0.097	0.082	0
8	0.545	0.236	0.582	0.036	0.073	0.073	0	0
9	0.680	0.200	0.533	0.053	0.013	0.080	0.120	0
10	0.647	0.265	0.500	0.029	0.059	0.147	0	0
11	0.659	0.183	0.378	0.110	0.098	0.146	0.073	0.012
12	0.791	0.308	0.670	0	0.011	0	0.011	0
13	0.581	0.062	0.597	0.217	0.039	0	0.085	0
14	0.579	0.104	0.584	0.182	0.117	0	0.013	0
15	0.795	0.136	0.580	0.227	0.023	0.011	0.023	0
16	0.817	0.075	0.550	0.283	0.025	0.025	0.042	0
17	0.682	0.205	0.614	0.091	0.091	0	0	0
18	0.696	0.087	0.696	0.217	0	0	0	0
19	0.768	0.268	0.609	0.094	0.029	0	0	0
20	0.683	0.254	0.667	0	0.079	0	0	0

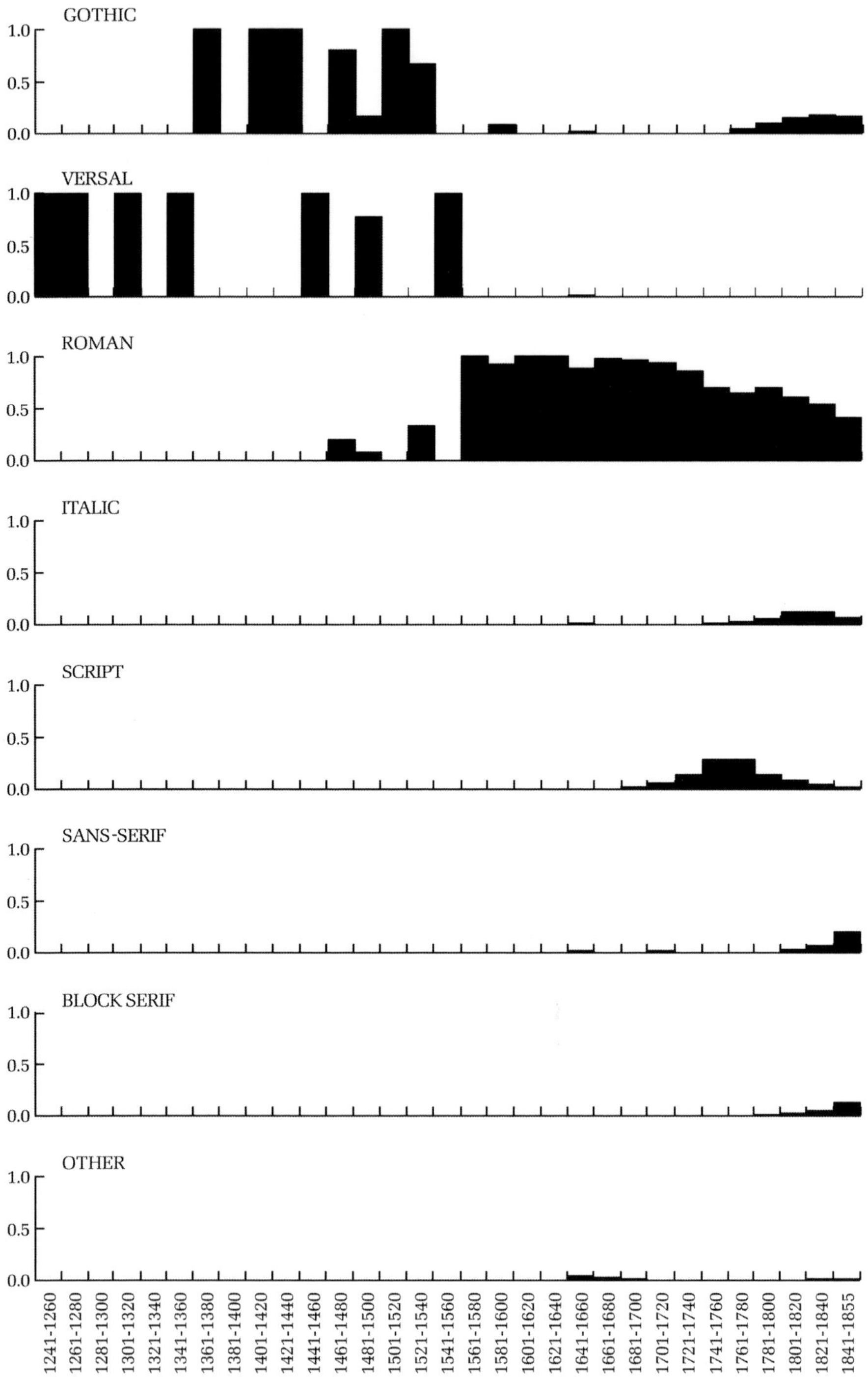

Figure 148

Fig. 148—The frequencies of eight lettering styles on Scottish gravemarkers 1241–1855.

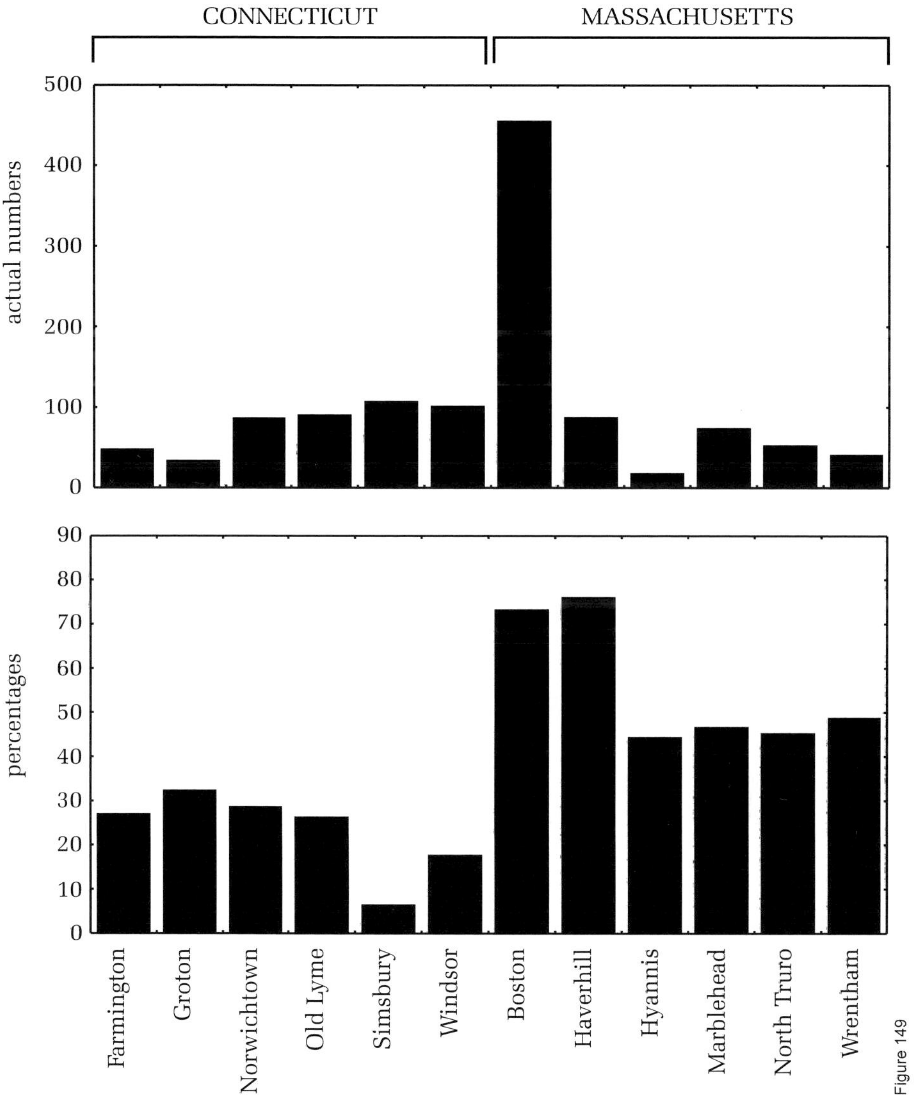

Fig. 149—Roman lettering on gravemarkers in Connecticut and Massachusetts, based on counts (above) and on frequencies (below).

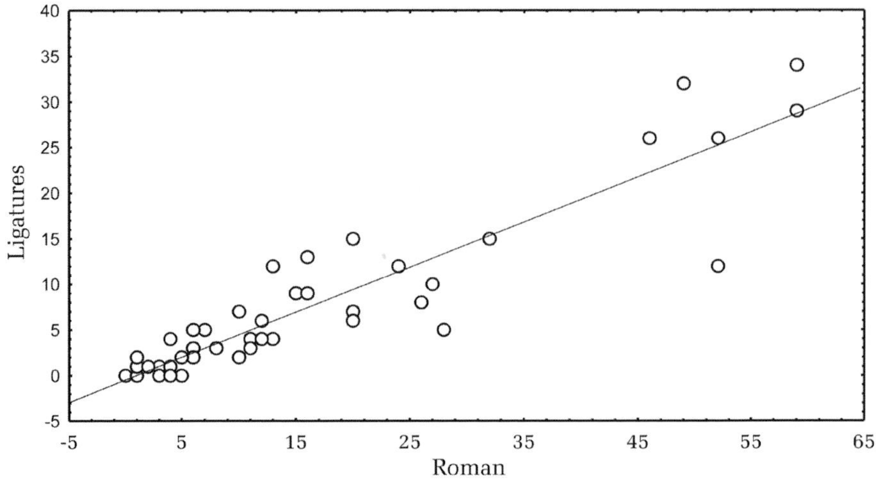

Figure 150

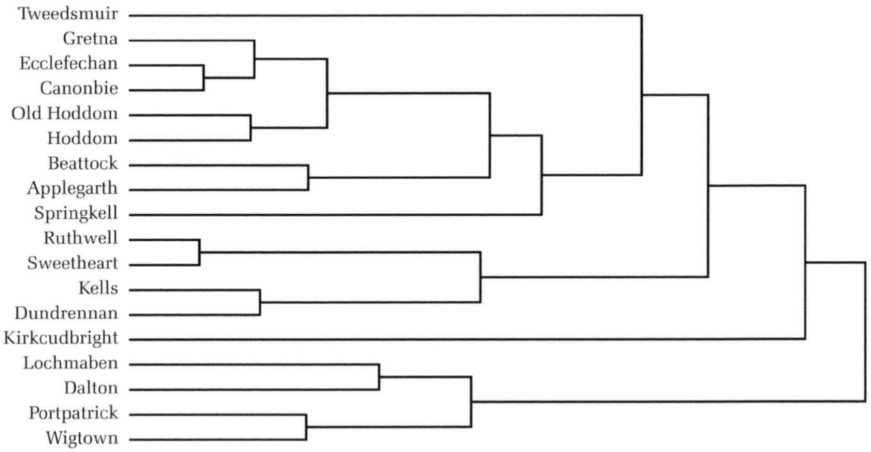

Figure 151

Fig. 150—Correlation plot showing the relationship between roman capitals and ligatures on gravemarkers in the counties of Cavan, Fermanagh, Monaghan and Tyrone, Ireland. The proximity of the circles to the regression line shows that there is a weak correlation.

Fig. 151—A joining tree or dendrogram produced from cluster analysis showing the relationships between gravemarkers based on lettering attributes in eighteen sites in south-west Scotland.

aim is to record the occurrence of a specific style or letterform, we cannot be certain of its absence in the sites that have not been explored. For example, even if 90% of the burial sites in a region have been surveyed and cursive lettering has not been found, we cannot say with certainty that it will not be found somewhere in the remaining 10%. We can only say that there is a high probability that it will not. Probability is a statistical concept that software can calculate easily.

Many statistical methods require the input of basic data in spreadsheet form, with variables (the lettering attributes) in columns and cases (each individual record) in rows, recorded as present (1) or absent (0), together with a code for missing data. If the data are entered in binary form, it is very easy to perform some basic calculations that, in many instances, will be as far as the researcher will want to proceed with the analysis. Once the frequencies of each attribute are calculated, the attributes can then be the variables and the burial sites the cases (Table 4). If actual measurements have been made, or other data types recorded, various methods can be used for their interpretation and analysis, usually through simple calculation. Counts tell us how many times a particular attribute occurs in the data record. This simple procedure was used in a study of different styles found on Scottish gravemarkers in twenty-year periods from 1241 to 1855. The change in the relative popularity of different forms over 600 years was demonstrated using a series of bar charts (Fig. 148).[121] In another study, the data from an analysis of gravemarkers in the burial sites of twelve cities and towns in Connecticut and Massachusetts, represented as simple counts, suggest that many more inscriptions in Boston are in capitals than anywhere else in the sample. This is misleading, however, as the number of gravemarkers recorded varies considerably from site to site, especially in the case of Boston, where the data were based on five separate burial grounds. Raw data often have to be converted into frequencies. In this case frequencies are more meaningful, as they explain the occurrence of an attribute as a proportion of the occurrence of another attribute, or of the total record or sample. The more extensive use of capitals in Massachusetts is clear in the bar chart based on percentages at each site (Fig. 149). This is significant, considering the trade in headstones throughout New England in the seventeenth and eighteenth centuries. The fact that there is a difference between the two states could suggest that the memorials in Connecticut were not supplied from source with the inscriptions already cut, these being added locally. It could also suggest that fewer imported headstones were used in Connecticut, where the local letter-cutters possibly used lower-case more often.

The relative differences between two or more sets of gravemarkers, using several variables from each, can be calculated by several algorithms, including Manhattan, Euclidean and Mahalanobis distances. Correlation and regression are slightly more complex concepts. We may want to find out if one attribute has some sort of relationship with another in the way it varies. For example, we may find through correlation analysis that in a

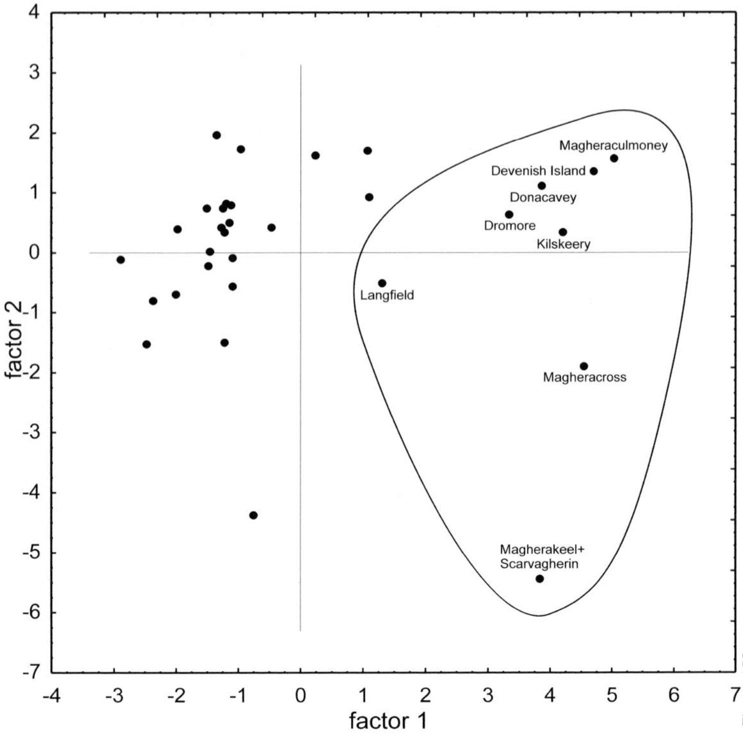

Figure 152

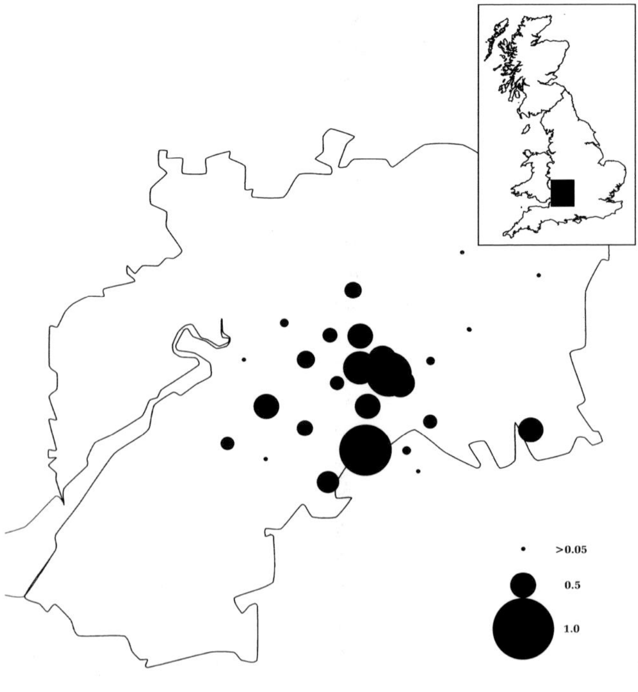

Figure 153

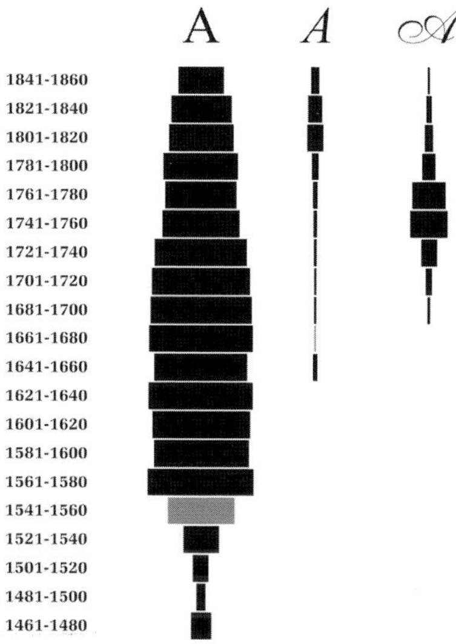

Figure 154

Fig. 152—Ordination showing the grouping of gravemarkers based on a factor analysis of letterform attributes in the counties of Cavan, Fermanagh, Monaghan and Tyrone, Ireland. The envelope illustrates the correspondence with the spatial distribution of burial grounds.

Fig. 153—Map of the frequency of gothic lettering on exterior brass plate memorials in Gloucestershire, England. Circle size corresponds with frequency.

Fig. 154—Spindle chart showing the relative frequencies of roman, italic and script letterforms in Scotland from 1461 to 1860.

specific site block serif lettering occurs much more often in inscriptions that are in relief lettering, or that ligatures are more common in inscriptions in roman capitals (Fig. 150).

Cluster analyses can represent the grouping of similar gravemarker data sets in the form of joining trees or dendrograms (Fig. 151). Some of the most useful multivariate methods for gravemarker inscription analysis come under the headings of principal components analysis (PCA) or its variant principal factor analysis (PFA), which can determine which attributes are contributing most to the differences between data sets. The distinction between these two related procedures has been misunderstood and questioned. Using only the more significant variables reduces the amount of data entry required for further studies. PCA and PFA can make comparisons between the inscriptions, based on a number of variables, from several burial grounds. They can then group these together according to their affinities, so producing what is, in effect, a classification of the cultural profiles of each group or cluster. This in turn can be compared with the spatial distribution of sites or any other a priori grouping of the artefacts. In a study of discoid gravemarkers at 32 burial sites in the Irish counties of Cavan, Fermanagh, Monaghan and Tyrone, PFA was used to explore the relationships between lettering and the distribution of gravemarker forms.[122] Eighteen letterform variables were identified and used in the analysis. The resulting ordinations demonstrated both that there was a relationship between letterform attributes and their spatial distribution and that the use of letterform as a cultural marker was more effective than the analysis of other morphological features (Fig. 152).

More often than not it is best to examine and present the outcomes of analysis in graphic form rather than as lists of numbers. Even if the final outcome of the analysis is a diagram or chart, retain the original data;

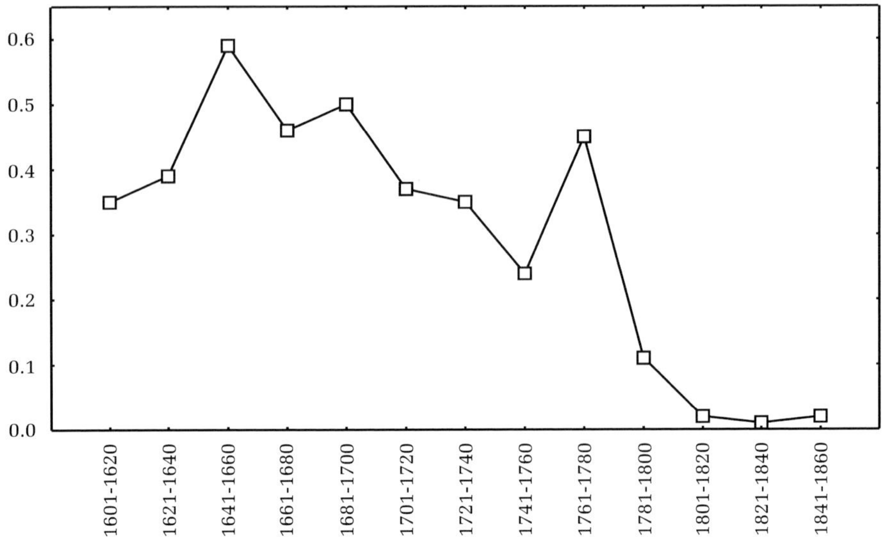

Figure 155

it may be useful in future studies. One of the most obvious methods of presenting the results of a survey of gravemarker lettering across a region is to map the distribution of the attributes, showing the relative frequency of each by circles or other symbols of varying size (Fig. 153). Readily available spreadsheets, as well as the more sophisticated statistical software packages, can produce a wide range of graphs and charts that elucidate numerical data. Column or bar charts display data values for different categories, usually representing actual numbers or percentages for each group. A variant of the bar chart is the spindle diagram, used extensively by archaeologists in seriation analysis. This is based on relative dating and displays the relative frequency as stacked horizontal bars of several artefact types over time. This type of chart has great visual impact and gives an instant graphic representation of temporal data. It is most useful when only a few artefact types are displayed (Fig. 154). Line graphs show the sequential increase and decrease of single or multiple data values in relation to changing conditions, such as a series of years (Fig. 155). Simple scatter diagrams plot two variables on the x and y (horizontal and vertical) axes to determine whether there is any evidence of correlation between the attributes. More complex scattergrams can be three- or even four-dimensional, when a complexity of variables (dimensions) has been collapsed into fewer variables (dimensions) so that the relationships between objects can be visualised more easily.[123] Ordinations, produced using principal components analysis (PCA), principal factor analysis (PFA), multidimensional scaling (MDS), discriminant analysis and some other statistical methods that can determine the similarities and differences between data sets, are special types of scatter diagrams in multivariate analysis. They are used to explore the nature of data sets to order objects so that similar ones are near to each other and dissimilar ones are further

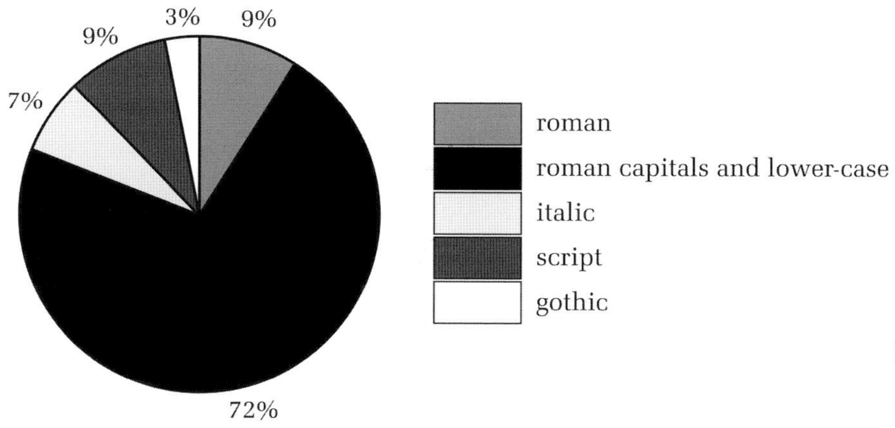

Figure 156

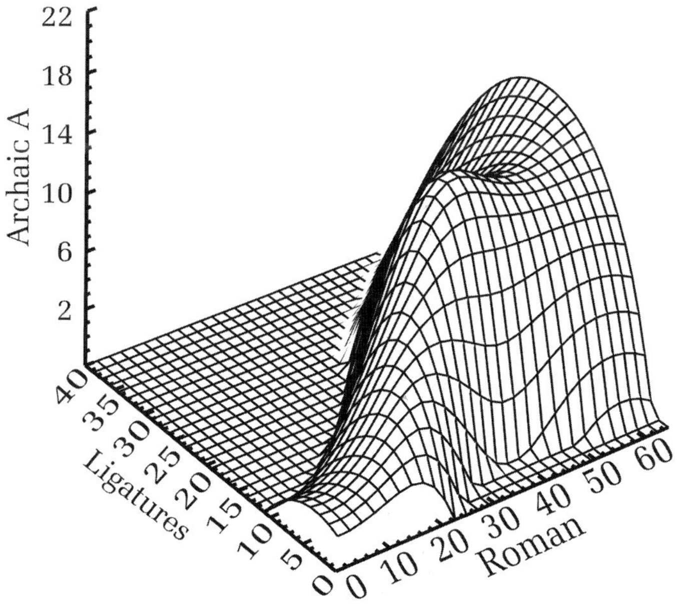

Figure 157

Fig. 155—Line plot showing the increase and decrease in the use of ligatures on Scottish gravemarkers from 1601 to 1860.

Fig. 156—Pie chart showing the proportions of different lettering styles on gravemarkers in Trinity Church Burial Ground, New York City, New York, USA.

Fig. 157—Surface plot showing the relationship between roman, ligatures and the archaic form of capital A in inscriptions on gravemarkers in Trinity Church Burial Ground, New York City, New York, USA.

apart. Pie charts display the contribution of each data value to the whole (Fig. 156). There are many other chart types, such as histograms, range plots and surface plots, that may be useful in gravemarker lettering research (Fig. 157).

Statistical analysis is only the means to an end. An objective evaluation of the statistical output should lead to a fuller understanding of the lettering and its wider context. Palaeography informs other disciplines, including material culture research, aesthetics, art history, social history, folk-life studies, archaeology, geography and genealogy. The data produced from statistical procedures could be quite different from what was envisaged and may not support a hypothesis. Part of the excitement of analysing gravemarker lettering data comes from encountering the unexpected. If everything was predictable, the pursuit would be very dull indeed.

CASE-STUDY: A COMPARISON OF THE LETTERING ON EARLY GRAVEMARKERS IN TWO IRISH BURIAL GROUNDS

The following is an example of a preliminary study of gravemarker lettering at two burial sites in the south of Ireland. The analysis is somewhat elementary, and very much more could be gleaned from the data collected. The case-study demonstrates some methodologies that can easily be applied to the inscriptions at almost any burial site to provide meaningful information that can be used as the basis for further study.

Introduction and methods

Regional variation in lettering styles on gravemarkers carved before the widespread use of specimen-books and letterforms based on typographic specimens is a phenomenon that can be detected throughout much of western Europe. The relationships between and the differentiation of attributes in closely adjacent localities can sometimes be achieved more objectively by methods other than simple observation. This is especially so in the case of the more subtle characteristics of the lettering. The burial sites at Buttevant, Co. Cork, and Galbally, Co. Limerick, in southern Ireland were chosen because they are geographically close enough for potential cultural interaction but sufficiently distant that some diversity could be expected. The sites are separated by a straight-line distance of 29km (eighteen miles).

The majority of the gravemarkers at Buttevant are headstones in the burial ground between the nineteenth-century St Mary's Church and the thirteenth-century Franciscan friary, with some within the ruins of the medieval building. The Galbally burial ground lies to the south of the town and surrounds the ruins of the thirteenth-century church. One significant difference between the two areas is that Galbally retains much toponymic

Table 5—Variables used in case-study with a description of their attributes. Significant differences are shown bold.

	Variable name	Attribute	*Frequencies* Buttevant	Galbally
1	MIXED	more than one style on same stone face	**0.505**	**0.339**
2	NOTMIXED	only one style used on same stone face	**0.495**	**0.661**
3	GOTHIC	gothic	0	0.008
4	VERSAL	letterform characterised by exaggerated entices on verticals and bulging curves (uncio-versal)	0	0
5	ROMAN	serifed letterforms excluding uncio-versal and block serif forms	0.757	0.839
6	ITALIC	distinguished from script by 'sloped roman' capitals	0.068	0.016
7	CURSIVE	cursive forms excluding script and italic	0.039	0.024
8	SCRIPT	script form emulating pen-written forms	0.136	0.097
9	SANS	non-roman letterforms lacking serifs	0	0
10	BLOCK	block serif forms including slab and Egyptian	0	0.016
11	OTHER	any form not including above	0	0
12	RAISED	relief lettering	0.097	0.161
13	INCISED	incised (intaglio) lettering	0.903	0.839
14	CAPS	capitals	0.175	0.121
15	CAPS_LC	capitals and lower-case	0.825	0.879
16	LIGS	ligatures present	**0.068**	**0**
17	NO_LIGS	ligatures absent	0.932	1.000
18	HT_MORE	height of letters greater than width	0.748	0.669
19	HT_EQUAL	height of letters approximately equal to width	0.252	0.331
20	HT_LESS	height of letters less than width	0	0
21	THIN	line width of letters approximating to the typographic style 'light'	**0.515**	**0.226**
22	MID	line width of letters approximating to the typographic style 'medium'	0.437	0.516
23	THICK	line width of letters approximating to the typographic style 'bold'	**0.048**	**0.258**
24	CAPMORE2	capital height greater than twice the x-height	0.624	0.759
25	CAPEQUA2	capital height approximately equal to twice the x-height	0.153	0.093
26	CAPLESS2	capital height less than twice the x-height	0.223	0.148
27	A_NORM	'normal' form of capital A	0.965	0.919
28	A_VLINE	crossbar of capital A in form of a V (broken)	0.018	0.081
29	A_V_BAR	horizontal line across top of capital A	0.017	0
30	B_IN	centre line of capital B touching vertical	0.960	0.884
31	B_NOT_IN	centre line of capital B not touching vertical	0.040	0.116
32	E_OUT	centre line of capital E approximately equal to upper and lower horizontals	0.031	0.037
33	E_IN	centre line of capital E shorter than upper and lower horizontals	0.969	0.963
34	M_LONG	centre V of capital M reaching baseline	**0.463**	**0.846**
35	M_SHORT	centre line of capital M not reaching baseline	**0.537**	**0.154**
36	R_STRGHT	leg of capital R straight	**0.424**	**0.175**
37	R_CURVED	leg of capital R upturned at end	**0.576**	**0.825**
38	W_NORM	'normal' form of capital W	0.797	0.716
39	W_2_VS	capital W comprising two Vs	0.203	0.284

evidence of past English influence, whereas Buttevant's post-medieval heritage is distinctly Irish.

Most of the gravemarkers at both sites, as in much of Ireland, are heavily encrusted with lichen, making both photography and later recording of attributes often difficult. As most of the attributes can be resolved from partial inscriptions, very few could not be included. The incised lettering of several inscriptions, especially at Galbally, had been painted, virtually destroying the integrity of the letterforms. When these could not be resolved with confidence, they were excluded from the data.

Every gravemarker dated 1840 or earlier was photographed digitally and the data entered into a *Statistica* spreadsheet. Thirty-nine attributes were recorded as being present or absent. Lettering used for the cipher IHS was not included. Several headstones at Galbally were clearly post-dated and were excluded from the data set. *Statistica* was used for all computations, although much less advanced software could have been employed. In total, 77 gravemarkers were recorded at Buttevant and 96 at Galbally. From these, 103 inscriptions or partial inscriptions with different lettering styles were identified at Buttevant and 124 at Galbally.

Analysis

Four lettering styles were identified on gravemarkers within the study dates at both sites: roman, italic, cursive and script. In addition, one example of block serif was noted at Galbally, dated 1837. Inscriptions in roman capitals and roman capitals and lower-case were recorded separately. The earliest dates for each style are detailed below.

	Buttevant	*Galbally*
Roman capitals	1603	1742
Roman capitals and lower-case	1702	1739
Italic	1806	1827
Cursive	1777	1818
Script	1775	1796

Actual numbers of inscriptions in each style for twenty-year periods from 1700 to 1840 are represented in the series of bar charts in Fig. 158. Inscriptions in roman far outnumber those in other styles, gradually increasing in frequency over the period. The percentages of each style in relation to the total number of inscriptions are similar at both sites (Fig. 159).

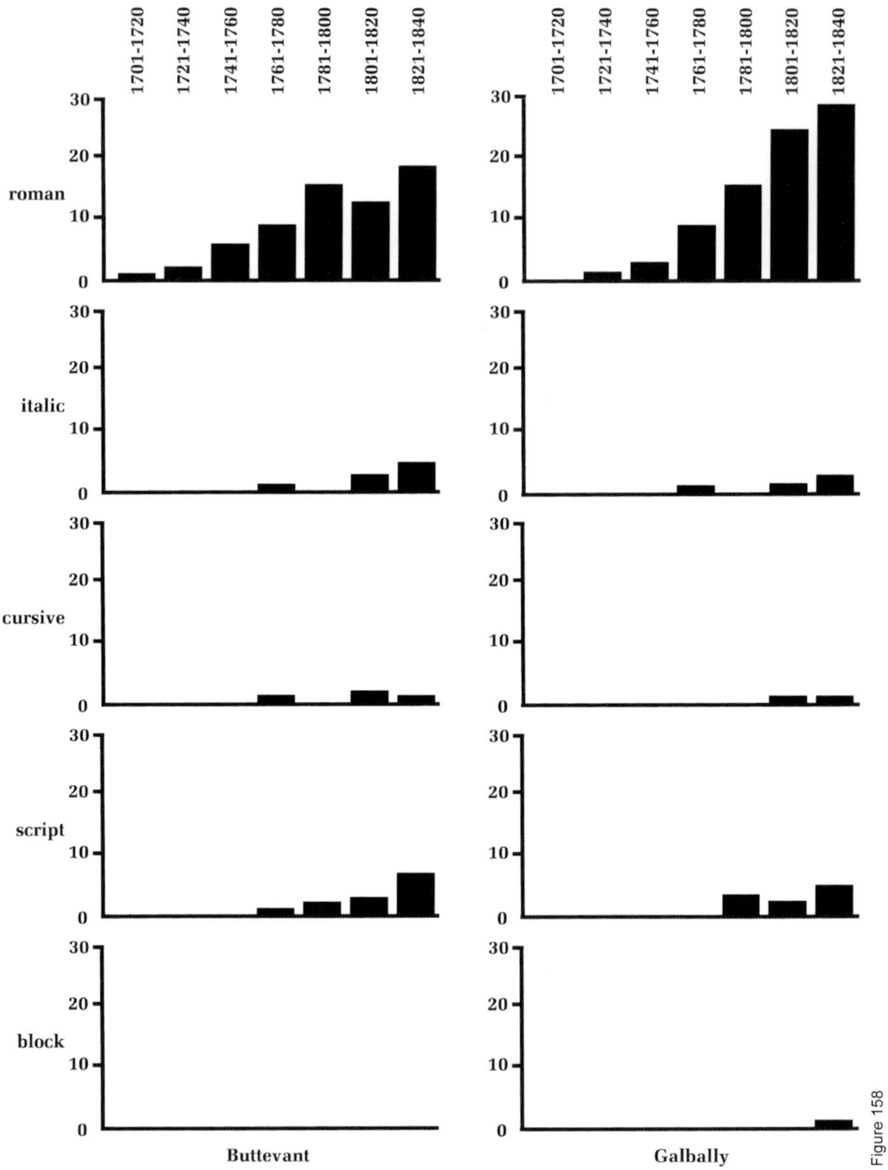

Fig. 158—The number of inscriptions in each lettering style from 1700 to 1840 at Buttevant, Co. Cork, and Galbally, Co. Limerick, Ireland.

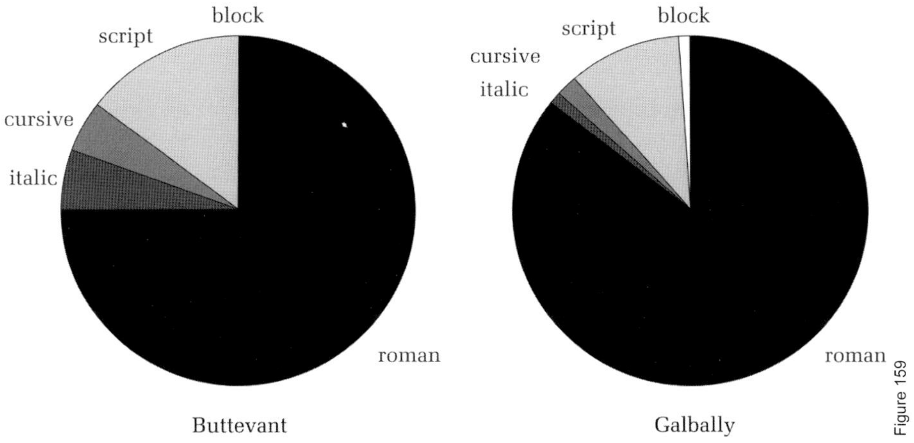

Fig. 159—The relative proportions of each lettering style at Buttevant, Co. Cork, and Galbally, Co. Limerick, Ireland.

The binary data were converted to frequencies for each attribute. Table 5 lists the variable names, their attributes and frequencies. Although the similarity between both sites in styles is also reflected in the statistical correlation coefficient for all attributes ($r = 0.93$: $p < 0.05$), there are some important differences in detail, both quantitative and qualitative. Gravemarkers with more than one style on the same face are much more prevalent at Buttevant, although the gravemarker with the most styles (four: roman, relief roman, script and relief script) is at Galbally, dated 1796. At Galbally, many more inscriptions are in a bold weight and half as many in light-weight lettering than at Buttevant. The more archaic forms of M with the short V and R with a straight leg are much more frequent there. Nearly 7% of Buttevant inscriptions have ligatures, whereas there are none at Galbally. The ligatures at Buttevant are NE (1775), HE (1747 as enlarged initial capitals, 1780, 1820), ME (1820, 1835) and THE (1804). The inscriptions on several headstones at Buttevant in relief capitals have the letters A and H with a crossbar formed from a series of small circles. Some also have the capital P with a descender.

At Buttevant, eight inscriptions are in relief roman capitals and only one in relief roman capitals and lower-case. At Galbally, only two are in relief capitals and thirteen are in relief capitals and lower-case. Also at Galbally, several headstones have the inscription in alternate relief and incised lines, a feature not so far found elsewhere in Ireland (Fig. 160).

There is a significant difference between the two sites in the inscriptional form of roman capitals and lower-case on many headstones. The roman at Galbally is 'modern' in style, with strong contrast between the thick vertical and thin horizontals and conspicuous hairline serifs. At Buttevant, the roman retains the strong vertical/horizontal contrast but the serifs are minimal, and in some instances completely lacking.

Conclusions

The high proportion of inscriptions with capitals more than twice the x-height and the W formed of two Vs corresponds with the general trend in the rest of Ireland in the eighteenth and early nineteenth centuries, a feature that distinguishes Irish inscriptions from contemporaneous inscriptional lettering in Scotland and England.

The distinctive forms of A, H and P at Buttevant, described above, are also found in other nearby burial sites in County Cork and probably represent the work of a single stonemason. The alternate incised and relief lines on several headstones at Galbally may be unique in Ireland. The iconography and decoration on these headstones differs, so they may not be the work of a single mason. This suggests that they may represent an element of a distinctive local material culture.

The relatively frequent occurrence of headstones with inscriptions in relief roman lettering is an extremely interesting feature of burial sites in parts of southern Ireland. The relative numbers of inscriptions in relief capitals, greater at Buttevant, and relief capitals and lower-case, greater at Galbally, fits the transect pattern (cline) from south to north identified in other studies, with the proportion of inscriptions in capitals and lower-case increasing northwards. One headstone at Galbally has part of the relief inscription in script.

Some of the characteristics of the lettering at Buttevant, especially the frequency of the archaic forms of M and R, suggest that lettering design is somewhat less advanced there in terms of style and in relation to lettering trends further north in Ireland.

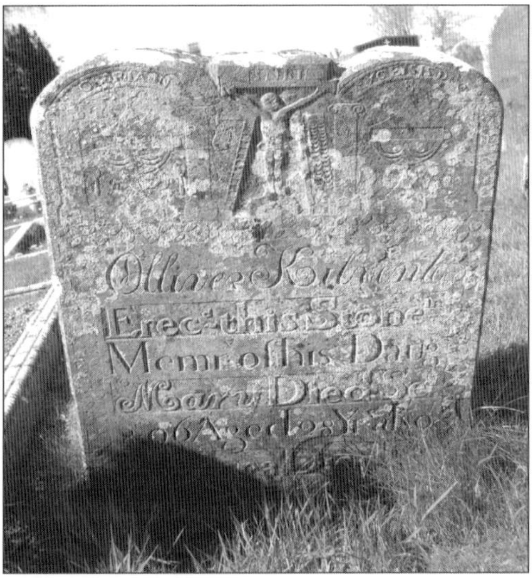

Figure 160

Fig. 160—Headstone with alternate lines of incised and relief lettering. Note the relief lettering in the word 'Mary'. Galbally, Co. Limerick, Ireland (1896).

CONSERVATION

No burial ground is frozen in time. Those that are still in use evolve and grow as more memorials are erected (Fig. 161). Closed burial grounds, i.e. those that no longer accept interments, become overgrown with vegetation unless they are regularly tended, and the gravemarkers develop a patina of moss and lichen (Fig. 162). To some, the abandoned graveyard is a blot on the landscape and would not stand in the way of their destruction. To others, it is a place with a unique atmosphere, a place to be treasured and sometimes a wildlife refuge. The following extracts illustrate the chasm between two opposing views on the future of burial sites and their gravemarkers.

> 'The churchyard is a doomed institution. The idea of consecrated ground will fall by the wayside as surely as other outdated superstitions, and land hitherto reserved for the dead will be released for the living. No one should mourn the gradual disappearance of the churchyard, except gravediggers and monumental masons, for whom its demise will be bad news economically. Monuments and other objects of historic or artistic value will quite properly be removed to museums . . .' (Bailey 1987, 183).

> 'It is important that as many historic stones as possible are preserved in their settings for future generations. Without them the nation's heritage can never be fully documented. The rural kirkyard, burial ground or urban cemetery can and should play a crucial role in embodying the specific and unique memory and history of a place. We need to conserve and even enhance the character of these valuable spaces within the

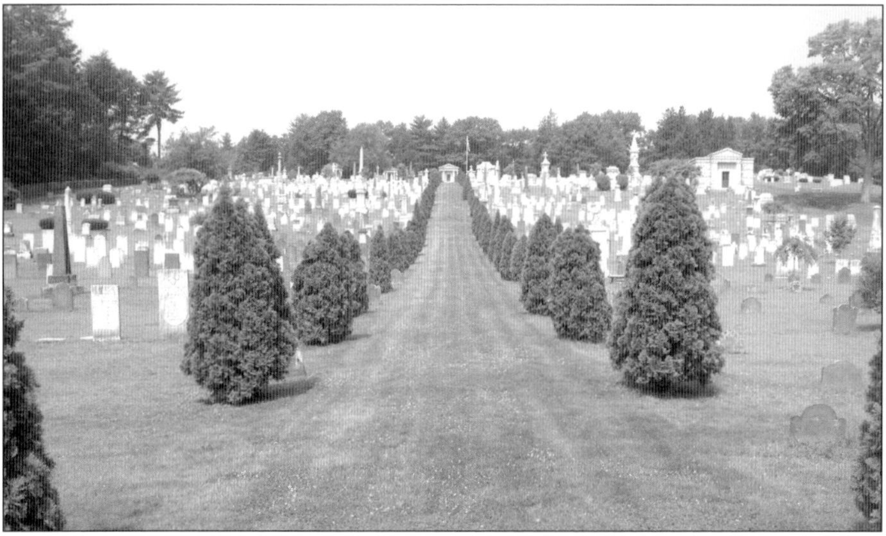

Figure 161

rural landscape or urban setting. We should be grateful that we have inherited so many fine works of art in our historic graveyards and that these documents in stone have been preserved for us to enjoy and learn from' (Maxwell *et al.* 2001, 4).

The first of these could be considered to be utilitarian, the second romantic. Opinions on the conservation and value of burial grounds and gravemarkers are inevitably coloured and informed by a number of factors, including legality and ownership, ethics, aesthetics, cultural significance, historical importance, and personal experience and involvement. Most recently, health and safety and costs have become issues that are determining the fate of many historic burial grounds in Britain and Ireland. The value of land has also led to some more extreme actions. Harborne Cemetery, Birmingham, was partially cleared in the 1960s to make way for a carpark. As recently as 2005, the headstones at Upwell Baptist Chapel, Cambridgeshire, were cleared with a bulldozer. There are bound to be conflicts in these complex situations that will not be addressed here, except where they impact on the contribution that gravemarker lettering can make to our cultural heritage and any consequent need to have inscriptions protected and conserved.

The impetus for burial ground and gravemarker conservation comes mainly from individuals, local groups and other informal organisations with an interest in their future. Detailed practical guides to the conservation, restoration and protection of burial grounds and their artefacts do not exist in many countries, and have never been produced by governmental departments or civic authorities. Where it occurs, this lack reflects both historical practice and/or an indifferent attitude towards conservation.

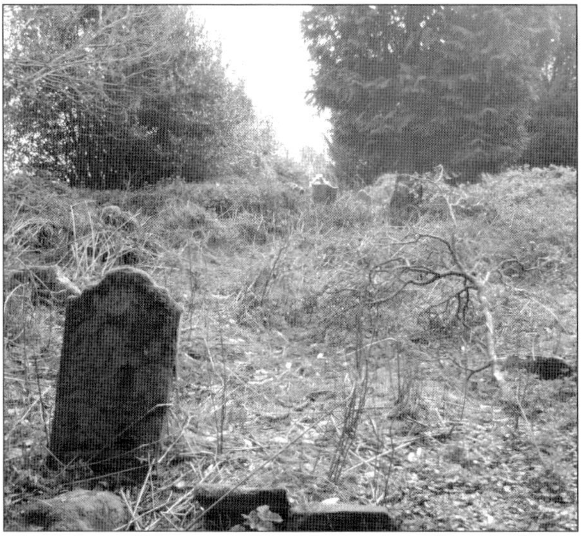

Fig. 161—Simsbury Cemetery, Simsbury, Connecticut, USA.

Fig. 162—Overgrown burial ground, Bahana (Whaley Abbey), Co. Wicklow, Ireland.

There are exceptions, notably in Scotland and Ireland.[124] Modern cemeteries are usually the responsibility of a local authority, sometimes with their management bound by local or national laws. One reason for the inconsistency in the degree to which older burial grounds are tended could be the differences in the ownership and maintenance responsibilities for both sites and memorials at national level. In the USA there appears to be no single approach, the responsibility being held by a local authority, the church or, if neither of these, by voluntary groups. In England the church looks after the burial grounds where these are adjacent to or associated with a parish or church building. Old Irish burial grounds are the responsibility of the local authority or the Church of Ireland. Local authorities maintain burial grounds in Scotland. German burial grounds are the responsibility of either the parish or civic authority. In many countries, the individual plots or lairs and gravemarkers are owned by the family of the deceased, either in perpetuity, as is the case in Britain, Ireland, the USA and Canada, or for a limited time, as in Germany, where the memorials must be removed at the end of the rental period.[125] A difficulty arises when the ownership can no longer be proved and the church or local authority can then retain, move or dispose of the memorial as they think fit, unless it is somehow 'listed' in a legally binding schedule.

Lettering on gravemarkers rarely features in published conservation discourses or guides and is usually marginalised as a relatively insignificant feature of the inscription. Usually, only the textual content is deemed important. Palaeographic and epigraphic study is frequently dismissed as a task for the art historian, a misplaced view that does not recognise the cultural significance of gravemarker lettering. Maxwell *et al.* are exceptional by including lettering in their list of criteria for an important gravestone, which they define as one that:

Fig. 163—Eroded raised roman and reconstruction of original form.

Fig. 164—Eroded incised roman and reconstruction of original form. Note that the letters are much finer (thinner) than would have been the case if drawn from a rubbing.

Fig. 165—Unusual effect of alveolar erosion on lettering, St Mary's Churchyard, Whitby, Yorkshire, England.

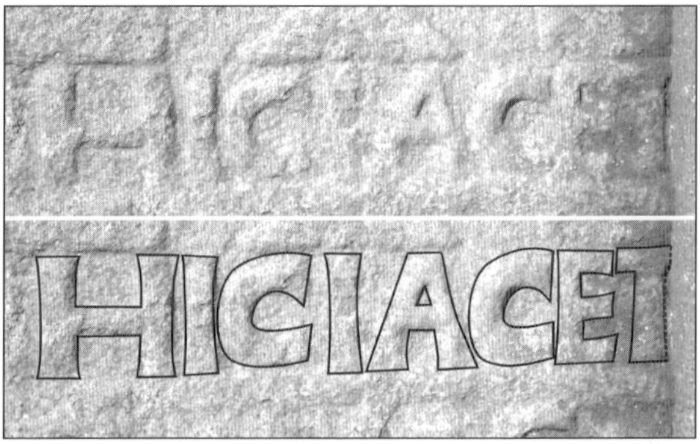

Figure 163

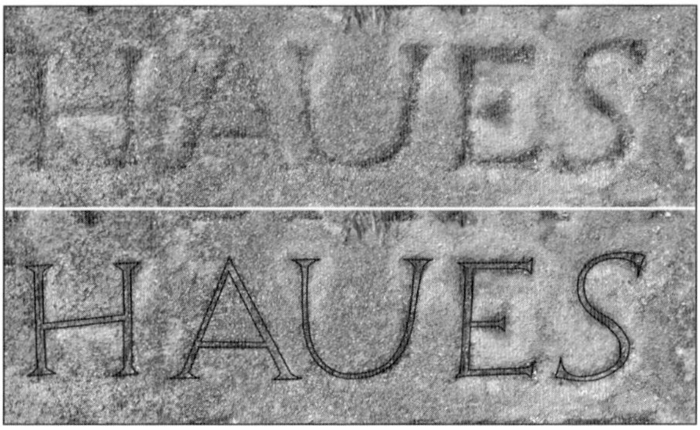

Figure 164

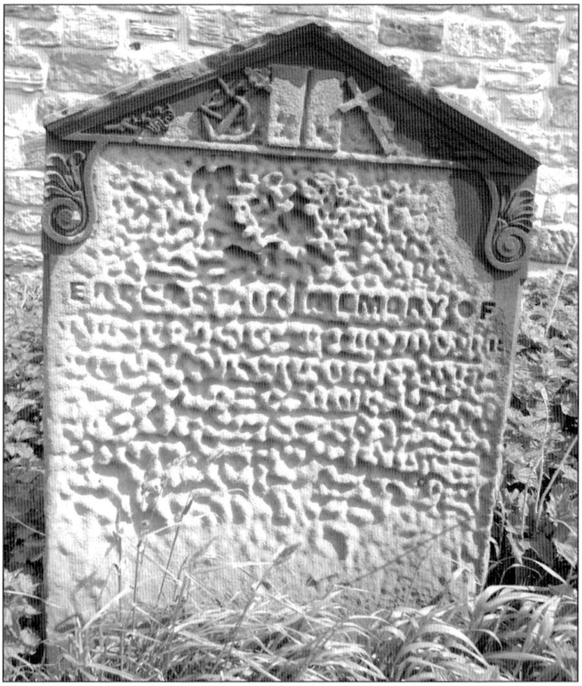

Figure 165

- is listed or scheduled;
- commemorates a person of recognised importance;
- is unique to that graveyard, for example in period, material, construction or design;
- contains significant carved detail or lettering;
- is one of the oldest in the locality;
- is one of a historic group of headstones;
- records a significant event;
- is otherwise unusual or representative.[126]

Those responsible for deciding the destiny of gravemarkers should follow this example.

Lettering is exposed to the same threats as the rest of the gravemarker. The cut of most inscriptions is usually very shallow compared with the sculpturing of the memorial and is likely to result in lettering being the first part of the artefact to be lost. Gravestones are susceptible to several natural processes that lead to their eventual destruction, including delamination, contour scaling, surface blistering and erosion.[127] These are mostly weather-induced, through wind and water penetration. Atmospheric pollution is also effective in the process. Deterioration can be accelerated, however, by human interference with the patinated stone surface. Some stone types vary in their durability. Generally sandstone, limestone and marble are the least durable. Slate and granite survive the elements best. Some sandstones and limestones are extremely hard-wearing and most coarser-grained granites deteriorate quickly. Gravemarkers made from certain other materials are even more prone to environmental attack. Wood rots very quickly, and only a few inscriptions on wooden markers have survived in areas of extremely low humidity. Cast iron rusts, and most inscriptions on iron markers have been completely lost. Lettering on so-called brass plates, made from a bronze-like alloy, has survived extremely well, many for more than 300 years. Only those made from inferior materials have been significantly damaged; otherwise the only change that has occurred is the development of a patina.

Deterioration of relief inscriptions can be detected by the loss of the crisp edges, sharp corners and the serifs of letters. The eroded lettering has a soft, rounded appearance, quite unlike its original form (Fig. 163). Incised lettering is affected quite differently. Erosion of the letters widens the lines and results in lettering that appears much headier (bolder) than it would have been when first cut (Fig. 164). A very unusual phenomenon can be seen on some memorials where the cutting of the inscription has protected the stone below, leaving it proud when the background has suffered from alveolar erosion (Fig. 165).[128]

Vandalism, both civic and by individuals, is a growing problem in many burial sites. Civic vandalism includes bad maintenance practice that poses a risk to gravemarkers or even to the burial site. Economics

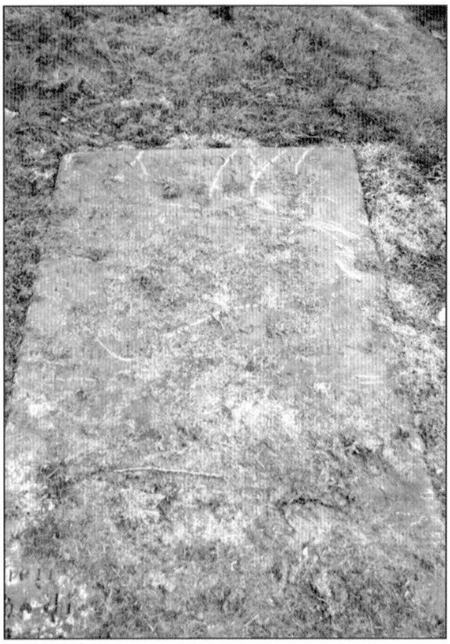

Figure 166

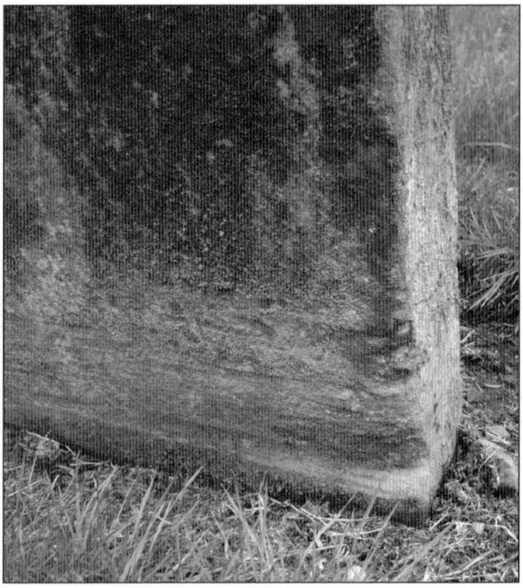

Figure 167

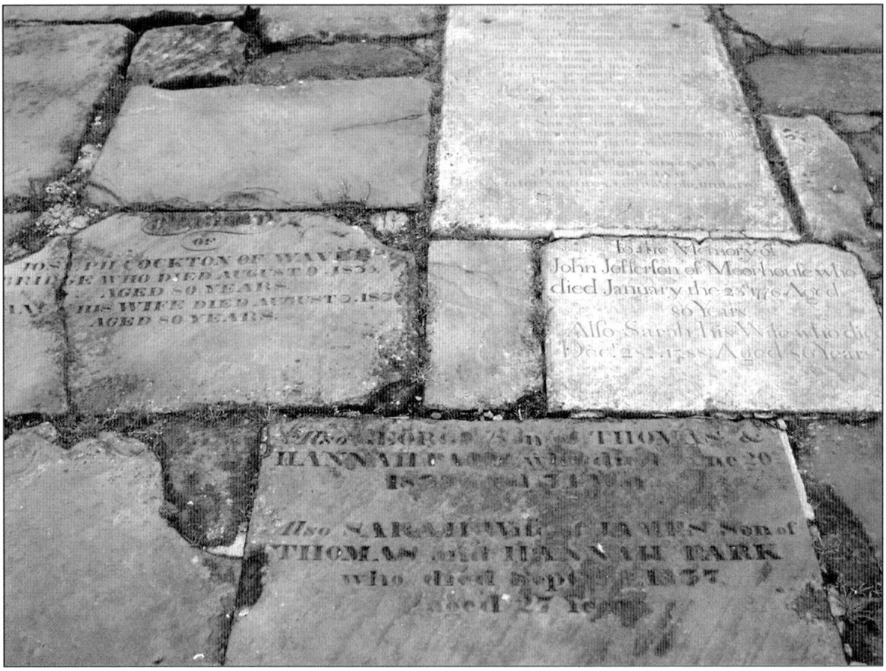

Figure 168

Fig. 166—Damage by lawn mower driven over the top of a ledger, Troqueer Churchyard, Dumfriesshire, Scotland.

Fig. 167—Damage by lawn mower to base of headstone, Terregles Churchyard, Dumfriesshire, Scotland.

Fig. 168—Headstones used as paving, St Mary's Church, Wigton, Cumbria, England.

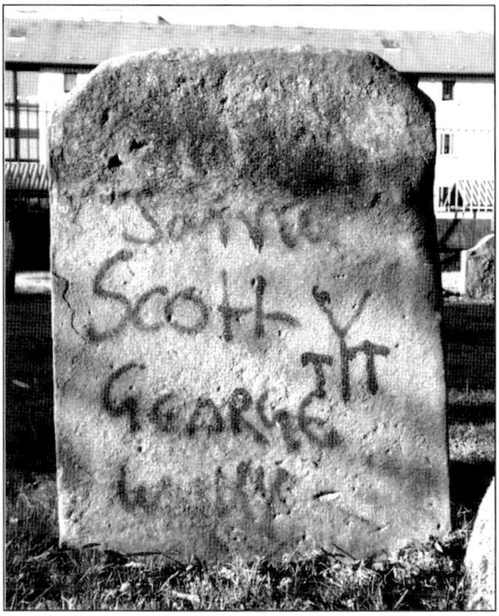

Figure 169

Fig. 169—Headstone defaced with graffiti, Govan Old Churchyard, Glasgow, Scotland.

often determines the means by which a graveyard or cemetery is looked after. Grass-cutting is often undertaken with motor mowers that are driven over ledgers and flattened headstones, and run carelessly against other gravemarkers, causing irreparable damage (Figs 166 and 167). Headstones are laid flat, supposedly for health and safety reasons but often, in reality, to make maintenance easier and less expensive. Other memorials are used as paving, frequently in areas where there is heavy foot traffic that inevitably and rapidly wears the inscription (Fig. 168). There is a view that the replacement of grass with gravel destroys the character of a graveyard. This could be preferable if the alternative is the ultimate defacement and destruction of the gravestones by maintenance machinery. In some urban areas, graffiti is a serious ongoing problem. Gravestones are spray-painted or otherwise damaged by individuals with little respect for what the memorials represent (Fig. 169).

Theft of old gravemarkers is a serious problem in parts of the USA. In New York in 1987, headstones fetched prices between $1,000 and $5,000. The stolen artefacts are being made into coffee-tables and headboards for beds. In 1985 it became a criminal act to steal a gravestone from a burial ground, punishable by up to ten years in prison. The law appears to have had some effect. Nevertheless, in Connecticut cemetery associations have replaced important headstones with concrete replicas and moved the originals to museums or locked vaults.[129]

The entire surface of some memorial stones was painted when originally erected. The use of paint on stone, even if this was the intention of the mason, is aesthetically unattractive (Fig. 170). The lettering of inscriptions on older gravemarkers should never be painted to make them more legible, or for any other reason (Fig. 171). The outlining of relief lettering is even less desirable (Fig. 172).

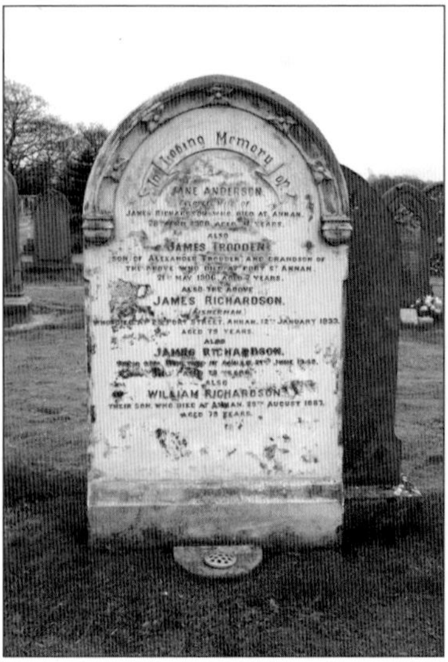

Figure 170

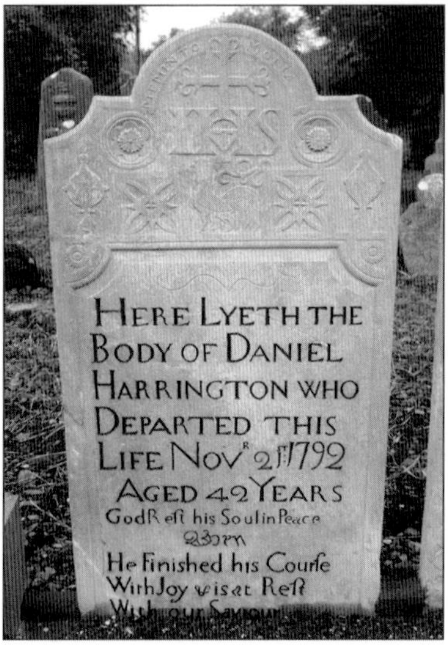

Figure 171

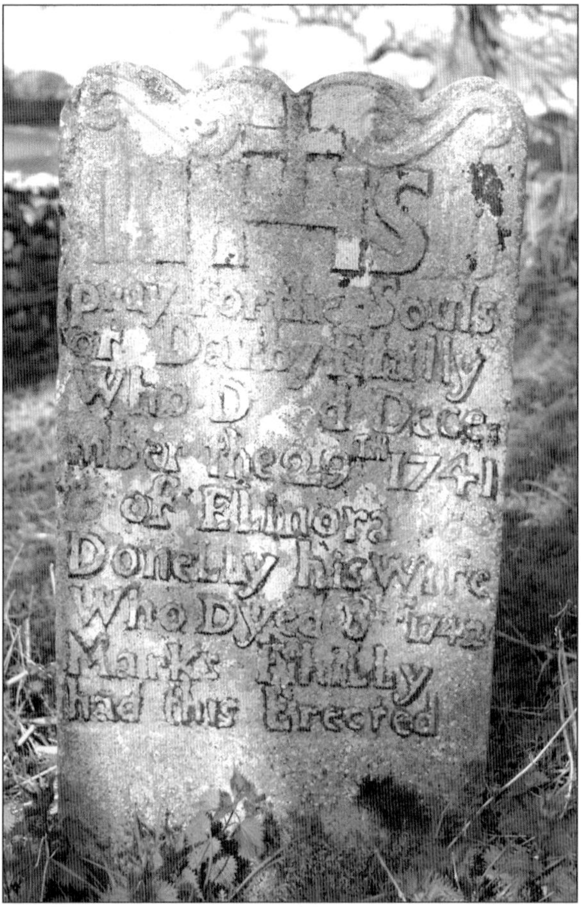

Figure 172

Fig. 170—Painted headstone, Annan Cemetery, Dumfriesshire, Scotland (1906–67).

Fig. 171—Painted incised lettering, Innishannon Burial Ground, Co. Cork, Ireland.

Fig. 172—Outlined lettering, Kiltoom, Co. Roscommon, Ireland.

Fig. 173—Volunteers cleaning gravestones with a pressure hose and brushes, Noordbroek, North Holland, Netherlands.

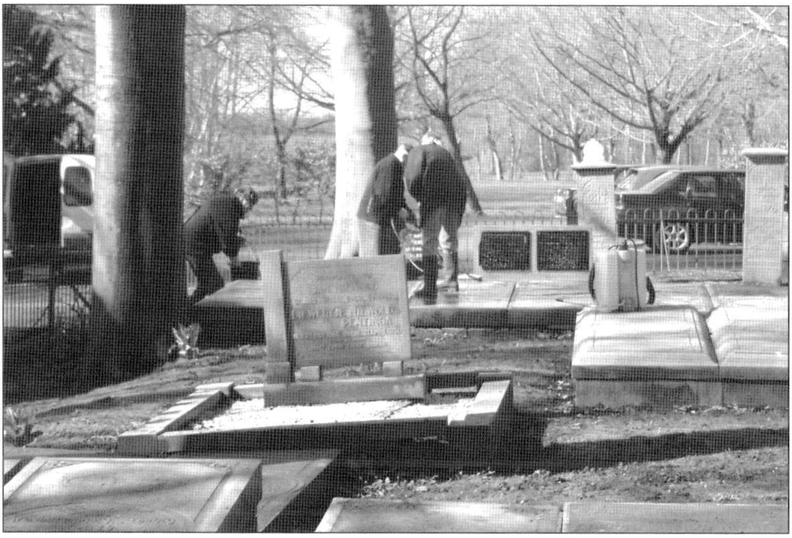

Figure 173

The current view of most conservationists is that gravemarkers should be cleaned only by those qualified to do so. It is easy to find instances where careless cleaning has accelerated the erosion process because the protective patina has been destroyed. We can sometimes find ourselves in the frustrating situation of doing nothing, when surface brushing would greatly enhance the legibility and clarity of the inscription in the short term. There are many instances where an inscription that is unclear because of surface contamination or vegetative growth will simply deteriorate to the point where the lettering will be completely destroyed if nothing is done about it. Usually, there is no will and/or finance to resolve the issue, and untrained volunteers often have to take on the work of maintenance (Fig. 173). Light surface deposits can be removed by brushing *very lightly* with a soft bristle brush. Wire brushes cause severe damage to stones. Cleaning compounds, liquids and powders should never be applied to a gravestone inscription to make it legible.

The relocation of gravemarkers is a contentious issue. In Germany and some other parts of continental Europe, the time-limit for ownership of burial plots results in a relatively rapid turnover of memorials. Some gravemarkers are relocated beside the church buildings or conserved in museums, but the majority are destroyed or reused. Several old burial grounds in Ireland have been cleared and the area redesignated as a park, e.g. Cabbage Garden, Dublin, and Arklow Abbeylands, Co. Wicklow, and the headstones repositioned on the perimeter of the land. The Arklow park is a pleasant recreational area (Fig. 174), but the headstones at the Dublin site have been badly damaged and vandalised (Fig. 175). A major project at Greyfriers Graveyard in Perth, Scotland, between 1999 and 2001 involved restoration of the graveyard, professional cleaning of several headstones and the relocation of a selected few under a canopied structure to protect

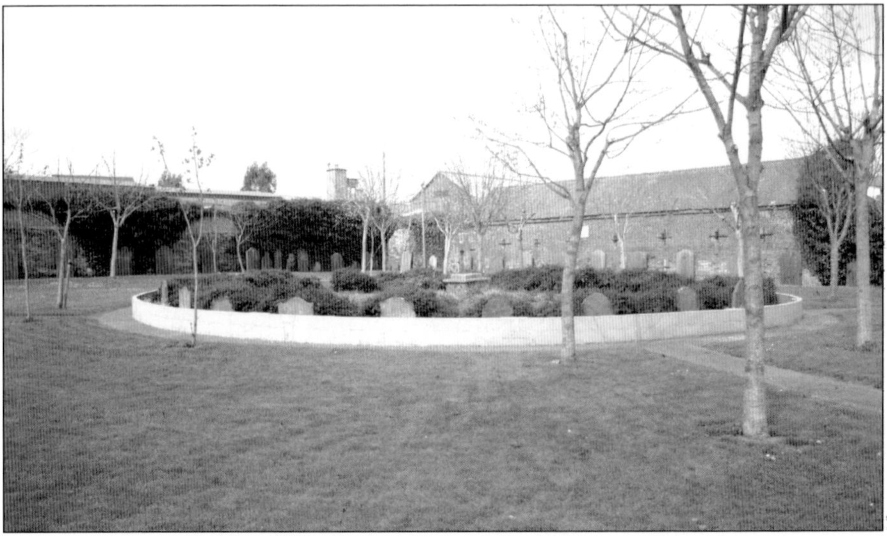
Figure 174

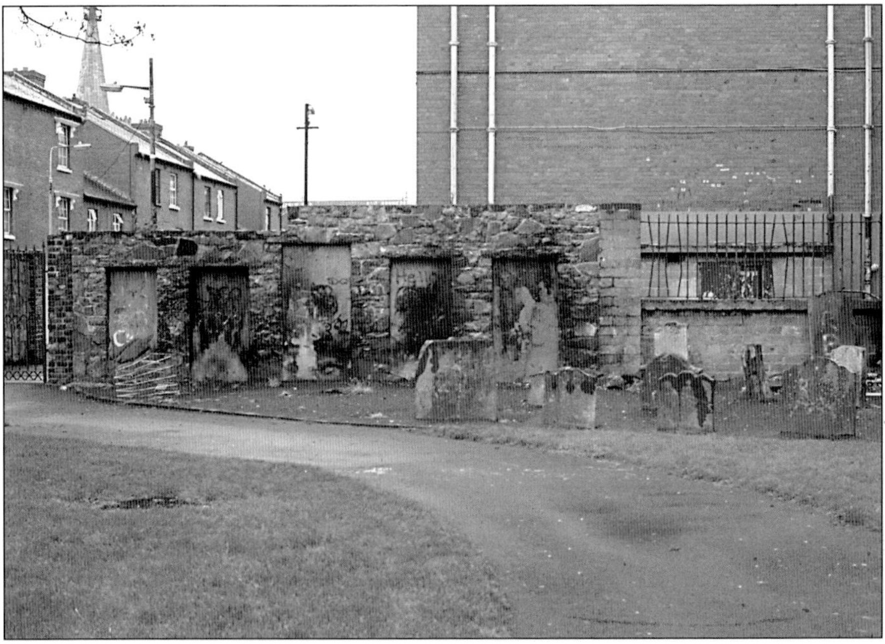
Figure 175

Fig. 174—Relocated headstones at Arklow Abbeylands Burial Ground, Co. Wicklow, Ireland.

Fig. 175—Vandalised relocated headstones, Cabbage Garden Burial Ground (partly Huguenot), Dublin, Co. Dublin, Ireland.

Fig. 176—Canopy built to protect important headstones, Greyfriers Burial Ground, Perth, Perthshire, Scotland.

Inscribed in remembrance

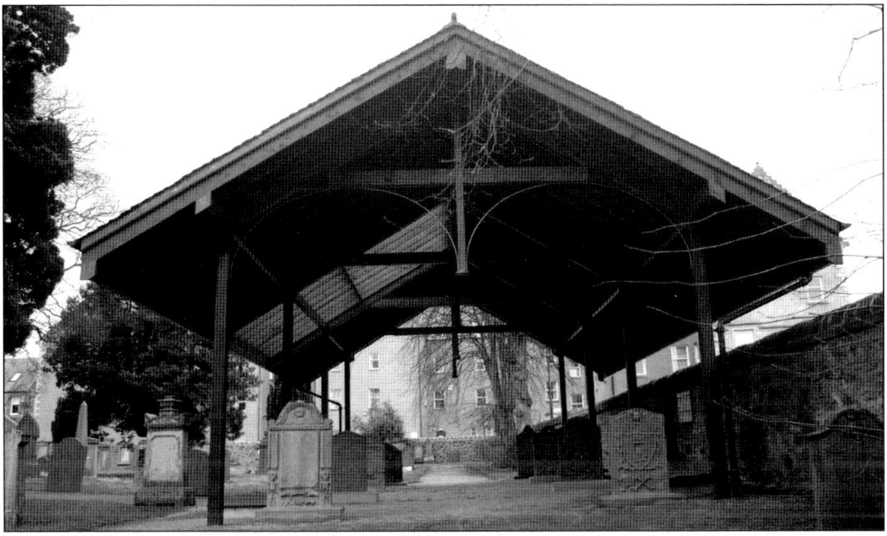

Figure 176

them from the elements (Fig. 176).

Lettering on gravemarkers raises no specific conservation issues, other than those that relate to gravemarkers as a whole.[130] On the other hand, restoration of inscriptions by recutting, even by expert masons, should never be attempted. The integrity of the original inscription should always be maintained. There are instances in Britain and Ireland where an inscription has been recut, although the practice was never widespread and was probably more common in the past than in recent years. Probably the best-known examples are those of the Scot Robert Paterson, known as 'Old Mortality', who, as well as carving and erecting post-dated Covenanters' headstones in southern Scotland, recut many older ones in the eighteenth century.

Both individuals and civic authorities should recognise the importance of lettering as a cultural resource. Official bodies should give it serious consideration when embarking on any conservation measure. Individuals should recognise its significance so that gravemarker surveys include detailed recording of letterform attributes and significant inscriptions are consequently recognised. These should be publicised and reported to appropriate local and national conservation authorities, such as English Heritage, Historic Scotland, the National Monuments Service in Ireland, Terebinth in the Netherlands, and state associations for the conservation of historic graveyards in the USA.

NOTES

1. Badham 2001. See Higgitt 1994, 1999 and 2000 for examples and references to other papers. Stone (1991, 11) and Schlereth (1985) point out the lost opportunities inherent in studying only the élite and unusual.

2. Bartram 1978.

3. Colas 1924, 9ff; Steilen 1938, 24–30; Timoney 2005, 26; Gilbert 1980, 68–75; Burgess 1963, 206–16; Willsher and Hunter 1978, 7; Runge 1979, 18–20; Willsher 2005, 22, 35, 36–7.

4. See the series of papers by Longfield (1943; 1944; 1945; 1946; 1947; 1948; 1954), Grogan (1998) and Mytum (2004a).

5. Burgess 1963 is one of the few exceptions, taking a more empirical approach to the subject.

6. The Monumental Brass Society has published a series of books on several English counties, each including a comprehensive inventory of both small plates and monumental brasses.

7. Thomson 2006, 22, 27.

8. The introduction of mechanical methods of gravestone manufacture was a gradual process, beginning with the use of rudimentary power tools in the eighteenth century to the currently used computer-driven cutters. The majority of inscriptions in Europe, the USA and Canada are now shot-blasted or laser-cut.

9. Enchev-Vidju 1994; see especially numbers 12, 25, 55, 121, 230 and 586.

10. Pektaş 2007, 70.

11. See Thomson 2002a; 2002b; 2004; 2005a; 2005b; 2006a; 2006b; 2006c; 2006d; 2007a; 2007b; 2008.

12. Curl 2004, 10.

13. In Ireland there was a requirement to set aside specific areas in cemeteries for Roman Catholic burials.

14. *Investigations at St John's Church, Co. Antrim*. Data Structure Report No. 6. Centre for Archaeological Fieldwork, Queen's University, Belfast (2002).

15. Fischer 1996.

16. Curl 2004, 10.

17. Williamson (1888, 304–9) details the context and establishment of the Greenock Cemetery. Jackson and Vergara (1989) describe the evolution of the cemetery in the USA.

18. Burgess 1963, 64–5.

19. Little 1998, 5; Willsher 2005, 29–36.

20. Thomson 2006c, 4.

21. Lees 1998, 51.

22. Bousquet 1980; Cardoso 2000; Colas 1924; Peralta Labrador 1996.

23. See Thomson 2006b for a summary.

24. Thomson 2005b, 428. Willsher and Hunter (1978, 2) suggested that the earliest Scottish headstone was dated 1623.

25. Trask 1978, 11. Although the Annapolis Royal headstone imported from Boston is the oldest extant in Canada, there are reliable accounts of what is believed to be a gravestone found by Francis Alger and Charles T. Jackson near a known early burial ground on the shores of Goat Island in the Annapolis Basin, Nova Scotia, in 1827. It measured about 76cm by 61cm (30ins by 24ins). The stone was deeply carved with the date 1606 and emblems believed to be a square and compass. It is thought to have marked the grave of a French mason, stone-cutter or carpenter who died that year. About 1887 it was set in a wall of the Canadian Institute of Toronto and was plastered over. The stone has not been seen since (Haywood 1924; Harris 1924; 1986).

26. See illustrations in Longfield 1943; 1944; 1945; 1946; 1947; 1948; 1954; Bremer 1990; Schreiber and Hanke 1985; Steilen 1938; Quedens 1984; Runge 1979.

27. Ludwig (1966) makes a detailed analysis of mortality symbols on those headstones. See also Barba 1954 and Graves 1988.

28. Farber and Farber 1988.

29. Thomson 2006a, 260–1.

30. Liubenova 1996, 119.

31. Little 1998, 42.

32. Thomson 2007b, 52–4.

33. Frankowski 1920, 179–82; Thomson 2007b, 49–50.

34. Thomson 2006a, 259–61, 269.

35. Langdon 1988, 9–11.

36. Blomqvist 1997.

37. There are several good examples in the Museum für Sepulkralkultur in Kassel, Germany.

38. Little 1998, 32–3; Ball 1977.

39. Little 1998, 5.

40. Robinson (1999, 107–15) illustrates many examples.

41. Sexton (1991, 31–46) illustrates and discusses wooden gravehouses in Louisiana.

42. Thomson 2008.

43. Although their books are now rather dated, Blight (1872) and Dexter (1938) catalogue and discuss wayside crosses in south-west England. King (1985) and Crawford (1907) do the same for Ireland.

44. Frazer and Oestreicher 1998; Böttger and Cardorff 2003.

45. Diringer 1968, 10–11; Walker 1987, 9–32.

46. Thomson 2003, 15.

47. Anderson 1969, 45.

48. Catich 1968.

49. Gray 1986, 78–108.

50. Jackson 1981, 129; Dalgleish and Fothringham 2008.

51. Burgess 1963, 214–16. Early gravestone design manuals include Butterfield 1847, Kelke 1851 and Rogers 1872.

52. Anderson 1969, 189–90.

53. *Ibid.*, 32.

54. Gray 1986, 26.

55. *Ibid.*, 121.

56. Etcheverry *et al.* (2004, 118) question their uniqueness.

57. Howarth (1952, 183–4) suggests that Mackintosh designed only two gravemarkers. He designed several, but did not always use the Art Nouveau-influenced letterforms in the inscriptions. The weathered inscription on the East Wemyss memorial has been replaced by a bronze plaque with very different lettering.

58. Gray, as long ago as 1960, discusses the influences of technology on the design of lettering on environmental structures but does not extend her discourse to gravemarkers.

59. Little 1998, 41, 48, 52.

60. Thomson 2002a, 368.

61. Burgess 1963, 257.

62. Duval and Rigby 1978, viii.

63. Burgess 1963, 258.

64. Duval and Rigby 1978, viii.

65. Forbes 1927, 18.

66. Burgess 1963, 293.

67. The Hickey monumental sculptors business still exists in Aherna, Co. Cork, after more than 250 years. See also note 4.

68. Possibly the most comprehensive study of a gravestone-carver is that of Messimer (2000), detailing the life and work of the Pennsylvanian mason Joseph Brownmiller (1807–95), who cut his first stone in 1825. Forbes (1927) identified 127 gravestone-carvers from New

England and gives fairly detailed biographies of some from Connecticut, Massachusetts, New Hampshire and Rhode Island. Other works on carvers in the USA include Blachowicz 2000, Cathcart 2002, Luti 2005, and Chase and Gable 1988 and 1990.

69. Trask 1978, 11.

70. Runge 1979, 15–16.

71. The stone erected at Ardtalnaig, on Loch Tayside in Perthshire, for the parents of Duncan McLaren is mentioned in a document dated 10 July 1791 held at the National Archives of Scotland (GD112/11/2/3/5). The text reads: 'Sending £8 [Scots] and 2 guineas . . . part borrowed money, the rest till Duncan Hagart the mason has a headstone made for writer's parents; "I want him to make a good holsome stone & as large as any at Kenmore, but most be but plean & my father & mothers names on & there edge & place of abod. When the stone is plased at Ardtalnaig you will pay Mr Hagart . . . I will require Mr Hagart to make the stone from £4 to £5 & the rest will be for a treate to the friends at the time of settling of it".' Willsher and Hunter (1978, 4–5) give an account of James Faichney.

72. For lists of signed gravestones and their carvers see Barley 1948, Beament and Dudley 2000, and Kelly and Williams 1982.

73. Forbes 1927, 12–16. Stone (1991, 9) reports the same practice in Long Island, New York State.

74. Willsher and Hunter 1978, 7.

75. Thomson 2006c, 7.

76. Bertram 1996.

77. Lack *et al.* 2005, vii.

78. Thomson 2005b, 423–42.

79. Little 1998, 31–2.

80. Little (1998, 180) suggests that one of the advantages of marble was permanence. This is not borne out by the examples from North Carolina.

81. See the series of Monumental Brass Society publications.

82. Thomson 2008, 131–41.

83. Cameron 1946, 110–31.

84. Trask 1978, 48–9.

85. *Ibid.*, 51.

86. Mytum 2004b, 96.

87. Thomson 2006b, 1; Gray 1986, 121; Anderson 1969, 102.

88. Bartram 1978 uses the term 'english letter' throughout.

89. Astle (1784, 146) illustrates the 'Modern Gothic'. Morrison (1942) coined the term 'uncialesque' and details the development of the gothic style in the north of Europe.

90. Moseley 1963.

91. Thomson 2002b, 115–25.

92. Higgitt 1999, 137–49.

93. Gray 1986, 86.

94. Runge 1979, 18–19.

95. Gray 1986, 151.

96. The inscription was considered to be the oldest in North America by Duval and Rigby (1978, 1), but it was preceded by the headstone of 1633 at Cambridge, Massachusetts.

97. Moseley (1963) discusses the term in a typographical context at length.

98. Thomson 2002b, 119.

99. Gray 1986, 156.

100. Frazer and Oestreicher (1998) illustrate many modern memorials with beautiful, well-designed lettering.

101. Many examples of good German design, utilising modern materials, are illustrated in Böttger and Cardorff 2003.

102. Heseltine (2001, 9–12) lists several sculptors and craftsmen and where their work was sold. Numerous papers in the journal *Church Monuments* detail the work of medieval sculptors and the extent to which their work was made for a range of clients in England and elsewhere.

103. One of the most inventive examples of ligatured numerals is on a headstone at Dundrennan Abbey in the Stewartry of Kirkcudbright, Scotland, where the '6' and '8' of 1685 have been combined.

104. Thomson, unpublished.

105. Thomson 2002a, 363–5; 2005b, 434.

106. Thomson 2006a, 256–8.

107. The word 'ye' in gravemarker inscriptions and manuscripts is often wrongly pronounced 'ye'. The thorn character (written as 'y') represents 'th' and the correct reading is 'the'. See Simpson 1973, 42, for details.

108. Small brass plates of the post-Reformation period have been studied far less than the larger monumental brasses. See Heseltine 2001, 13.

109. Pocius 1981, 5–6.

110. Little 1998, 13.

111. O'Keeffe (2001, 165) illustrates the pediment of a headstone carved by Byrne. Longfield (1945) appears to have been unaware of this memorial.

112. Barley 1948.

113. Pathuis (1977) details memorial texts on a range of artefacts, including gravemarkers, wall plaques, silver, bells and furniture. Dunning (1967) and Gray (1986, 142–4) illustrate examples of lettering on other artefacts. Lettering on hammered coins of the thirteenth to seventeenth centuries was similar in style to contemporary lettering on gravemarkers; see Spink 2007, 149–308; 2003, 15–86.

114. Both Burgess (1963) and Little (1998) give far more credence to non-vernacular gravemarkers.

115. Bartram (1978) illustrates very few truly vernacular gravemarkers.

116. Thomson 2006b, 7–8.

117. Sabrowsky (2006) provides a comprehensive illustrated catalogue of all gravemarkers in Oldenburgerland, north-west Germany. Schreiber and Hanke (1985) illustrate all the gravemarkers on the Friesian island of Föhr, and Quedens (1984) does the same for the island of Amrum.

118. Ebdon 1985 is an easy-to-understand introduction to basic statistical procedures. For more advanced techniques see Baxter 2003. The documentation for *PAST* is a good introduction to some advanced statistical procedures (see note 119).

119. The *Statistical Package for the Social Sciences* (*SPSS*) is a modular package by SPSS Inc., Chicago. *Statistica* is also modular and is a product of StatSoft Inc., Tulsa. *Statgraphics* is a graphically based statistical suite by StatPoint Inc., Herndon. The free software package *PAST* by Hammer, Harper and Ryan provides several easy-to-use advanced techniques that can be used for gravemarker lettering analysis.

120. Stone 1991; Deetz 1996.

121. Thomson 2002a, 357–62.

122. Thomson 2006a.

123. Three-dimensional charts can be represented on a two-dimensional plane but are clearer using stereograms. Four-dimensional objects, however, must be shown three dimensions at a time, or by algorithmic procedures such as rotation or slicing.

124. Maxwell *et al.* 2001; FitzPatrick 1995.

125. The situation in Germany is extremely complex but includes some innovative ideas. Important older gravemarkers can be officially listed. The *Grabmalpatenschaft* was established so that a person could adopt a gravemarker for his or her own use. After a twenty- to thirty-year period, the gravemarker must be re-adopted or removed.

126. Maxwell *et al.* 2001, 13.

127. *Ibid.*, 27–35.

128. *Ibid.*, 33.

129. Hamilton 1987.

130. See Maxwell *et al.* 2001, 48–66, for a detailed account of good practice for the restoration of gravemarkers.

Anderson, D.M. 1969 *The art of written forms. The theory and practice of calligraphy.* Holt, Rinehart and Winston, New York.
Anon. 2002 *Investigations at St John's Church, Co. Antrim.* Data Structure Report No. 6. Centre for Archaeological Fieldwork, Queen's University, Belfast.
Astle, T. 1784 *The origin and progress of writing.* J. White, London.
Badham, S. 2002 The contribution of epigraphy to the typological classification of medieval English brasses and incised slabs. In J. Higgitt, K. Forsyth and D. N. Parsons (eds), *Roman, runes and ogham. Medieval inscriptions in the insular world and on the Continent*, 202–10. Shaun Tyas, Donington.
Bailey, B. 1987 *Churchyards of England and Wales.* Robert Hale, London.
Ball, D.B. 1977 Wooden gravemarkers: neglected items of material culture. *Tennessee Folklore Society Bulletin* **43** (4), 167–85.
Barba, P.A. 1954 *Pennsylvania German tombstones. A study in folk art.* Pennsylvania German Folklore Society, Allentown.
Barley, M.W. 1948 Slate headstones in Nottinghamshire. *Thoroton Society Transactions* **52**, 69–86.
Bartram, A. 1978 *Tombstone lettering in the British Isles.* Lund Humphries, London/ Watson-Guptill, New York.
Baxter, M. 2003 *Statistics in archaeology.* Hodder Arnold, London.
Beament, J. and Dudley, E. 2000 *In blessed memory . . . Incised headstones of North and West Devon and North Cornwall 1650–1860* [exhibition catalogue]. Exeter School of Art and Design, University of Plymouth, Exeter.
Bertram, J. (ed.) 1996 *Monumental brasses in art and history.* Allan Sutton/Monumental Brass Society, London.
Bickham, G. and Bickham, J. 1741 *The universal penman.* London.
Blachowicz, J. 2000 William Coyle: father of the Plymouth carving tradition. *Markers* **17**, 32–108.
Blight, J.T. 1872 *Ancient crosses and other antiquities in the west of Cornwall* (3rd edn). William Cornish, Penzance.
Blomqvist, P.-O. 1997 *Gravvardar av metall i Pojo.* Ekenäs Tryckeri, Ekenäs.
Böttger, C. and Cardorff, P. 2003 *Mein letztes Wort. Der Grabstein als Visitenlarte.* Schwarzkopf and Schwarzkopf, Berlin.
Bousquet, J. (ed.) 1980 *Les stèles discoidales. Archéologie en Languedoc* (special issue, 1980), 67–80.
Bremer, J.T. 1990 *Oorkonden in steen. 17e en 18e eeuwse grafzerken op de oude begraafplaats van Huisduinen/Den Helder.* Uitgeverij Pirola, Schoorl.
Burgess, F. 1963 *English churchyard memorials.* Lutterworth Press, London.
Butterfield, W. 1847 *Instrumenta ecclesiastica.* Van Voorst, London.
Cameron, H.K. 1946 The metals used in monumental brasses. *Transactions of the Monumental Brass Society* **8**, 110–31.
Cardoso, G. 2000 *Estelas medievais e modernas do Cadaval.* Arqueologia do Cadaval 2. Museu Municipal Cadaval, Cadaval.
Cathcart, A.M. 2002 The Rule family: Vermont gravestone carvers and marble dealers. *Markers* **19**, 214–39.
Catich, E.M. 1968 *The origin of the serif. Brush writing and Roman letters.* Catfish, Davenport.
Chase, T. and Gable, L.K. 1988 Seven initial carvers of Boston 1700–1725. *Markers* **5**, 210–32.
Chase, T. and Gable, L.K. 1990 *Gravestone chronicles I. Some eighteenth-century gravestone carvers and their work.* New England Historic Genealogical Society, Boston.
Colas, L. 1924 [1923] *La tombe Basque.* Société des Sciences, Lettres, Arts et Études Régionales de Basque (Bayonne), Paris.
Crawford, H.S. 1907 A descriptive list of early Irish crosses. *Journal of the Royal Society of Antiquaries of Ireland* **37**, 187–239.
Curl, J.S. 2004 A short history of the cemetery movement in Europe. In S. Berresford, *Italian*

memorial sculpture 1820–1940. A legacy of love, 10. Francis Lincoln, London.

Dalgleish, G. and Fothringham, H.S. 2008 *Silver made in Scotland*. NMSE-Publications, Edinburgh.

Davis, C.T. 1899 [1969] *The monumental brasses of Gloucestershire* [facsimile edition]. Kingsmead Reprints, Bath.

Deetz, J. 1996 *In small things forgotten. An archaeology of early American life* (new edn). Doubleday Anchor, New York.

Dexter, T. 1938 *Cornish crosses, Christian and pagan*. Longmans, Green and Co., London.

Diringer, D. 1968 *The alphabet. A key to the history of mankind* (3rd edn). Hutchinson, London.

Dunning, G.C. 1967 Late medieval jugs and lettering. *Medieval Archaeology* **11**, 233–41.

Duval, F.Y. and Rigby, I.B. 1978 *Early American gravestone art*. Dover, New York.

Ebdon, D. 1985 *Statistics in geography. A practical approach* (2nd edn). Wiley Blackwell, London.

Enchev-Vidju, I. 1994 *Bälgarskj naroden kräst*. Akademichno Izd-vo Prof. Marin Drinov, Sofia.

Etcheverry, J., Duvert, M., Etchehandy, M. and Labat, C. 2004 *Les stèles discoïdales et l'art funéraire basque. Hil harriak*. Lauburu/Elkarlanean, Bayonne.

Farber, D. and Farber, J.L. 1988 Early Pennsylvania gravemarkers. *Markers* **5**, 96–121.

Fischer, N. 1996 *Vom Gottesacker zum Krematorium: eine Sozialgeschichte der Friedhöfe in Deutschland*. Boehlau, Wien.

FitzPatrick, E. (ed.) 1995 *The care and conservation of graveyards*. The Stationery Office, Dublin.

Forbes, H.M. 1927 *Gravestones of early New England and the men who made them, 1653–1800*. Houghton Mifflin, Boston.

Frankowski, E. 1920 *Estelas discoideas de la Península Ibérica*. Museo Nacional de Ciencias Naturales, Madrid.

Frazer, H. and Oestreicher, C. (eds) 1998 *The art of remembering*. Memorials by Artists, Saxmundham.

Fry, E. 1828 *Specimen of modern printing types by Edmund Fry, letter founder to the King*. Edmund Fry, London.

Gilbert, L. 1980 *A grave look at history. Glimpses of a vanishing form of folk art*. John Ferguson, Sydney.

Graves, T.E. 1988 Pennsylvania German gravestones: an introduction. *Markers* **5**, 60–95.

Gray, N. 1960 *Lettering on buildings*. Architectural Press, London.

Gray, N. 1986 *A history of lettering. Creative experiment and letter identity*. Phaidon, Oxford.

Grogan, E. 1998 Eighteenth-century headstones and the stonemason tradition in County Wicklow: the work of Dennis Cullen of Monaseed. *Wicklow Archaeology and History* **1**, 41–63.

Hamilton, R.A. 1987 Ersatz tombstones replace the historic. *New York Times*, 12 April 1987.

Harris, R.V. 1924 The masonic stone of 1606. *The Builder Magazine* **10** (10), 295–8.

Harris, R.V. 1986 Freemasonry in Canada before 1750. In *The papers of the Canadian Masonic Research Association 1949–1976* **1** (31), 564–5. The Heritage Lodge No. 730, Cambridge.

Haywood, H.L. 1924 Studies of masonry in the United States: part 1. The early traditions. *The Builder Magazine* **10** (9), 277–8.

Heseltine, P. 2001 Engravers of monumental brasses. *Proceedings of the Monumental Brass Society* (2001), 9–13.

Higgitt, J. 1990 The stone cutter and the scriptorium: early medieval inscriptions in Britain and Ireland. In W. Koch (ed.), *Epigraphik 1998: Fachtagung für mittelalterliche und neuzeitliche Epigraphik, Graz, 10–14 Mai 1988*, 149–62. Österreichische Akademie der Wissenschaften Philosophisch-Historische Klasse, Denkschriften.

Higgitt, J. 1994 Monasteries and inscriptions in early Northumbria: the evidence of Whitby. In C. Bourke (ed.), From the Isles of the North. *Proceedings of the Third International Conference on Insular Art*, 229–36. HMSO, Belfast.

Higgitt, J. 1999 Epigraphic lettering and book script in the British Isles. *Bayerische Akademie der Wissenschaften* **117**, 137–49.

Higgitt, J. 2000 The dedication inscription. In J. Geddes (ed.), *King's College Chapel, Aberdeen, 1500–2000*, 66–73. Maney Publishing, London.

Howarth, T. 1952 *Charles Rennie Mackintosh and the Modern Movement*. Routledge and Kegan Paul, London.

Hueppi, A. 1968 *Kunst und Kult der Grabstätten*. Walter-Verlag, Olten.

Jackson, D. 1981 *The story of writing*. The Parker Pen Company, London.

Jackson, K.T. and Vergara, J. 1989 *Silent cities. The evolution of the American cemetery*. Princeton Architectural Press, New York.

Kelke, W.H. 1851 *The churchyard manual intended chiefly for rural districts*. C. Cox, London.

Kelly, S. and Williams, A. 1982 'And the men who made them': the signed gravestones of New England. *Markers* **2**, 1–103.

King, H. 1985 Irish wayside crosses 1600–1700. *Post-Medieval Archaeology* **19**, 13–33.

Lack, W., Stuchfield, H.M. and Whittemore, P. 1998 *The monumental brasses of Cumberland and Westmoreland*. Monumental Brass Society, London.

Lack, W., Stuchfield, H.M. and Whittemore, P. 2005 *The monumental brasses of Gloucestershire*. Monumental Brass Society, London.

Langdon, A.G. 1988 *Old Cornish crosses*. Cornwall Books, Exeter.

Lees, H. 1998 *Porch and pew. Small churches of the Cotswolds*. Walnut Tree Publishing, Dursley.

Lees, H. 1993 *Hallowed ground—churchyards of Gloucestershire and the Cotswolds*. Thornhill Press, Cheltenham.

Little, M.R. 1998 *Sticks and stones. Three centuries of North Carolina gravemarkers*.University of North Carolina Press, Chapel Hill and London.

Liubenova, I. 1996 *I grobovete umirat*. Akademichno Izd-vo Prof. Marin Drinov, Sofia.

Longfield, A.K. 1943 Some 18th century Irish tombstones. I. Introduction. Dennis Cullen of Monaseed. *Journal of the Royal Society of Antiquaries of Ireland* **73**, 29–39.

Longfield, A.K. 1944 Some 18th century Irish tombstones. II. Miles Brien. *Journal of the Royal Society of Antiquaries of Ireland* **74**, 63–72.

Longfield, A.K. 1945 Some 18th century Irish tombstones. III. James Byrne and his school. *Journal of the Royal Society of Antiquaries of Ireland* **75**, 76–88.

Longfield, A.K. 1946 Some 18th century Irish tombstones. IV. J. Butler, Hugh Rogan, David Doyle, etc. *Journal of the Royal Society of Antiquaries of Ireland* **76**, 81–8.

Longfield, A.K. 1947 Some late 18th and early 19th century Irish tombstones. V. Subjects not related to the Crucifixion. Saints and scenes by Kehoe, at St Mullins, and by an unknown carver, at Termonfeckin. *Journal of the Royal Society of Antiquaries of Ireland* **77**, 1–4.

Longfield, A.K. 1948 Some late 18th and early 19th century Irish tombstones. VI. East County Louth. *Journal of the Royal Society of Antiquaries of Ireland* **78**, 170–4.

Longfield, A.K. 1954 Some 18th century Irish tombstones. VII. Clonmel, Kiltoom, Seir Keiran, etc. *Journal of the Royal Society of Antiquaries of Ireland* **84**, 173–8.

Ludwig, A.I. 1966 *Graven images. New England stonecarving and its symbols, 1650–1815*. Wesleyan University Press, Middletown.

Luti, V. 2005 Eighteenth-century gravestone carvers of the Upper Narragansett Basin: George Allen. *Markers* **22**, 108–59.

Maxwell, I., Nanda, R. and Urquhart, D. 2001 *Conservation of historic graveyards. Guide for practitioners 2*. Historic Scotland, Edinburgh.

Messimer, C. 2000 *Known by the work of his hands*. The Pennsylvania German Society, Kutztown.

Morrison, S. 1942 *Black letter text*. Cambridge University Press, Cambridge.

Moseley, J. 1963 English vernacular. *Motif* (Winter 1963–4), 3–55.

Mytum, H. 2004a Graveyard survey of West Ulster. *Church Archaeology* **5/6**, 110–12.

Mytum, H.C. 2004b *Mortuary monuments and burial grounds of the historic period*. Manuals in Archaeological Method, Theory and Technique. Kluwer Academic/Plenum Publishers, New York.

O'Keeffe, D. 2001 Instruments of passion on the gravestones of South Tipperary. *Tipperary Historical Journal* (2001), 155–74.

Pathuis, A. 1977 *Groninger gedenkwaardig heden. Teksten, wapens en huismerken van 1298–1814.* Van Gorcum, Assen.

Pektaş, K. 2007 *Adilcevaz çevresindeki mezar taşlari.* Zero, Istanbul.

Peralta Labrador, E.J. 1996 Las estelas discoideas gigantes de Cantabria. In *La arqueologia de los Cántabros.* Actas sobre la Primera Reunion de la Edad del Hiero en Cantabria, 313–41. Fundación Marcelino Botin, Santander.

Pocius, G.L. 1981 Eighteenth- and nineteenth-century Newfoundland gravestones: self-sufficiency, economic specialization, and the creation of artefacts. *Material History Bulletin* **12**, 1–16.

Quedens, G. 1984 *Die alten Grabsteine auf dem Amrumer Friedhof.* Jens Quedens, Amrum.

Robinson, D. 1999 *Saving graces. Images of women in European cemeteries.* Norton and Co., New York.

Rogers, F. 1872 *Designs for monuments, head-stones, mural tablets, and church-yard crosses.* London.

Runge, W. 1979 *Sprechende Steine. Grabstelen im Oldenburger Land von 1600 bis 1800.* Heinz Holzberg, Oldenburg.

Sabrowsky, M. 2006 *Grabstelen und Grabplatten im Oldenburger Land aus dem 17 und 18 Jahrhundert* (CD-ROM). Wilhelmshaven.

Schlereth, T. 1985 Material culture studies: a symposium. In S. Bronner (ed.), *Material Culture* **17**, 2–3.

Schreiber, E. and Hanke, D. 1985 *Friedvoller Hasen. Dokumentation aller alten Grabsteine auf dem Kirchof von St. Johannis in Nieblum auf Föhr.* Edel Verlag, Duisburg.

Sexton, R. 1991 Don't let rain fall on my face: French Louisiana gravehouses in an anthropo-geographical context. *Material Culture* **23** (3), 31–46.

Simpson, G.G. 1973 *Scottish handwriting 1150–1650. An introduction to the reading of documents.* Bratton, Edinburgh.

Spink 2003 *Coins of Scotland, Ireland and the islands.* Spink, London.

Spink 2007 *Coins of England and the United Kingdom* (42nd edn). Spink, London.

Steilen, D. 1938 *Norddeutsche Grabmalkunst.* Arthur Geist, Bremen.

Stone, G. 1991 Material evidence of ideological and ethnic choice in Long Island gravestones. *Material Culture* **23** (3), 1–29.

Thomson, G. 2002a Research in inscriptional palaeography (RIP). Scottish tombstone lettering 1241–1855: methodology and preliminary analysis. *Proceedings of the Society of Antiquaries of Scotland* **131** (2001), 349–73.

Thomson, G. 2002b Script lettering on Scottish tombstones: origins and influences. *Scottish Tradition* **27**, 115–25.

Thomson, G. 2003 *Digital calligraphy. How to create perfect lettering from your desktop.* Watson-Guptill, New York.

Thomson, G. 2004 *Scottish kirkyards and tombstone lettering* (CD-ROM). Privately published.

Thomson, G. 2005a Inscribed in remembrance. *Ancestors* (December 2005), 43–7.

Thomson, G. 2005b Research in inscriptional palaeography (RIP). Tombstone lettering in Dumfries and Galloway. *Proceedings of the Society of Antiquaries of Scotland* **135**, 423–42.

Thomson, G. 2006a Irish discoid gravemarkers and inscriptional lettering. *Breifne* (2006), 247–73.

Thomson, G. 2006b The cultural significance of lettering on gravemarkers. *Borderlines* **1** (2), 1–12.

Thomson, G. 2006c Tombstone lettering in Scotland and New England—an appreciation of a vernacular culture. *Mortality* **11** (1), 1–30.

Thomson, G. 2006d Irish discoid gravemarkers. *Archaeology Ireland* **20** (3), 10–14.

Thomson, G. 2007a We're all doomed! . . . to an eternity of gravestones with spelling errors. *DGBLife* **3** (January 2007), 30–3.

Thomson, G. 2007b Scottish discoid gravemarkers. The origins and classification of a rare type of artefact. *Markers* **25**, 44–65.

Thomson, G. 2008 Lettering on small brass plates. *Transactions of the Monumental Brass Society* **22**, 131–41.

Thornely, J.L. 1893 *The monumental brasses of Lancashire and Cheshire*. William Andrews, Hull.

Timoney, M.B. 2005 *Had me made. A study of the grave memorials of County Sligo from c. 1650 to the present*. TASKS, Keash.

Trask, D. 1978 *Life how short. Eternity how long. Gravestone carving and carvers in Nova Scotia. An illustrated study*. The Nova Scotia Museum, Halifax.

Walker, C.B.F. 1987 *Cuneiform*. Reading the Past Series. British Museum, London.

Williamson, G. 1888 *Old Greenock embracing sketches of its ecclesiastical, educational and literary history*. Alexander Gardner, London.

Willsher, B. 1985 *Understanding Scottish graveyards. An interpretative approach*. Council for Scottish Archaeology, Edinburgh.

Willsher, B. 2005 *Understanding Scottish graveyards* (new edn). Council for Scottish Archaeology, Edinburgh.

Willsher, B. and Hunter, D. 1978 *Stones. A guide to remarkable eighteenth century graveyards*. Canongate, Edinburgh.

INDEX